Going the Distance

Going the Distance

The Teaching Profession in a Post-COVID World

LORA BARTLETT
ALISUN THOMPSON
JUDITH WARREN LITTLE
RILEY COLLINS

HARVARD EDUCATION PRESS
CAMBRIDGE, MASSACHUSETTS

Paperback ISBN 9781682539439

Library of Congress Cataloging-in-Publication Data is on file.

Published by Harvard Education Press,
an imprint of the Harvard Education Publishing Group

Harvard Education Press
8 Story Street
Cambridge, MA 02138

Cover Design: Patrick Ciano
Cover Image: Calvin Chan Wai Meng via Getty Images

The typefaces in this book are Minion Pro and ITC Stone Sans.

Dedicated to all teachers who taught during the historic coronavirus pandemic, especially the seventy-five teachers who generously shared their journey with us.

Contents

1

Teachers' Work in a Time of Crisis

Have you ever broken a teapot by pouring boiling water into it? The crack that appears is the result of thermal shock caused by the stress of the sudden change in temperature. The likelihood of cracking depends on the material composition of the teapot, the production process, the presence of other stressors, and the extremity of the temperature difference. Porcelain is more resistant to thermal shock than ceramic, but both are vulnerable given certain circumstances. This is why it is advisable to warm a teapot before adding boiling water, but even a warmed pot will break if structural weaknesses are already present. Preventing breakage requires a slow gradual pour, careful attention to process, and a well-made container.

For the teaching profession, the pandemic was much like pouring boiling water into a teapot. The public health stress posed by COVID-19 was the hot water that rapidly engulfed all sectors of American society, producing an unprecedented level of shock to personal, professional, and public life. The pandemic dramatically affected America's public schools and schoolteachers, with modified instruction extending well into the following school year in many areas and effects on teaching and learning still felt more than three years later.[1] Preexisting vulnerabilities of the teaching profession compounded the strain. Over more than two decades, teaching had suffered declines in status and compensation together with tightened policy and bureaucratic controls over teachers' work.[2] The likelihood of teachers making it through the stress of the pandemic with their occupational commitment intact was shaped by those vulnerabilities, the nature and extent of other stressors, the presence or absence of established professional communities, and the availability of supportive working conditions characterized by respect and influence.

In spring 2020, the shock of the initial disruptions revealed the strengths of the K–12 teacher workforce as teachers emerged, second only to health workers, as "first responders" directly supporting families and children. Community recognition of teachers' capacity to respond with care and competence earned them widespread respect in those early days. But the heroic framing of the spring was tarnished in the fall when teachers' reluctance to return without adequate safety measures left them often feeling vilified, compounding teacher stress and reducing career satisfaction.

Over the next two academic years, schools and communities struggled to regain some sense of normalcy while still contending with fluctuations in pandemic threat. The pandemic exposed and exacerbated existing social and educational inequalities, heightening the urgency of learning from the success and failures of the pandemic response. Official responses to the public health crisis—and especially the length of time taken to return fully to in-person learning—prompted questions and debates about the responsibilities accorded to schools and the obligations of the teachers and other adults who work in them.[3]

Going the Distance draws on the pandemic experience of seventy-five elementary and secondary school teachers in the United States who participated in the Suddenly Distant Research Project, a study spanning more than two years. Their experience, and the impact it had on their career plans and commitment, has led us to take up the question of how to stimulate a needed transformation in the appeal of the teaching profession and the conditions in which teachers work. The book delves into the pandemic experience of classroom teachers as they first adapted to abrupt school closures and then to the tumultuous, sometimes contentious, and often extended process of returning in person to the classroom. Teachers' stories, elaborated in multiple interviews and in the lengthy comments appended to surveys, supply a vivid portrayal of teaching in and through crisis.

Teachers' struggles to navigate the serious disruptions of the COVID-19 pandemic underscore the importance of a robust and respected teacher workforce, capable of pursuing the ambitious goals of public education during ordinary times and up to the task of responding quickly and capably in times of crisis. Even as it details the many challenges that teachers faced, the book places special emphasis on those teachers who succeeded in "going the distance"—emerging from the pandemic experience with their commitment to teaching intact—and on the conditions that enabled them to do so. The insights derived from those teachers offer lessons for strengthening and supporting a profession that many had judged to be in peril prior to the pandemic, and for bolstering an institution—public education—considered under political threat.[4]

In the wake of the pandemic, numerous articles and news reports speculated on the added effects of the pandemic on teacher recruitment and retention, both of which had declined in preceding years.[5] In one article, focused on teacher attrition prior to the pandemic, authors posited that "schools' staffing problems are expected to worsen in response to the COVID-19 pandemic and its impact on the economy. . . . COVID-19's related challenges for teachers, such as safety and added stress, may also increase voluntary attrition, reducing the supply of teachers."[6] Yet the same article, analyzing data from the nationally representative Schools and Staffing Survey of a decade earlier, found that "strong teacher voice, supportive work environment, fewer school problems, and greater teacher morale significantly reduce teacher attrition."[7] That is, working conditions matter to the likelihood that teachers will remain in teaching.[8]

In *Going the Distance*, we acknowledge the concern for whether teachers stay or leave but also argue that simply attending to patterns of retention and attrition will be insufficient to understand the significance of the pandemic for the teaching profession and for individual teachers' career perspectives and decisions. Among the teachers in our study, some remained satisfied with their teaching careers more than two years after the onset of the pandemic; we derive important insights from the supports that sustained their commitment. Others stayed in teaching reluctantly, frustrated with their work environment and disengaged from the work of teaching but trapped by financial constraints; these "stuck stayers" offer a cautionary tale to those who might think of teacher retention as an unalloyed good, while also reinforcing the role of working conditions in teacher satisfaction. Finally, there are teachers whose career commitment was broken and who left, despite a professed love of the classroom, and who might have stayed had conditions beyond the classroom been more favorable.

Going the Distance opens a window into the experience of K–12 teachers as they taught in, through, and beyond a crisis of large magnitude. The study's longitudinal design enabled us to follow the experiences of seventy-five teachers in nine states from the school building closures in March 2020 through two full school years. Lengthy semi-structured interviews yielded rich narrative detail and helped us grasp the extent to which teachers' experiences varied over time and within and across states, districts, and schools. A sequence of five surveys, spread over two years, supplemented the interview data and revealed both systematic commonalities and context-specific differences in teacher experience and perspective. This rich corpus of data supplies a deep and detailed picture of teachers' lives as they worked in and through crisis, revealing both supports for and risks to teacher commitment, and provides the starting point for a vision of a robust and resilient teaching profession.

A PERSPECTIVE ON DISASTERS AND CRISES

To aid us in considering how the pandemic may have affected long-standing relationships between teachers' work contexts and outcomes of interest—including career commitment and retention—we turned to the social science literature on the study of disasters and crises. In conceptual frameworks and empirical research dating back decades, disaster events are portrayed as occurring in the context of existing social, cultural, and policy systems; such occurrences rise to the level of crisis as they are "socially amplified."[9] An event can trigger a crisis but is not, in and of itself, necessarily a crisis. It is the context in which an event occurs, in combination with the interpretation of the event and existing capacity to respond, that ameliorates it or amplifies it into a crisis. Crisis scholars refer to this as the *reception* and *response* to the event. The potential for crisis exists in the intersection of the three: reception, event, and response.

In one empirical example, disaster theory explains the dramatic difference in deaths between the 2003 heat wave disaster in France (15,000 deaths, mostly in Paris and mostly low-income elderly living alone) and an even bigger heat wave in 2019 (1,500 deaths in Paris, a tenfold reduction). In 2003, the heat wave event was socially amplified by the context of its reception, including the isolation of the elderly both socially and physically in buildings not equipped to protect from heat. The slow-moving emergency response further amplified the event to a crisis, hampered by poor planning, citizen inexperience, and the August "vacation culture" in France.[10] By 2019, the National Heatwave Plan (adopted in 2004) had dramatically improved the city's capacity for an effective reception by means of enhanced community awareness of risk to the isolated elderly, an array of greening programs to reduce urban heat, thermal insulation upgrades, and an improved heat wave response plan (event cancellations, public health announcements, cooling rooms, extended pool hours).[11]

A historical and sociological analysis of 2005's Hurricane Katrina in New Orleans orients us to the pre- and post-event "landscapes of risk and resilience that produce differing degrees of vulnerabilities."[12] In considering the severity of storm damage and the variability of consequences along economic and racial lines, that analysis presents resilience as the "adaptive capacity of a social system or unit to withstand shocks and protect against other hazards by reorganizing and innovating" and risk as the threat of harm from preexisting trauma, challenge, and inequity.[13] In New Orleans, differing degrees of vulnerability to storm damage risk and resilience existed in relation to urban public disinvestment, private investment priorities, racist policies, and residential segregation. A tangible example of this landscape occurred in response to a devastating 1965 hurricane-related flood when New Orleans built levees to ostensibly reduce recurrence risk.[14] Unlike the response to the Paris heat wave, post-event mitigation efforts in New Orleans actually increased flood vulnerability by draining swamplands for residential development, setting the scene for greater destruction by Hurricane Katrina.[15] Neighborhood resilience, especially in the capacity to rebuild post-Katrina, was mediated by resident income, community networks, and municipal support. Lower income, predominantly African American neighborhoods in flood zones, beset with insurance redlining, were less resiliently positioned to adapt and rebuild than more affluent and predominantly white neighborhoods privileged in recovery processes. The resulting loss of homes, many owned for generations, devastated long-established communities.[16]

Crisis results when the context, conditions, and response to a trigger event amplify the potentially negative consequences to a point of significance. The *landscape of risk and resilience* framing moves beyond individual explanations and calls attention to structural and contextual factors of vulnerability. Much like thermal shock and the survival of teapots, vulnerability—of people, places, and, in the case of teachers during the pandemic, professions—to unfavorable outcomes is related to risk and resilience.

But unlike many natural disasters such as the European heat wave incidents and US hurricanes, the COVID-19 pandemic is categorized by crisis theorists as a new form of "transboundary" crisis, one that spreads rapidly across national, organizational, and societal boundaries from an ambiguous source, threatening a large or potentially large number of victims, "disrupting the social fabric of different social systems."[17] Often in transboundary crises, the established conventional responses to threat are insufficient. Successful response to transboundary crises requires both macro-level leadership and emergent adaptive behavior at multiple levels simultaneously—including the local level. Local capacity to assess and respond on the ground is a key component of effective response that requires horizontal coordination.[18] Teachers' close relationships to students positioned them ideally for this emergent response role: assessing needs (well-being, technology, learning), sustaining communication, and adapting systems and practices.

The social science research on disasters and crises accords little attention to the role of teachers and schools. However, an Annenberg Institute working paper, citing Hurricane Katrina as an example, maintained that schools may form a locus of first response. The authors write, "When an external crisis strikes, schools must shift their practices suddenly—often in ways that are impossible to anticipate. Teachers are 'first responders in tragedy,' and schools are integral to both the first-line and long-term post-disaster response."[19]

The COVID-19 pandemic also stimulated a reconceptualization of "focusing events," defined as sudden and unexpected disasters that may, under some conditions, motivate policy and social changes.[20] In a recent formulation, researchers characterize COVID-19 as a "slow-onset, long-duration" disaster likely to reveal its harms (and opportunities) over an extended time.[21] The Paris heat wave and Hurricane Katrina examples demonstrate—and the pandemic crisis reinforces—how crises may expose social fissures and problems of inequity, pointing to the need for social, policy, and institutional change. In the case of COVID-19, social fissures and problems of inequity centered squarely on schools. The present study presents an opportunity to fill a significant gap in the social science research by centering teachers' perspectives and experiences in the context of system-level responses to the pandemic by schools, school districts, and states.

The conceptual orientations to the social construction of crises and the particular characteristics of transboundary crises call attention to teachers' relative risks and resilience as they navigated potentially crisis-triggering events. In the case of pandemic-modified schooling, teachers' vulnerability to career consequences is directly related to their work landscape. In this book, we consider the degree to which a public health crisis developed into a teaching profession crisis. We find five aspects of the COVID-19 school and teaching profession landscape significant for teacher career risk and resilience: 1) the sociopolitical framing and structural conditions of the teaching profession before and during the pandemic; 2) the rationales employed by national, state, and local education actors as they mobilized a response, including the metrics used to convey (or downplay) a crisis interpretation of events; 3) the nature of system-level responses in the form of policies, programs, and practices established at the state and local level; 4) educational, social, and economic resources marshaled by and for teachers, students, and families; and 5) teachers' emergent behavior, including the role of existing and newly formed networks in supporting teachers.

A MOMENT IN TIME: SETTING THE SCENE

One way to think of the arrival of the COVID-19 virus in the United States is as an event—an event that could have played out in any number of different ways in relation to public health, public schools, and the experience of teachers. This event took place at a moment in time characterized by tight control over teaching practice and a narrowed conception of teaching work, together with a society deeply divided by political and ideological differences.[22] This context shaped the response to the event, determining the degree to which it constituted a crisis: a health crisis, a schooling crisis, and a teacher workforce crisis.

A Troubled Teaching Profession in 2020

Teachers navigated the pandemic at a particular moment in the history of the teaching profession. Notably, the pandemic arrived on the heels of two decades of high stakes accountability and managerialist reform that marginalized teachers' influence on educational goals and policies and affected teachers' career orientation, satisfaction, and commitment.[23] The educational response to COVID-19 was shaped in part by this moment in the teaching profession while also disrupting it.

Ushered in by the No Child Left Behind Act in 2001, the standards and accountability movement's equation of pedagogical uniformity with educational equity shifted curricular and pedagogical decision-making away from the classroom. State content standards, and associated standardized tests, narrowed and siloed academic subjects. As authority over content and pedagogy shifted away from local classrooms, expectations of teachers shifted, too. Increasingly, teachers were assessed on their demonstrated fidelity to centrally adopted curriculum guides and gains in student tests scores.[24] This centralization of authority increased pressure on and scrutiny of teachers' work even as it decreased their professional discretion over the shape and focus of their work days and classrooms.[25] In 2020, only one in five US teachers could say they were very satisfied with their work, fewer than 40 percent of parents viewed teaching as a desirable career for their children, and enrollment in teacher education programs had dropped.

Part of the explanation for a dramatic decline in the appeal of and satisfaction in a teaching career lies in the parallel declines in teachers' working conditions as manifested in reductions in teacher pay, respect, and authority.[26] In the decade before the arrival of COVID-19, the wages of other college-educated workers rose about 10 percent while teachers' wages were stagnant or declining.[27] And while there is substantial evidence associating occupational respect and prestige with job satisfaction, decision-making authority, and supportive working conditions, the fact that not even half of US teachers felt respected in 2018 suggests they also did not have access to the working conditions associated with satisfaction and prestige.[28]

This portrait of the profession depicts the overall trends preceding the onset of the pandemic—and yet it also collapses substantial variation within the profession. For example, although national trends capture the decline in teacher unionism, teacher union capacity varies immensely between and within states.[29] Even where unions are constrained by legal prohibitions on collective bargaining, automatic dues collection, and strikes, teachers demonstrated during the 2018 Red for Ed movement that they could organize collectively for better working conditions.[30] Even when occupational dissatisfaction is statistically high, there are still many teachers who find their teaching careers very satisfying and students who enroll in teacher education programs.[31] Tight controls over and narrow conceptions of teachers' work are not uniformly felt, and some teachers work in schools where they are actively engaged in stewarding professional practice collaboratively with supportive leaders and colleagues. These context variations are well understood to matter in terms of teacher recruitment, support, job satisfaction, and retention, with some working contexts better positioned to foster teacher commitment.[32]

The COVID-19 disruptions served as a spotlight shining back in time, bringing a new perspective on a decades-long landscape of reform efforts that tightened central control, standardized content and curriculum, externalized learning assessments, and intensified teachers' work while constraining their professional discretion.[33] The teaching profession in 2020 was both vulnerable, in a precarious moment, and yet also resilient, strongly positioned in some places to navigate the challenges of pandemic-modified schooling and ameliorate its effects on teachers' careers.

A Society Divided

Societal division has a long history in the United States, but the COVID-19 pandemic surfaced at a moment of particular discord, with a political discourse increasingly polarized and polarizing. "Americans have rarely been as polarized as they are today," according to one research brief published in the first year of the pandemic.[34] Some analysts, writing at the same time, noted, "Divisiveness in American politics is certainly nothing new—nor is it always a bad thing. A healthy democracy requires a regular contest of ideas, and bipartisanship can sometimes mask deep social inequities."[35] Yet they, and others writing more recently, agreed that the divisions have grown steadily starker, more rigidly defined, and more closely attached to political party affiliation over the past thirty years, resulting in the erosion of social trust.[36]

An effective response to crisis arguably relies on the element of social trust: citizens trusting each other to act in mutually supportive ways and trusting professionals to have both the expertise and the ethical commitment to do what is needed. As the spread of COVID-19 led to school closures nationwide and then to decisions about a return to in-person instruction, it would be reasonable to expect both health-care experts and teachers to count among those trusted professionals. The initial education policy response to COVID-19—the nearly universal closure of public schools to stem the spread of the virus in mid-March—appeared to reflect just such a level of social trust, deference to public health experts, and faith that schools and teachers would step up to help students and their families.

However, the trajectory from school closure to school reopening soon laid bare the social and political fissures so prominent in much news coverage. As we elaborate in chapter 4, a brief period of coordinated activity gave way to a fracturing of system response at the federal, state, and local level. One survey-based study of public preferences for a return to in-person schooling found that support for reopening generally increased by early 2021 but that differences in support were attributable to political orientation: "School reopening, as a salient education policy, was uniquely politicized during the pandemic."[37] A research brief titled "School Reopening Plans Linked to Politics Rather than Public Health" found school district reopening plans in late July 2020 statistically correlated with county-level voting patterns in the 2016 presidential election—and to have no relationship with the county-level incidence of new COVID-19 cases.[38] Researchers at Michigan State University analyzed school district reopening plans in relation to county-level COVID-19 rates, voting patterns in the 2016 presidential election, local teacher union strength, and public opinion survey data regarding support for in-person instruction. They found "political partisanship is a much larger factor in school district reopening plans than local public health data on COVID-19 risk."[39] More specifically, they found that districts in counties with a higher Democratic vote share in 2016 were significantly less likely to open in-person schooling in fall 2020. Further, there was a large partisan divide in public opinion regarding whether districts should be offering in-person instruction that fall even if COVID-19 cases were still present in the community, with only 25 percent of Democrats but 78 percent of Republicans expressing agreement. Summing up their analyses, the authors conclude, "Although we might hope that local decision-making was more responsive to local health threats, it was instead more responsive to citizen and interest group views."[40]

In the early months of 2020, then, the pandemic erupted in a society under strain and in a key social institution—public education—whose workforce was precariously positioned to contend with a major crisis. In that moment, as COVID-19 began to take its relentless toll, teachers emerged among the first responders.

LAUNCHING A STUDY OF TEACHING IN CRISIS

The Suddenly Distant Research Project had its origin in the experiences of the authors at the onset of the pandemic. As the lead author, Lora Bartlett, recalled in an essay for *Education Week*,

> One week before the start of the spring quarter, my university announced all instruction would be remote and directed faculty to "take classes online." I was scheduled to teach a 300-student undergraduate course, often the first education course taken by aspiring teachers. It was a class I had taught a dozen times but I felt overwhelmed. I had never taught anything online. I was unfamiliar with the technology, unprepared pedagogically, and unsure of my students' current realities. Overnight, I went from expert to novice. Meanwhile, my twin daughters were enduring the abrupt transition of their senior year from the lively reality of track meets, theater productions, and group projects to full days sitting and Zooming from our dining room table. They felt isolated and struggled to focus. Their teachers worked hard to reach through the computer and appeared tireless in their daily presentations, though I was sure most were new to teaching remotely and had their own home and work stress. This made me wonder what more was happening behind the scenes for teachers as they worked to meet the challenges of the moment.[41]

Bartlett's experience inspired her to recruit a team of scholars and educators to study the realities of pandemic teaching in order to learn from classroom teachers about their experiences and what it could signify for the future of the teaching profession. Alisun Thompson, whose spring 2020 included navigating the loss of classroom placements for her student teachers, recognized the substantial learning demands teachers faced in real-time adaptations. Judith Warren Little's decades of research on the policy and organizational contexts of teachers' work attuned her to the broader implications of this moment. And Riley Collins brought to the project her interest in labor dynamics and her prior experience with labor-management processes in both union and district positions.[42] Together, the team initially conceived of a modest activity—seeking perhaps fifty teachers to interview in summer 2020—that would illuminate the experience of K–12 teachers as they pivoted overnight to teaching from a distance. The team designed a short recruitment survey and circulated it through known teacher groups and networks. The planned scope of the study, and the evident need for it, expanded significantly when the recruitment survey quickly yielded responses from more than 750 teachers from over forty states and the District of Columbia. Clearly, teachers thought there was something to be learned from the experience of going suddenly from classroom teaching to teaching from a distance.

The research team narrowed the study to nine focal states selected to provide variation in teacher labor union strength, a possible factor in state and local policy decisions, and in COVID-19 death rates reported by the CDC as of mid-July 2020, a possible factor in crisis response (see figure 1.1).[43] The designation of labor union strength was based on a comparative study of teacher unions in the fifty states and the District of

Figure 1.1 COVID-19 deaths versus teacher union strength*

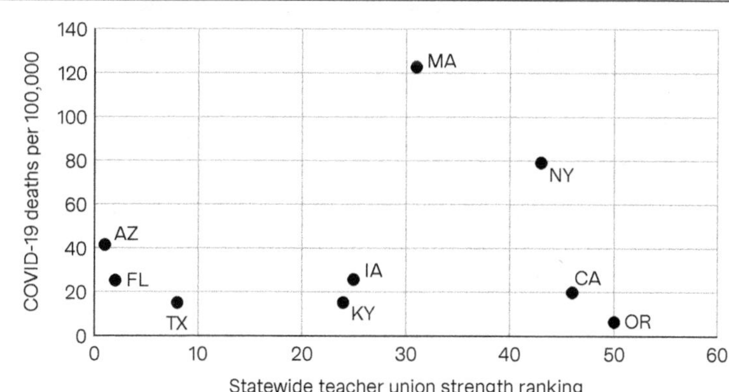

* Statewide union rankings are based upon Winkler et al.'s (2012) state-by-state comparison of teacher union strength; COVID-19 death rates are given per the Centers for Disease Control and Prevention as of July 23, 2020.

Columbia published in 2012.[44] That study's detailed comparisons ranked each state by union strength and provided the most comprehensive point of departure for our sample selection at the time. Oregon, New York, and California were ranked among the highest third of teacher union strength among all states; Arizona, Florida, and Texas were in the lowest third; and Iowa, Kentucky, and Massachusetts fell in a middle category of teacher union strength.[45]

Across the nine states, seventy-five teachers were selected to provide diversity in school level (elementary, middle, high), geographical setting, and demographics (race, gender). The resulting sample, although not statistically representative, mirrored the demographic profile of the US teacher workforce (see table 1.1). And it was a manageable number for a small research team to study.

A first round of interviews, conducted between July and September 2020, invited all seventy-five teachers to share their experience with the sudden pivot to teaching from a distance. Teachers provided an account of how their local community was affected by and responded to the pandemic and how the school closure unfolded, including any guidance or directives they received from the school, district, union, or state. They recounted details of their workday and workweek during the remaining weeks and months of the school year. They supplied a portrait of what form instruction took and the nature of their interactions with students and families. Teachers provided an estimate of how much new academic content they introduced and offered their judgment about how many—and which—of their students were able to engage meaningfully with that content. They described any support they had received, including professional development related to new technologies and other aspects of teaching from a distance. Finally, teachers conveyed their understanding of the arrangements and expectations they would likely encounter as schools attempted to reopen in fall 2020.

A focal group of thirty-six teachers provided three additional interviews conducted in late fall 2020, summer 2021, and summer 2022. The choice to restrict subsequent interviews to thirty-six teachers represented a trade-off. Although it would have been ideal to continue interviewing

Table 1.1 Teacher sample and focal teachers in comparison to US teacher workforce demographics, 2017–2018*

	Gender and race		Grade level		Geography			Years of teaching		
	Female	White	9–12	PreK–8	Urban	Suburban	Rural	1–10	11–20	>20
Teacher sample (N=75)	76%	72%	45%	55%	31%	40%	25%	37%	36%	27%
Focal teachers (N=36)	81%	76%	47%	53%	39%	28%	28%	33%	36%	31%
US teachers 2017–2018**	77%	79%	49%	51%	29%	39%	21%	37%	40%	23%

* The US and research sample teacher experience data do not map directly as the experience percentages are reported by NCES as 0–9 and 10–20 years while the research sample used 1–10 and 11–20 years.
** *Source:* USDOE NCES, https://nces.ed.gov/programs/coe/indicator/clr.

the full sample of teachers, the more limited group enabled a small research team to complete each wave of data collection and preliminary analysis in a timely manner. The focal teachers were selected to reflect both positive and negative responses to local reopening plans for fall 2020 as well as other sources of variation (school level, community type, teacher demographics). In the three additional interviews spanning nearly two years, the focal teachers offered detailed accounts of their teaching lives: the nature of the teaching day; their relationship with students, fellow teachers, administrators, and parents; their professional learning needs and opportunities; the professional workplace culture of their schools and districts; the district and school approach to mitigating the COVID-19 threat; and the degree to which teachers were able to exercise voice and influence as schools returned to in-person instruction. Presented with the themes emerging from the research as of summer 2021, teachers commented on whether and how the themes reflected their own experience and circumstances, enabling the research team to deepen its understanding of state and local variation. In the final interview, conducted at the end of the 2021–2022 school year, teachers helped flesh out our understanding of their pandemic experience by telling the story of how they had come to be a teacher and by considering whether they would now recommend a teaching career to others. In that last interview, teachers also reflected on what they saw as potentially lasting changes inspired by the pandemic experience and on lessons learned—or yet to be learned.

Over thirty months, spanning two full school years, the team also conducted five surveys with the full sample. All surveys queried teachers about their instructional mode, what they found most and least satisfying about their work at the time, significant challenges they faced, and any changes to their career plans. Selected surveys included additional items related to sources of teacher support; the focus and perceived usefulness of professional development; teachers' ability to use most or all of their preferred instructional methods; plans for standardized testing and teacher evaluation; vaccine access and safety protocols in place; school staffing challenges; the level of professional respect teachers felt from the district, school administration, community, and students; the level and type of union advocacy; and the degree to which teachers felt that district and school decisions were informed by teachers' experience and judgment. Teachers often added lengthy written comments to more fully explain or elaborate on their response to specific items. The pattern of survey responses formed the basis of some questions posed in interviews conducted at the end of the 2020–2021 and 2021–2022 school years.

Throughout the study, in both interviews and surveys (and sometimes via emails sent in between) teachers offered richly detailed accounts of their experience and thoughtful reflections on the meaning of the pandemic for teachers, their students, and public education more broadly. It was not uncommon for interviews to last ninety minutes or more and each round of surveys produced a response rate of 97 percent. Teachers' participation in the study over more than two years resulted in an extensive corpus of data that enables us to examine the significance of the pandemic for the teaching profession and public schooling.

A Foundation in Prior Research on Teachers' Work

We situated the study in research on the teaching profession, the teacher workforce, the organizational and policy contexts of teachers' work, and teachers' professional identities and career trajectories, with emphasis on the conditions that shape attraction to the profession, support or limit teacher development, and bear on teacher satisfaction and commitment. That body of research speaks to the conditions that enable teachers to pursue school improvement and instructional innovation, cope with major policy shifts, or respond effectively to exogenous shocks like natural disasters.[46] It provided a foundation for questions regarding teachers' pandemic experiences and their consequences for teachers' professional identity, sense of efficacy, and career commitment. More specifically, prior research on teachers' work attuned us to the likely role of school workplace culture, including the strength or weakness of collegial ties, professional learning resources, school and district leadership, and teacher voice in differentiating teachers' experience of teaching during an extended pandemic.

Based on a large body of research on teachers' school-based professional relationships, we anticipated that teachers whose prepandemic workplace culture was marked by strong, improvement-oriented collegial norms and practices would be able—even at a distance—to rely on school-based colleagues for information, ideas, and social support. We further expected, based on advances in the study of teacher networks, that teachers whose professional connections extended to groups and networks beyond the school would be better positioned to seek out instructional resources and social support than teachers whose relationships were more insular. We judged that districts and schools with a well-developed professional development infrastructure and existing investments in technology would be best positioned to help with the rapid pivot to remote teaching but also expected—based on decades of research on professional development—that schools would vary widely with respect to teachers' access to professional learning opportunities that they considered both timely and responsive to their interests. Finally, prior research speaks consistently to the significance of district and school leadership in sustaining or eroding teachers' engagement and commitment. We expected that teachers who could count on clear and timely communication, sensitivity to issues of workload, access to meaningful professional development and other supports, and inclusion in decision-making would be more likely to remain engaged with and committed to teaching. Considering the likely significance of workplace conditions in a time of crisis, we feared that those who lacked such supports, including effective and responsive leadership, would be especially vulnerable to stress, disengagement, and burnout.[47]

Altogether, we anticipated that the conditions in which teachers worked before and during the pandemic would significantly affect the degree to which they were satisfied with their jobs and motivated to continue in teaching. Taking account of prior research, we asked these questions: In what ways might previously well-documented relationships between workplace conditions and teacher workforce outcomes persist or change at a time of unprecedented disruption in the ordinary structures and routines of teaching, learning, and schooling? How might those relationships vary by context? How might the experience of teaching in and through crisis inform future policies and practices in ways that could bolster the professional standing of the teaching profession and strengthen the ability of teachers to achieve success both in times of calm and times of crisis?

Together, the available body of research on teachers' work and the teaching profession, together with conceptual and empirical research on crises and disasters, guided our investigation of teachers' work in the context of an extended pandemic. What adaptations or innovations were teachers able to make—or constrained from making—in contending with pandemic teaching? What working conditions sustained and supported teachers' sense of efficacy, or eroded it, as schools and communities grappled with an extended pandemic and recovery? How and to what extent did teachers' experience of teaching during a pandemic stimulate new career plans and decisions?

LEARNING FROM TEACHERS

The chapters that follow draw on the narratives that teachers provided through interviews and surveys, supplemented by documentary evidence derived from news accounts and from official pronouncements and regulations. Together, these sources supply the evidence for five key findings that then serve as the basis for our thinking about postpandemic changes.

First, teachers, as emergent actors, adapted quickly and creatively in the face of crisis, drawing on their professional knowledge, skill, and judgment and on their individual and collective initiative to pivot to remote teaching. Chapter 2, The Face of Pandemic Teaching, portrays the work teachers did to manage the early disruption of school closures, to adapt to changing circumstances over the following weeks and months, and to wrestle with new challenges as schools, districts, and communities pursued a return to normal.

Second, the pandemic teaching experience took a toll on teachers' enthusiasm for teaching and their career commitment. Those who left—and some who stayed—spoke to their realization that teaching lacked the kinds of institutional supports needed to help them reap the rewards of classroom teaching. Yet after two years of pandemic-era teaching, some teachers could be deemed "satisfied stayers." Chapter 3, Career Commitment in and

Through Crisis, traces the career trajectories that unfolded over the course of two years, detailing whether, how, and why the pandemic led teachers to change or maintain their career perspectives and plans.

Together, chapters 2 and 3 invite an investigation of the landscape of risk and resilience that affected teachers' career stances and decisions. That landscape included large-scale system responses to the pandemic, the local community, district, and school contexts in which teachers worked and the degree to which and means by which they were able to exercise voice and influence.

In a third key finding, system-level responses created significant and shifting conditions for teachers' work. Following a briefly unified response in mid-March 2020, when the president's announcement of a national health emergency drove school closures in all fifty states, system-level responses at the national, state, and district level quickly fragmented in ways that strongly affected teachers. Chapter 4, The Significance of System Responses, focuses especially on the growing significance of state-level messaging and decision-making as the pandemic and pandemic responses evolved in the weeks and months following widespread school closures.

The fourth finding centers on the influence of local working conditions, demonstrating the importance of workload and workplace culture in teachers' career perspectives and decision-making. Chapter 5, The Power of the Local, delves into the powerful influence of local working conditions on how teachers experienced pandemic-era teaching. The chapter highlights the importance of workload, workplace relationships, and district and school leadership to teachers' engagement with teaching and to their career plans and perspectives.

Finally, the study underscores the place of teacher voice in teachers' satisfaction with their work. Chapter 6, The Value of Teacher Voice, reports the generally limited voice and influence that teachers experienced as districts and schools planned for reopening, while also noting the role of union advocacy, grassroots organizing, and locally constructed avenues for voice where they existed. The chapter makes the case for the importance of teacher voice to teachers' satisfaction with the plans and processes established for reopening schools.

The five data-based chapters form the basis of two concluding chapters. Chapter 7, The Great Realization, synthesizes the study's overall findings and connects those findings to teachers' new occupational perspectives and to prior research on conditions of organizational commitment. It offers insights and implications into the relationship among policy context, working conditions, and teacher exit, voice, and loyalty. Chapter 8, Supporting and Sustaining a Crisis-Ready Profession, imagines an ecology of a teaching profession well prepared and well supported both to pursue the multiple and ambitious goals often expressed in official pronouncements *and* to adapt skillfully, creatively, and effectively in the face of crisis.

Going the Distance portrays the many challenges that teachers encountered over more than two years of contending with a crisis of long duration but also pays tribute to the professional expertise and adaptability that teachers demonstrated. Those who left and those who would like to leave underscore the cost of low public regard and weak working conditions—made especially visible in a crisis—to teacher commitment. For those teachers, the image of the fragile teapot seems apt, a fragility rooted in the structural conditions of their work. Teachers who were satisfied to stay, even after the added stress of a pandemic, highlight the conditions of professional respect and support that enable teachers to reap the rewards of teaching in ordinary times and to respond effectively in a time of crisis. Those supportive conditions, more akin to a sturdy teapot, require policies and practices that value and acknowledge teachers as professionals and that supply them with the resources to do the job well.

Going the Distance is ultimately a hopeful book. The seventy-five teachers whose narratives populate the text offer clear guidance for policy and practice. Their stories point to the importance of public messaging geared toward responsible and respected professionals, manageable workloads and reasonable work-life balance, high-quality instructional resources, a collaborative workplace culture, timely and responsive professional learning opportunities, well-prepared and effective leadership, positive parent and community relationships, productive avenues for teacher voice, and decent compensation. Supplying those conditions, we argue, offers the strongest assurance of a teacher workforce prepared to go the distance.

2

The Face of Pandemic Teaching

For students and teachers throughout the United States, mid-March 2020 marked the start of a massive and unprecedented disruption as school districts everywhere moved to respond to pandemic-related fear, challenge, and loss: loss of life, as the death toll rose from virus transmission; loss of public trust; and loss of the comfort of familiar patterns of daily life. In education, that loss was felt most acutely in the disruption to the daily life of schools: the energy of classroom activity, informal exchanges among teachers in hallways and staff rooms, after-school social and sporting events, and the visible presence of school leaders. Announcements of school building closures were understandably ambiguous about next steps, but all were clear that school would suddenly look vastly different.

As detailed in chapter 1, emergent crisis behaviors include on-the-ground responses by the people closest to the impact. Early in the pandemic, teachers were among those "first responders" as they worked to assess local needs and locate displaced students in an exercise of virtual search and rescue. Teachers reached out to students, established routines, built networks, used new technologies, and rebuilt teaching from the ground up. When pandemic-modified schooling extended from that first spring into one full school year and then another, teachers adapted to shifting instructional modalities, varied safety protocols, changes in student engagement, and a plethora of new policies, systems, and structures.

Pandemic teaching evolved from the initial disruption to the many adaptations teachers made throughout modified schooling in 2020–2021 to the nearly universal return to in-person schooling in the 2021–2022 school year. The daily lives of teachers, the dilemmas they faced, and the solutions they implemented made visible the realities of pandemic teaching.

DISRUPTED: SPRING 2020

Teachers didn't just leave classrooms in spring 2020; they also left behind the school schedule, attendance requirements, curriculum expectations, familiar instructional routines, grading practices, and state assessments. In most places, teachers were tasked with figuring out how to keep students connected with the school, what and how to teach, and often even when to teach. A job centered in the intense, interactive space of the classroom was transformed overnight into a desk-based job done in isolation from home. And its central preoccupations changed overnight as well.

Care, Contact, and Connection

As in most emergencies, the early days were characterized by an emphasis on survival. An ethic of care predominated, as teachers' first undertaking was to establish contact with students, confirm their safety, and determine the family's needs for food and technology support. Elementary school teacher Nella Worth was in her second year of teaching in spring 2020.[1] Her large urban district in Texas prioritized meeting families' basic needs first and then addressing infrastructure for remote learning. She explained, "We had a week of 'just contact families,' so the district would say, 'What's important is your safety and your health.' And [the district] is just so huge but they did a phenomenal job at distributing food. That was their top priority. And then they started distributing technology to kids" (August 2020).

Teachers were asked to maintain regular contact with families and to keep students engaged, sometimes logging contacts on a daily or weekly basis. For example, teachers in a suburban Florida middle school were urged by administrators to "just try to keep the kids engaged, do those Zoom calls. And so it wasn't a learning environment. It was a hold on and stay connected environment." Elementary teacher Jessica Holm in New York City recalled, "Initially it was a big shift from being in the classroom, being in the middle of units, and then being told to forget about academics and just call your families." The shift was easy for a few but difficult for most. For everyone, it was a change in what it meant to be a teacher.

As schools entered into remote learning, districts directed teachers to "give grace." Many established "no harm policies" that made student attendance optional and failing grades prohibited. These constraints, while understood and even supported by most teachers, proved challenging. Taylor Brennan, an Iowa middle school teacher, was in her fourth year of teaching. Her district, like many others, adopted a policy that year-end grades were to be determined solely by classroom performance prior to mid-March. Try as she might, she could not get her students to sign on to Zoom meetings. Exasperated, she sent out a poll to get student feedback and consider what she might do differently to boost participation. Her students assured her, "It's not personal. It has nothing to do with what you're doing." Ms. Brennan understood from the survey that students were not going to attend class voluntarily that spring regardless of what she did to lure them there.

Content, Pedagogy, and Curriculum

Restrictions on new academic content were a prominent component of the no-harm policies established in the first weeks of the shutdown. School leaders attributed this move to students' uneven access to technology and the related stress of the pandemic that might affect student participation and performance. With standardized testing suspended, teachers adapted their curriculum coverage, deciding what was essential and what could be cut. Most teachers (75 percent) introduced some new content, and a few reported introducing all new content.[2] Yet all acknowledged that not all their students—and in some cases very few—accessed that content. A common refrain about new content was that it was "made available" but few students engaged with it. Nearly all teachers, including those who had introduced substantial new content, taught less content than they would have otherwise and made selective decisions about what to prioritize.

Content coverage was also affected by the constraints of remote teaching as teachers cut out material that did not lend itself readily to online instruction. Iowa middle school teacher Judy Aldrich explained that "physical science definitely needs to be taught hands-on instead of something online." Similarly, math teacher Leslie Spark in Florida abandoned a unit she had begun on probability, explaining that "probability was such an abstract concept that I went back to the lead [math] teacher and I said, we're getting nowhere. You know, there were no manipulatives at home." Francisco Vargas, a veteran California math teacher, was known as someone who got students talking together about math, working collaboratively to explore concepts. He tried many ways to sustain his pedagogical commitments to mathematical discourse and student sensemaking. When his efforts faltered, he found himself becoming a talking head on Zoom, focusing on procedures and providing explanations. He lamented, "I got good at exactly the kind of teaching I don't believe in."

Despite these challenges, teaching happened in spring 2020. It didn't look the same as before the pandemic, nor did it look the same everywhere. Teachers found knowledge where they could and as they needed it. A veteran Texas high school science teacher tapped into online teaching networks to develop the skills and knowledge she needed to adapt to online teaching. New instructional practices emerged, like the online guided reading protocol redesigned by Kentucky teacher Nancy Walsh. Committed to ensuring her kindergarten students would not lose ground in their emergent reading skills and despite her complete newness to Zoom, Ms. Walsh modified a strategy that typically requires a teacher sitting with four or five students around a small table. It wasn't easy but she made it work by collaborating with a classroom assistant to rotate students through virtual stations using Zoom's breakout room function. A seventh-grade team of teachers in Texas launched a weekly two-hour trivia game based on the curriculum to lure their students into their previously empty Zoom classrooms.

Long Days, Desk Jobs, and Blurred Boundaries

Teachers reported longer and intensified workdays: not merely working more but also adjusting to the novel demands of pandemic teaching with the associated stress of a world health crisis. Like many telecommuters before them have found, working from home often means working all the time. Most teachers (87 percent) had work schedule autonomy and only 40 percent were required to work a set number of daily hours. Still, teachers routinely worked past their previously defined contract day to meet student needs.

Teachers contoured their schedules to students, making themselves available at irregular and extended times. In spring 2020, teaching asynchronously from home, suburban high school science teacher Eve Nowak found the conventional school day meaningless.[3] Students worked online at all hours, including the middle of the night. During traditional school hours, Ms. Nowak posted lessons and graded student work but then was on call well into the evening. She described continually monitoring her phone, iPad, and Google Classroom with a reminder application running so she wouldn't miss a student contact. She ate dinner each night to the sound of pinging alerts but her workday still wasn't done: "After dinner, guess where I am again? I'm back on the computer because I have a kid that can't figure out how to type into a Google Slide. So there I am, five, six o'clock at night and I'm fielding questions from students answering and trying to troubleshoot . . . and that would go on until nine or ten o'clock at night. I'm getting little messages on my phone" (July 2020).

In many ways, Ms. Nowak couldn't imagine doing it any other way. After twenty-two years of teaching in the same school district, living close to New York City, she was aware that many of her students' families were affected by the pandemic. Determined to do all she could to support students, she was also tired, worn down by the unrelenting need.

Many teachers found themselves suddenly working a "desk job" they never expected or wanted. Accustomed to moving all day amid the immediacy of the classroom, they found themselves staring at a computer screen for long hours as they searched for resources, posted lessons, and connected online with students and colleagues. Reports of teaching from kitchen counters and bedrooms, with notes posted warning their families to be quiet, rivaled stories of teaching from closets, garages, and even cars. Lori Perenno set up her remote classroom in her bedroom, the only available space in the Arizona home she shared with her remote-working husband and two school-age children also learning online. She worked closely with her fourth-grade team to tackle the steep learning curve of online teaching. When one struggled with new technology, they would all "hop on Zoom" to figure it out together. Ms. Perenno felt anchored to her computer, as it was the lifeline to her teacher community, the remote classroom for her fourth-grade class, and the means of providing technology tutorials for parents: "It was bad. Stressful. I felt like I was tied to the computer, which I'm not used to."

The disruption of schooling did not end in that spring, but the focus changed over time. As the pandemic stretched into the next school year, attention shifted from mitigating the stressful experience of the shutdown to adapting structures and practices to the changing conditions. New content had to be taught, academic testing was returning, and communities had to figure out how to educate students under the shifting reality of schooling during a pandemic.

Ongoing questions and contentious debates, about child transmission rates and the safety of in-person schooling, added to the uncertainty of the pandemic. School board meetings, traditionally poorly attended, attracted scores of parents queuing up for public comment. Across the country, teachers and parents rallied on issues related to school reopening, instructional modality, and masking. As summer gave way to the beginning of the 2020–2021 school year, teachers tried to prepare for the new school year with few certainties and amid intense community conflict.

ADAPTED: THE 2020–2021 SCHOOL YEAR

A contentious political landscape divided communities in debates about reopening schools. Some who had lauded teachers as heroes in the spring now portrayed them as the obstacles to school reopening, demanding that teachers return to buildings as "essential workers." Even as COVID-19 numbers surged in fall 2020, media accounts opined that schools were not major sources of spread and urged schools to open and remain in-person.[4]

Exhausted from pandemic disruptions yet feeling more confident with the experience and knowledge they had developed, teachers looked to the new school year for stability and continuity but found little in the way of predictability or familiar routines. Remote teachers faced a computer screen "sea of blank boxes," with few of their students turning on their cameras and many disengaged. Those teaching in person navigated COVID-19 mitigation strategies, quarantining students, and learning to teach with a new set of protocols and restrictions. In person or remotely, schools struggled with student attendance, well-being, and ongoing fluctuations in plans.

No classroom looked as it had prior to the pandemic, and all teachers—whether remote, in-person, or hybrid—worked to modify their instructional practice. A few fortunate teachers had the whole of 2020–2021 to hone their new knowledge and skill in one modality. But most teachers adapted over and over again as their schools rode the waves of virus surges and navigated numerous shifts among in-person, hybrid, and online teaching (see figure 2.1). Being ever poised to pivot was a defining feature of that tumultuous school year and pivot they did. Only 11 percent (8) of project teachers taught in schools that maintained a single mode of schooling, 57 percent (40) experienced one to three changes in school instructional configuration, while 31 percent (22) taught in schools that shifted modes from four to nine times. Some teachers started the school year remotely then shifted to in person or hybrid when their school started to bring students back to campus. Others who started fully in person experienced shifts to remote or hybrid, often necessitated by spiking virus transmission rates or related absenteeism.

These modality changes intensified and added uncertainty to teachers' work lives. Teachers were on high alert for the next change. In some places, unions negotiated a planning day for teachers before each teaching modality change. For others, the change often arrived without warning and allowed little preparation time. While shifting modalities exacerbated the

Figure 2.1 Number of school instructional mode changes, 2020–2021 (N=70)

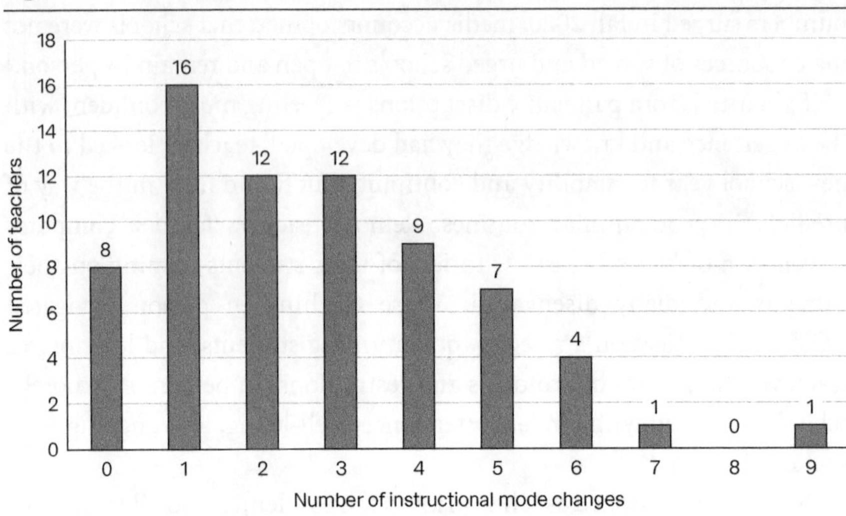

challenges of adapting instructional practice, each modality required adaptation from both the spring 2020 pandemic teaching experience and prepandemic norms; teachers were still building the classroom as they taught in it.

The Evolution of Remote Teaching

Most teachers began the 2020–2021 school year more experienced with teaching in a remote context.[5] All but a few had by then used online platforms like Zoom, and even those who were limited to an asynchronous model were accustomed to meetings on a virtual platform. But online teaching changed significantly that fall. The new school year resumed with a swift return to schooling structures that were put on hold in the spring. It was expected that content instruction would resume and the no-harm policies that characterized schooling in the spring would be discontinued. It was common for the regular bell schedule to be used, with only a five-minute "passing period" between Zoom classes. Teachers and students were expected to start the school year as if it were any other; they may not be in buildings, but school was back in session.

That fall, fourth-year Oregon high school teacher Noelle Cruz was starting her school year online. While she agreed with Oregon's state guidance and her school district's decision to remain remote until COVID-19 cases declined and a vaccine was available, she desperately missed being in class with her students. Identifying as a teacher of color with strong ties to her rural community, Ms. Cruz was drawn into teaching to make a difference in the lives of her Latino students: "I didn't feel seen in high school, so the equity work and just making sure that every kid can just be themselves as they walk through the door, it's really what fires my work." But making connections with students proved very difficult through a computer. In her five synchronous online sections of ninth-grade English language arts, Ms. Cruz found that few students would turn on their cameras. She taught her classes staring at "thirty-six blank boxes with their names below. And you're like, 'Hello, hello? Are you there?' It's like that. That feels like my life." Close relationships with her students proved elusive in this digital and distancing domain. Pre-COVID, she shared, teaching was "part of my heart," but now teaching was breaking her heart.

Attempts to reestablish "normal" schooling was a common response to the uncertainty and disruption that characterized the initial pandemic response in March 2020. Returning to a remote school day that looked more like a traditional school day was one way to get schooling back on track. Unlike spring 2020, during the 2020–2021 school year almost all remote teachers taught synchronous online classes.[6] For some teachers, like suburban Oregon elementary school teacher Imani Johnson, this meant that they were logged into their remote classrooms with their students for the entire school day. Ms. Johnson told the parents of her fourth graders, "You just need to get them signed in online in the morning, and we will take it from there."

Fall 2020 synchronous instruction was very different from the synchronous instruction of the spring. Spring synchronous classes looked like the Fun Fridays when California special education teacher Liz Darcie toured her students through her home garden or the lively games of Kahoot! that Leanne Edwards and her colleagues organized to attract their middle school students to remote class meetings. In fall 2020, remote synchronous teachers were teaching grade-level content to new cohorts of students after months of disruption. This required ongoing development of online teaching methods and approaches while contending with the Zoom fatigue that accompanied a full teaching day logged on to a computer.[7]

In summer 2020, when asked about her return preference for the upcoming school year, high school English teacher Casey Wright was conflicted. Living in an urban center in Northern California that was experiencing a COVID-19 spike, she worried about colleagues in high-risk groups and their exposure to the virus. Yet she really didn't want a repeat of the spring 2020 remote teaching experience. She explained, "It was just so hard last year that I was like, ugh, no. I just don't want to do this again." When the district announced an all-remote opening with a forecast of remaining remote until numbers declined or there was a vaccine, she leaned into the challenge, adapting her highly interactive teaching strategies for a remote context. Still, she missed her students, not knowing what some of them looked like because they wouldn't turn on their cameras in her Zoom classroom. By March 2021, Ms. Wright reported feeling "much better" about her remote teaching because she was "still doing things that are intellectually stimulating—having interesting discussions, Socratic seminars, even some acting, while discussing big ideas." Reflecting back on the year in June 2021, she said, "Despite the distances created by teaching on Zoom, I forged some really lovely relationships with students and feel like I still kept the core values of my pedagogy." Ms. Wright's perseverance at adapting her instructional practice resulted in a satisfying year for her and academic learning for her students despite pandemic disruptions.

In-Person Teaching: Back in the Classroom but Far from Normal

Jennifer Donegal, a Florida elementary teacher, started the 2020–2021 school year teaching entirely in person.[8] All summer she worried about how to reduce her family's virus exposure while teaching. After much deliberation, Ms. Donegal and her husband decided one of them should stay home to keep their three-year-old out of day care. As their health-care insurance came from her teaching job, they decided Ms. Donegal would keep teaching. While the plan made sense, she worried about the logistics of masking fourth graders, sustaining three feet of spacing, and not bringing the virus home despite the close daily contact with twenty-five ten-year-olds in a school community of six hundred.[9] To her relief, her fourth graders adjusted to COVID-19 safety protocols and "from the outside, things appear[ed] almost normal." More challenging was reconciling safety mitigation protocols with her teaching style: clustering students to work in groups, to share materials, and to collaborate on projects was impossible to do given the safety protocols. Describing the aspect of teaching she felt least satisfied with that fall, Ms. Donegal reported, "It's impossible to be a good teacher from three feet away."

While in-person teaching might seem like the closest thing to "normal" teaching, it required significant adaptations and posed distinct dilemmas for teachers. Teachers worked to make adjustments that would adhere to safety protocols while still engaging students in meaningful learning. Classrooms formerly organized in collaborative groups with shared materials were restructured with masked students facing forward in rows using their own set of nonshareable math manipulatives or markers. Although teachers were happy to be reunited with their students and were reminded of the relational rewards of teaching, very little of the 2020–2021 school year felt normal. Jane Farley, a high school teacher in New York, acknowledged that safety protocols were comforting, but they also dampened the joy she usually witnessed among her students as they came in masked and silent. Her once-bustling classroom was quiet and distant, not a scenario she was accustomed to in her six years of teaching. In Iowa, Ruth Cartwright's history students were reluctant to talk to each other. Ms. Cartwright said, "It's so quiet. It's like these masks are a barrier. The kids don't look at each other. They don't talk."

Jennifer Donegal also faced the dilemma of how to engage students safely within the parameters of safety protocols, but she resolved it by prioritizing her preferred teaching methods over the safety protocols. She described needing to choose between "being a good teacher" and "being a good citizen." In the beginning of the year, she worked hard to keep students socially distanced. She kept students in rows and prohibited shared materials. But as the year wore on her resolve diminished: "So my instruction had to change because I was just like, I just can't do this. I'm going back to the pre-pandemic ways. So now my kids work in small groups, and I pass out papers, and I collect papers. So, in the sense of instruction, it's exactly what it was pre-pandemic because I can't, I can't teach that (socially distanced) way" (December 2020).

Ms. Donegal faced a choice: "There's the me that's just a citizen living through the pandemic and trying to do what we need to do and trying to follow the rules and stop the spread. And then there's the me that's the teacher and I need to do what's best for my kids." Faced with that choice, she decided her dedication to being a teacher was more important; she taught the way she believed she should and did what she could to make sure she and her students were safe.

The Multiple Meanings of Hybrid Teaching

Florida high school social studies teacher Sarah Weaver was told the 2020–2021 school year would start hybrid, but exactly what that meant was unclear. Initially she was assigned to teach two versions of each class, an online version and an in-person version. This setup required that she shift between modalities from one period to another, with students enrolled in one version or the other. Just as the school year started, her school adopted a different form of hybrid. In this new form, all of Ms. Weaver's classes were populated with both in-person and remote students together synchronously. This rapid pivot was followed by a juggling act that even the most seasoned teacher would find daunting. To reach students at home and in class, Ms. Weaver had at least three devices going at all times. She synced a desktop computer with the smartboard for dual-mode slide projection. She used her school laptop to watch for student emails and her personal laptop to interact remotely with students through Microsoft Teams. Blending at home and in-person students together in the same class was challenging. It was "not ideal," but it was also "the reality right now," so she soldiered on, "trying to do the best [she could]."

After twenty years in the classroom, she learned new tools like Jamboard to keep her high school students engaged. In November 2020, when asked what aspect of teaching she felt most satisfied with, Ms. Weaver replied, "nothing."

Hybrid teaching was a common school mitigation strategy employed in pandemic modified schooling. Many saw it as a middle ground solution, providing families with options to remain remote or to go partly or fully in person. Hybrid schooling, however, was far from uniform.[10] We found it useful to have subcategories to capture the variation in hybrid models. Throughout, we refer to these as parallel, alternating, and blended. Parallel hybrid maintained two offerings made up of different groups of students and teachers, one online and one in-person. In parallel hybrid, teachers taught in just one mode. Alternating hybrid required teachers to plan for two distinct instructional modes and adapt their instruction for both in-person and remote students but never at the same time. Blended hybrid mixed remote and in-person students into the same classes, requiring the teacher to teach in both modalities simultaneously. Teaching in-person and remotely required different pedagogical approaches. Teachers assigned either an alternating or a blended mode described working "double-time," needing to adapt their lessons for two contexts. While both alternating and blended hybrid intensified teachers' work, blended hybrid demanded far more from teachers—often more than they could give. As Texas chemistry teacher Claire Macalister put it, blended hybrid was "the worst" by far. "Because the teacher can't be doing both, they just can't. They physically cannot do it. You're going to burn them out, and I'm not talking a little burnt out. I'm talking quitting and never coming back."

A common adaptation for teachers teaching in a blended hybrid model was to focus on the in-person students in the classroom and post asynchronous work for the students who were remote. Chelsea Doyle and her colleagues in rural Kentucky tried to spread their attention to both groups of students simultaneously but quickly abandoned this as it was "absolute chaos." The remote students couldn't hear her instructions, so she was constantly shifting between working solely with either group. Exhausted and frustrated, she and her colleagues regrouped and decided something had to change. They ended up meeting with their remote students during homeroom, assigning them asynchronous work, and then leaving them to complete the work independently. Although this adjustment mediated the teachers' workload and stress, academic coverage for their students was significantly reduced: "The virtual kids? We just cut out a bunch for them. When we realized that it wasn't going to work with us being on the same page, we all just sat down and said, 'OK, what do my kids absolutely have to be able to [do to] move on to the next class or move on to next year?' So I cut out a lot of stuff that I had my in-person kids do that was good and helped them but I just didn't make my virtual kids do the same" (December 2020).

Frustration with the hybrid model was exacerbated by some teachers' lack of input into modality selection and systemic inattention to the workload issues and student learning limitations. Arizona teacher Cora Donner, frustrated with the lack of consultation, pointed out, "Had they asked a teacher, we could have told them it just wasn't going to work." In some states, unions negotiated protections in collective bargaining agreements. In the lead-up to the 2020–2021 school year, Imani Johnson reported, "Our union is at the table bargaining a lot of things [about the proposed hybrid model]. And one of the things is it feels all of a sudden like maybe we have 1.5 or 2 jobs."

That first full year of pandemic teaching is best characterized as a year of uncertainty, change, and adaptation. Whether in-person, remote, or some form of hybrid, classrooms were hardly recognizable from their pre-COVID form. Adapting to the changing educational landscape intensified teachers' work in complexity, working hours, and workload. At the end of that school year, 68 percent of teachers reported overwork and exhaustion as a significant challenge, and more than half experienced a diminished sense of success and increased cynicism about being a teacher.

In addition to instructional challenges and adaptations, teachers also struggled with a growing sense of estrangement from their communities. Feelings of being connected in a common endeavor, focused on surviving a global pandemic, were replaced with a sense of alienation. Janet Featherstone in Florida described the sense of "one for all and all for one" in the spring being replaced by mounting political tensions about schools reopening and debates about mask mandates. Teacher Leanne Edwards in Texas commented, "I've left every single one of my social media accounts. I just can't stand to see how people are talking about teachers." Pandemic teaching had taken a toll on teachers in almost every way imaginable, and it wasn't over.

But the end of the 2020–2021 school year also offered hope. By then, all project teachers had access to the vaccine, 84 percent were vaccinated, and most schools anticipated in-person teaching reopening that fall. Teachers were exhausted, but they also looked forward to a summer of rest and then what might feel more like the schooling of prepandemic days.

RESUMED: THE 2021–2022 SCHOOL YEAR

The second year of pandemic teaching, 2021–2022, looked and felt more familiar. Almost everyone was back in person, students could interact more freely, and most teachers were once again using their preferred methods.[11] Teachers felt better about their teaching and welcomed the resumption of traditional structures of schooling. Californian elementary school teacher Linnea Harris celebrated "making in-person connections with students, after fifteen months of remote learning, and seeing students bond with their friends again" as the most satisfying aspect of her year. Teachers were proud of the growth they saw in their students and proud of their successes. Connections with students, both relationally and academically, restored teachers' enjoyment of teaching.

However, while teaching was returning to familiar structures and routines, teachers continued to struggle with the demands of pandemic teaching. To the surprise of many, that school year was harder than the year before. Sixty-one percent of teachers reported more stress, and the majority were still working beyond prepandemic workloads. Overwork and increased stress took a toll on teachers' well-being and efficacy: two-thirds of teachers continued to feel a diminished sense of success as a teacher and half felt increased cynicism about being a teacher. This led to a lot of questioning about purpose, goals, and priorities. So much was resumed: students and teachers were back in buildings, sports programs and other activities had been reinstated, Zoom cameras were no longer an issue. But so much was also changed: talk of learning loss was everywhere, substitute teachers were in short supply, students were unfocused, and anxiety issues figured prominently in classroom interactions, while expectations of teachers were high. Teachers were both relieved to have resumed normal schooling and yet increasingly aware that the challenges of pandemic teaching were not resolved.

Reunited with Students

Restored relationships with students and a return to teaching practices gave teachers a glimpse into what recovery from the prior year and a half could mean. For Claire Macalister, connections with her students and the enjoyment of classroom teaching sustained her through the pandemic. When asked in summer 2022 how she made it through the pandemic still feeling positive about teaching, Ms. Macalister responded, "I think the biggest thing is that my students thank me every day. My kids will say, 'Hey, Ms. M. This was really cool today.'" The beginning of the new school year reminded her of the reason she became a teacher: "Like I watched it today. This was my twenty-second first day of school and I call it buy-in. I can tell when kids buy in. They start participating. They put down their phones. They start listening, they start talking to each other. They smile. They relax."

Fall 2021 saw teachers back in closer contact with their students, restoring their enjoyment in the small moments that make teaching enjoyable. Carl Graham, an Oregon elementary school teacher was happy to reinstate "Star of the Week," a routine that helped him build community in his elementary classroom. Emily Kline, a science teacher in Massachusetts, started the 2021–2022 school year worried about teaching Anatomy, a course she had only taught once before. But it turned out to be her favorite class of the year because of her students' enthusiasm: "The kids were just really, really fun, a great group. They were all friendly with each other and we were able to laugh and joke around but still also get stuff done." After almost a full year of remote teaching, she was happy to be "in front of bodies who could actually be sitting next to each other or near each other, to be able to see group work and interpersonal relations happen." Francisco Vargas was relieved "not to have to beg them to turn their cameras on" and was "just happy to be in the same room with students," able to work in his math classroom in ways that felt familiar. Don Granger in Texas was relieved that attendance in his class was back to normal and attributed that to his methods for teaching literature in person. "Students like my class. I'm very energetic, charismatic, and active in the classroom. At the end of *Hamlet*, I'm bruised all over because I die every time someone dies. It's just that kind of fun thing. There's a lot of discussion in my room again that they get to take part in as we go through the literature and make meaningful connections with them" (July 2022).

Resumed relationships with students had both relational and pedagogical benefits for teachers who had struggled throughout the pandemic with low student engagement and strained connections.

Normal Structures and Expectations

The rewards of connections with students were countered by pressures to return to a prepandemic norm of schooling that nonetheless felt out of reach. Getting "back to normal" meant a return to accountability pressures and instructional interventions. These initiatives added to teachers' workloads and denied the lasting implications of the pandemic. For Jennifer Donegal, this translated to a pacing guide for her fourth-grade students that did not take into account their disrupted previous year. Carla Morrison, a Massachusetts elementary teacher, had to cope with the implementation of new academic assessments and testing protocols. Ms. Morrison attributed her increased stress to the unexpected introduction of a new math diagnostic program in fall 2021. Without warning, and with only a two-hour professional development session, teachers were expected to transition immediately to the new system. Similarly, an Arizona school district launched new standards-based report cards in that fall. Cora Donner explained that a group of teachers implored district leadership to hold off on the implementation; their concerns fell on deaf ears as the district moved forward with the new report card with minimal implementation support for teachers. Returning to normal without recognizing the toll the pandemic had taken left teachers feeling frustrated and their efforts for the past year unappreciated.

Resumed and sometimes expanded accountability pressures were compounded by the social and emotional toll that the pandemic had also taken on students. Teachers were eager to help students but often found the push to get students "up to grade level" ignored or gave cursory attention to students' needs and the consequences of the pandemic for students' academic and social-emotional development. High school teacher Sarah Weaver remarked, "Last year, for students who had been out of school for a year and a half, sometimes more, it was just, 'back to normal.' You're going to get tested, tested, tested, tested." This pressure was felt across all grade levels. Nancy Walsh had taught in the same school for her entire career, giving her a unique perspective for considering differences in student behavior. Her kindergarten students did not know how to engage in the classroom, absenteeism was high, and behavior problems occurred daily; the level of student need far surpassed anything she had experienced in her twenty-one years of teaching. Addressing these needs had to precede any substantive learning, but Ms. Walsh felt pressed to keep pace with a prepandemic pacing guide that did not address this new reality.

Meredith Nathan, a Massachusetts middle school teacher, taught special education students in a self-contained classroom. Ms. Nathan was used to modifying instructional materials for her students and, after twenty-one years of teaching, was normally able to make pacing adjustments to keep up with district expectations. But it wasn't a normal year, and her already high-need students had even higher needs in the that school year. Her school added more benchmark testing, and when she tried to accelerate instruction to keep up with district demands, her students "wouldn't act out but would tell [me] in different ways, 'Oh, you're pushing me too hard' or 'You're going too fast' or 'I'm not ready for this.' " She felt caught in the middle between administrators who were saying, "Keep up, do this, do this, do this," and students who were telling her, "I'm not okay. I'm not ready yet. I'm not here yet." This pressure was exacerbated by lack of support. Her district lost a special education administrator, and a shortage of paraprofessionals "made everything harder because I didn't have the support systems that I was used to." Ms. Nathan ended the year declaring it the hardest of her twenty-one-year career in teaching.

A New Normal for Teachers

Some teachers indicated that the experience of pandemic-era teaching shifted their priorities and practices in notable ways, offering pandemic lessons for a "new normal." For many, digital tools were now an integrated aspect of their teaching, an impressive feat given that at the beginning of the pandemic 49 percent of project teachers reported no experience with online teaching and only 3 percent reported substantial experience.[12] Claire Macalister, previously technology averse, created an interactive digital notebook by collaborating with a colleague she met in a Facebook group formed during the pandemic. Ms. Macalister was certain the notebooks would become a permanent addition to her instructional repertoire.

Both pedagogical and practical rationales drove changes in teachers' practice. Learning management systems were now de rigueur; teachers used them to track grades, organize lessons, communicate with classes, and keep absent students connected to the classroom. Judy Aldrich developed instructional video production skills during remote teaching and used those skills to "flip" her classroom once back in person, posting lectures online for students to watch for homework so that class time could be used for hands-on lab work. Kindergarten teacher Nancy Walsh did not see much use for virtual tools with her young students but did plan on using Chromebooks more regularly and ensuring students and families could log into Google Classroom "in case we have to quarantine."

The experience of navigating the challenges of the pandemic also brought teachers' core values and priorities into clear focus, especially around the importance of building relationships with students, families, and colleagues. California teacher Summer Diaz planned to continue the parent newsletters she instituted with the families of her middle school students and anticipated continuing to use the communication apps she had relied on to reach parents. Teachers described a heightened commitment to community building and more awareness of students' social and emotional wellbeing. Florida teacher Sarah Weaver described a "seismic shift" to her teaching philosophy from being a rigid stickler for deadlines to a teacher who led with connection:

> It's taught me to be more accepting. Because I used to be, "This is the day it's due and it's ten percent off every day after you turn it in." And I just don't care anymore. I mean, I care that the student turns in the work but I'm much accepting. "If something's going on, just send me an email and we'll work it out." So, I used to care—of course I cared about my student and the relationship we had. But I was like, "You've still got to do that work." But now, I'm more like, "How are you?" before we even get to the work part. (August 2022)

Collegial relationships and the power of teacher teams also took center stage. Lori Perenno had always appreciated having a group of colleagues that she got along with but the pandemic moved collaboration from a nice "extra" to a core part of her teaching, "The planning piece—the way we lay everything out and work on it together. I told my team at the end of the year, 'We can't change this.' That's been a good thing from COVID, definitely." Teachers who attributed their survival of the pandemic to the support they received from their colleagues reported "never going back" to more independent or self-reliant modes of teaching. The relational work of teaching—with students and with colleagues—was cemented as a priority in postpandemic teaching.

THE ADDITIONAL CHALLENGES FOR PARENTING TEACHERS

School closures during spring 2020, and disruptions to in-person schooling throughout the pandemic, took a devastating toll on working parents. With the elimination of childcare for young children and the move to distance learning for school-age children, working parents found themselves juggling the demands of their jobs with the needs of their children without any of the customary supports. Numerous accounts during the pandemic shared an unsurprising truth: working parents were stressed, and the burden of working the first and second shift simultaneously fell disproportionately to working mothers.[13] Challenges faced by working mothers are particularly salient in teaching, a profession that is largely female and historically considered "family friendly." But the rules changed in March 2020. Teaching became difficult to sustain for working parents as schedules conflicted, boundaries between home and work dissolved, and workloads multiplied.

Thirty-one of the seventy-five teachers had school-age children living at home during the pandemic (41 percent). Challenges were compounded for the nearly one-third of parenting teachers with children under five and the 16 percent with special-needs children. Similar to the demographics of the US teacher workforce, most of the parenting teachers were women (84 percent). During the spring 2020 school closures, almost all parenting teachers had a partner or spouse also working remotely from home but less than a quarter of those partners shared the responsibility of caring for children or overseeing their schooling.[14] Parenting teachers were mostly on their own to navigate the overlap of work and home life.

Variation in teaching demands had a significant influence on the experiences of parenting teachers. In some cases, teachers were afforded the latitude to make their own logistical decisions about their teaching schedules. For example, teachers who could decide if and when to hold synchronous class meetings could schedule teaching and childcare responsibilities around one another. This was the case for Arizona teacher Fred Marino, who was one of the few teachers whose spouse was not working remotely. Because his husband was an essential worker, Mr. Marino was solely responsible for childcare during the day for their two special-needs children. To meet both his family needs and teaching responsibilities, Mr. Marino organized his classes asynchronously, planning and posting lessons at night for his high school chemistry students. This type of flexibility was common that first spring; of thirty-one parenting teachers, twenty-four reported having flexibility to organize their teaching day as they saw fit. While this made teaching while parenting logistically possible, it also created the conditions for overwork and exhaustion.[15]

Not all teachers had such schedule flexibility in the early days of the pandemic, and almost none had it in the fall. Forced to choose between teaching their students and supervising their own children's education, parenting teachers made uncomfortable compromises. Iowa high school teacher Rachel Larsen shared that she felt "deep guilt" over prioritizing her students' needs and her teaching work over the learning needs and supervision of her own school-age children: "The biggest problem was not a loss for my school kids as it was for my own kids with just not having much supervision. You know, they played a lot of video games. They didn't get assistance from me just because I'm a teacher. It was kind of like, 'Good luck. You know? I've got all this stuff (to do). I've got to grade and I've got all these phone calls I've got to make, and I need you to be quiet. So, yes, you may play Minecraft for the next three hours' " (August 2020).

Experience level was no guarantee against stress and remorse. Even parenting teachers with well-established success balancing work and home found it challenging. Imani Johnson had successfully balanced teaching and parenting for thirteen years. She described the dilemma of feeling unsuccessful in both roles: "Feeling horrible as a parent and feeling crappy as a teacher and then there's a pandemic. And I don't want people to get sick."

The stress of parenting and teaching during the pandemic was compounded for parenting teachers and remained an issue into the 2020–2021 school year. Some found themselves managing synchronous remote classes with mounting expectations for themselves and their children. Others struggled to cobble together childcare as they returned to in-person teaching while their children were still remotely learning. In fall 2020, more than half of parenting teachers identified managing distance learning or childcare as a significant challenge, and three in four reported overwork and exhaustion as a challenge. The idea that teaching is a career that allows a healthy balance of work and family life might always have been exaggerated, but during pandemic-modified instruction any semblance of balance was rare and fleeting. Parenting teachers, like all parenting workers, faced greater challenges than nonparenting workers. But unlike most parenting workers, parenting teachers were stretching to care for their own children as well as their students, mostly feeling undersupported in both efforts.

CONCLUSION

The arc of pandemic teaching, from the early closures of schools in March 2020 to the first year of fully resumed teaching in 2021–2022, did not follow a simple bell-curve trajectory from prepandemic routines to disruption and then back to normal. Each new development of the pandemic brought with it unique challenges that demanded new adaptations from teachers. Teachers' dexterity and ease at navigating those challenges—to pivot when necessary—was supported or diminished by the contexts in which they were working. All teachers were expected to adapt their teaching to the rapidly changing conditions, but some were supported more than others. The conditions that teachers encountered—the amount of flexibility they enjoyed, the number of instructional modality changes they endured, the nature of their obligations to work and to family, the resources they could count on, and the extent to which their voices were heard—all had significant bearing on their recovery from crisis and the way in which they came to look at a career in teaching. Teachers' perspectives on being a teacher, together with the decisions they made as the pandemic unfolded or were considering making as the crisis began to wane, form the focus of chapter 3.

for teaching children as well as their students' mostly feeling unsupported in such efforts.

CONCLUSION

The arc of pandemic teaching, from the early closure of schools in March 2020 to the full year of [illegible] remote teaching in 2020–2021, did not follow a simple bell-curve [illegible] from [illegible] routines to disruption and then back to [illegible] development of the pandemic brought with it unique challenges that demanded new adaptations from teachers. Teachers' [illegible] navigating those challenges—[illegible] if necessary—[illegible] supported or [illegible] the [illegible] in which they were working. All teachers were expected to adapt their instruction [illegible] others. The conditions that teachers encountered—the amount of [illegible] the number of [illegible] changes [illegible] of their obligations to work and to family, the resources [illegible] and the extent to which [illegible] in teaching [illegible] being a teacher, together with the decisions they made [illegible]

3

Career Commitment in and Through Crisis

Teaching during the pandemic was challenging for everyone, and yet those challenges affected teachers' careers in different ways. Some teachers found the challenges too much and left the profession. Some stayed in teaching reluctantly while seeking ways to exit, while others stayed because they saw no alternative. A few moved to new schools or districts, seeking more supportive conditions. Yet still others—those we came to call Satisfied Stayers—made it through all the turmoil with their professional commitment intact. For those teachers, the pandemic was disruptive and stressful, but they navigated it like a snowstorm-filled winter: difficult while it lasted, demanding much from them, and leaving damage in its wake. But like all seemingly endless winters, it eventually gave way to the renewal of spring. Two years after the onset of the pandemic, their hearts were still in the work, and they were happy to be teaching again in familiar ways and places. Understanding what made it possible for these teachers to go the distance is as important as understanding what eroded the commitment of others.

Policy makers, educators, and researchers all turned their attention to teacher turnover in the wake of the pandemic, finding evidence in several states that teachers' expressed intention to leave and teacher attrition rose markedly in the 2021–2022 school year.[1] While it is useful to track those metrics, teachers' stories provide insight into career perspectives and decisions that go well beyond retention and attrition statistics. The Leavers' stories illuminate what made teaching intolerable to previously committed teachers. Stories told by Satisfied Stayers—those who were staying by choice and with sustained commitment—highlight teachers' individual and collective capacity to navigate stressful situations, even extreme ones like a lengthy pandemic. And the stories of everyone in between, including the teachers who moved schools in an effort to stay and those who stayed while planning to exit, speak to the personal and professional conditions that shape teachers' attachment to the teaching profession.

CAREER PLANS CHANGED AND UNCHANGED

The pandemic upended the career commitments and plans of forty-three of the seventy-five project teachers, nearly 60 percent. These teachers, all of whom entered the pandemic with long-term intentions to remain, were found at every career stage, grade level, and community type. They successfully endured the disruption of school closures in spring 2020, longed to be back in the classroom, and initially conveyed their intent to remain in teaching. Yet the events of the ensuing weeks and months eroded their commitment, leading some to leave or move and others to wish for a way out. Some responded by leaving the profession, others moved to a new school, and still others stayed on as they planned to pursue career changes.

Nonetheless, the remaining thirty-one project teachers managed teaching during the pandemic without any lasting effects on their intended career path (see figure 3.1).[2] Their long-term career plans remain unchanged by pandemic teaching experiences, although two moved to new schools, one took a scheduled retirement, one left as planned to raise a family, and two stayed only for lack of an alternative. The remaining twenty-five teachers, one-third of the whole sample, taught in the same classrooms from March 2020 through spring 2022 and expressed satisfaction about staying in those classrooms. These are the teachers who stayed the course, teaching through and beyond the pandemic. Their stories

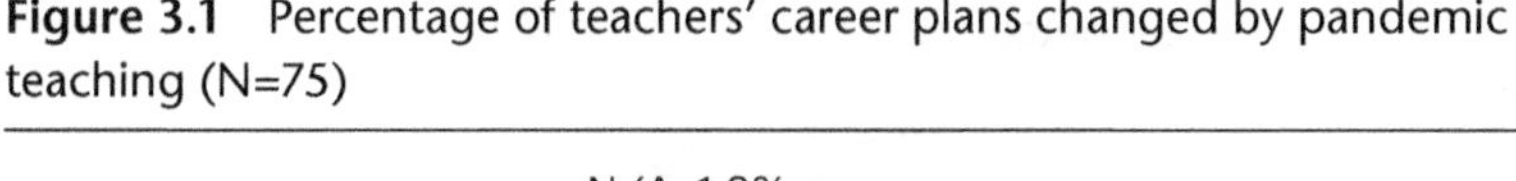

Figure 3.1 Percentage of teachers' career plans changed by pandemic teaching (N=75)

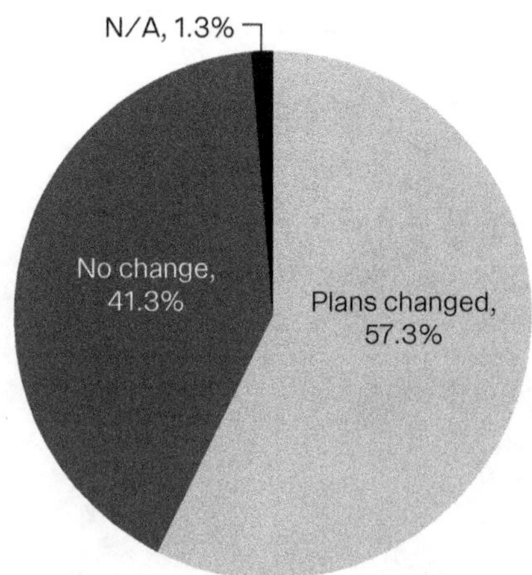

illuminate the capacity to sustain through times of crisis and, as such, have much to inform us as to what it takes to make it through turbulent times.

The sections that follow delve into teachers' stories of leaving, moving, and staying.[3] The stories convey the complex personal and professional circumstances that shaped teachers' career choices as they taught—or tried to teach—in and through crisis. Those complexities surface with special clarity in the distinction that emerges between teachers we term Dissatisfied Stayers and those we designate as Satisfied Stayers. Together, the stories of the Leavers, Movers, Dissatisfied Stayers, and Satisfied Stayers point toward the system and school-level conditions that prove crucial in generating teacher capacity and commitment in ordinary times and capitalizing on them in times of crisis (see figure 3.2).

The Leavers

Fully one-fifth of the project teachers left the teaching profession between summer 2020 and summer 2022. Fears about the health risks associated with COVID-19 and related frustration and anxiety about adequate safety

Figure 3.2 Teacher career outcomes as of summer 2022 (N=75)

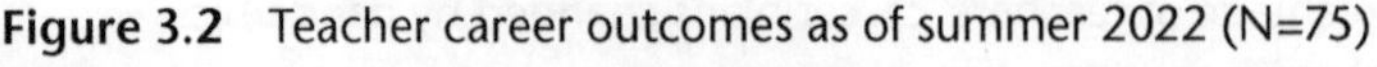

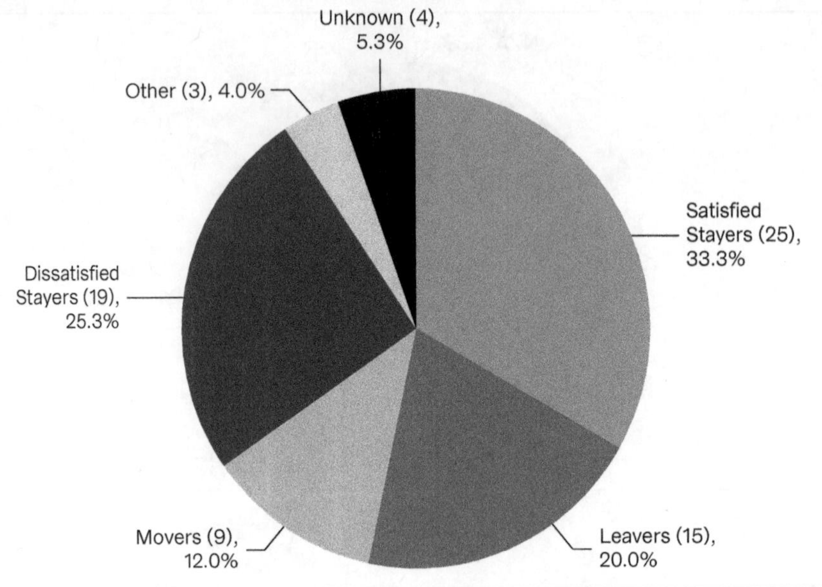

protocols drove the earliest exits, while later departures express a tale of cumulative challenge and exhaustion. Throughout, teachers expressed concerns about trust, respect, and the conditions needed to ensure student learning.

Early Exits: A Matter of Risk and Safety The earliest exits—two teachers in Iowa and one in Florida—reflected teachers' deep concerns over a lack of safety protocols in districts where administrators and school boards pushed hard for an early and full return to in-person teaching. In August 2020, high school chemistry and physics teacher Natalie Lehrer quit her job in rural Iowa after learning of her district's plans for reopening. As a science teacher, Ms. Lehrer was well aware of the health risks and deeply disturbed by what she saw as leaders' lack of concern for teacher safety: "Our district opted to go back face-to-face, 100 percent of the students in the building, with no mask mandate. The school board clarified that teachers were not allowed to make their own classroom rules requiring masking, either. I resigned. My resignation was based entirely on the lack of regard of the school board and superintendent for teacher and staff safety" (Fall 2020).

At the same time, fifteen hundred miles away in Florida, chemistry teacher Sophie Blum resigned for almost identical reasons. With a PhD in microbiology, she had a better understanding than many of epidemiology and public health issues. Dr. Blum decried her urban district's plan to return to school buildings as ill-informed, irresponsible, and unsafe: "It's an airborne virus. The infection rate is very high. If you interpret the data the way it should be interpreted, there is just no other conclusion to come to right now than, at least in Florida, it's irresponsible for our leaders to be pushing us in (to in-person teaching)." Most upsetting to Dr. Blum was the school board's seeming indifference to teachers' concerns, framing teachers as frontline workers who should be prepared to take on a high level of risk.

While Ms. Lehrer and Dr. Blum both quit preemptively and in what each considered a form of public protest against their district's plans, Iowa social studies teacher Rachel Larsen made significant personal sacrifices to teach in person at her rural school in fall 2020. With a husband in a high-risk health category, she was determined not to bring the virus home. At school, she wore a mask and shield and installed plastic screens between student desks. At home, she isolated from her husband and school-age children, changed clothes immediately after school, and restricted herself to a separate part of the house. She missed her family even though they were nearby—just never close enough to hug.

At first, things at school went better than she had anticipated. Teaching in a mask with barriers between students was awkward and there were instructional challenges, but community transmission rates stayed low and few at school got sick. She felt less effective as an instructor, thwarted by the mask and barriers, but she was keeping her students and her family safe and the trade-offs felt worth it. However, a post-Halloween virus spike made in-person teaching suddenly feel more threatening. She was appalled when, shortly before Thanksgiving, the school board voted to change the metrics they had established to remain fully in person. The rationale offered publicly made the decision even worse. A member of the school board asked, at a streamed meeting, "How many teachers are going to big family get-togethers for Thanksgiving, but yet they're claiming that they're scared of COVID and complaining that they want us to go online?" Ms. Larsen felt that the board's dismissive attitude toward teachers disregarded and derided the sacrifices she had made to keep teaching. Thanksgiving dinner at her house was eaten from opposite table ends in the garage with the roll-up door open, all of them bundled up to stay warm. After a short leave of absence, Ms. Larsen resigned. The decision was "heartbreaking," but "I feel like I gave up spending time with my family to have other people just disregard it. I mean, I feel like I gave so much of myself."

These early Leavers highlighted the fear and uncertainty surrounding the early weeks and months of the COVID-19 crisis. Nonetheless, at the end of the 2020–2021 school year, seventy-one of the seventy-five project teachers were still in the classroom. Nearly all, when asked what had been most satisfying during that first full school year, identified some aspect of classroom life (even when that "classroom" was online). They wrote of building relationships with students, supporting them both emotionally and academically. They expressed pride in their greater sophistication and effectiveness with technology, and pleasure at reconnecting with colleagues. Yet the list of satisfactions found a distorted mirror in an inventory of disappointments—the students they could not reach, the limited academic growth, the frustration of chairs in rows or behind shuttered cameras. Presumably, those disappointments would wane with the eventual return to in-person teaching, but other disappointments—especially disappointments with workload demands and with school and district-level decision-making—spoke to more systemic issues beyond the classroom, issues that came to weigh heavily in teachers' career deliberations.

Year Two Exits: Cumulative Stress, Disrespect, and Exhaustion A bigger wave of exits occurred in the second pandemic year—a year that teachers widely proclaimed as still more stressful.[4] The cumulative stress of pandemic teaching, persistent exhaustion, and a growing dissatisfaction with working conditions conspired to create a working reality many teachers deemed unsustainable.

By summer 2022, ten more project teachers had left the profession, citing both COVID-related decision-making and other working conditions. For these Leavers, the decision to exit emerged gradually over time. None of them had been planning to leave prior to the pandemic.[5] But the experience of pandemic-modified schooling, complicated further by social and political conflicts in some states and communities, eroded their will to stay in the profession.

In summer 2020, reflecting on her experience during the shutdown, rural Kentucky elementary teacher Frances Carter said, "I spent a lot of time really reflecting on whether I could continue teaching, and I came up with the conclusion that there's nothing else I would rather do. Even though this is hard, it's temporary. It might be a long temporary, but it's still temporary." In summer and fall 2020, she spent time seeking out professional development opportunities and felt pleased at "re-engaging with learning new things and feeling a little better that I can do this." She found what she considered very useful support from colleagues, tech specialists, the school librarian, and teachers in both new and existing teacher networks. But by March 2021, teaching in a blended hybrid mode with both in-person and remote students at the same time, she checked off a long list of significant challenges including overwork and exhaustion, a lack of student engagement, criticism from parents, inadequate safety protocols, and poor district communication. She reported a diminished sense of success and a growing level of cynicism. Ms. Carter lamented "how exhausting and challenging this year has been and how it has broken me as a teacher. How we have been expected to pull off unbelievable things with little appreciation or acknowledgment." And in June 2021, explaining her decision to leave after twelve years of teaching, she wrote, "I have never felt more defeated, exhausted, and just done as I did this year."

Ms. Carter might well be considered an unexpected Leaver, having found some substantial support but then a cumulative set of stresses and challenges that culminated in her departure. She was not alone. In spring 2020, suburban Kentucky elementary teacher Emma Thorsen was a third-year teacher who identified as "particularly passionate" about teaching English language learners. During the first months of the pandemic, her teaching commitment deepened as she focused on expanding students' access to technology and maintaining communication with them and their families. She felt a sense of purpose, teaching in a place and time where she was most needed. But as the 2020–2021 year wore on, her workload and stress levels increased. In early March 2021, her school shifted from completely online to hybrid instruction and by June 2021 she said, "This is the first time in my life where I truly felt burnout as an educator." Her circumstances worsened when an enrollment decline resulted in her transfer to a new school. She struggled with being a new teacher at the school. When she got COVID-19 in January 2022 and was out sick for ten days, her coworkers—strained by a substitute shortage—pressured her to teach remotely even while sick. When she returned, her principal blamed her for some extreme student behavior problems during her two weeks of sick leave. That was a turning point for Ms. Thorsen, and she subsequently left in search of a job outside teaching.

This second-year leaver trajectory of cumulative stress is well captured in the experience of Iowa social studies teacher Sam Stewart. In summer 2020, Mr. Stewart was in his ninth year of teaching and considered teaching his calling. Two years later, in 2022, he had left teaching, attributing his exit to a disregard for public school teachers conveyed by the state and local approach to reopening schools and compounded by the "demonization of teachers prevalent nationwide but including Iowa."

In summer 2020, Mr. Stewart described himself as an "activist teacher" motivated to "create positive impacts through teaching focused on promoting justice and anti-racism." As a white teacher, he saw teaching in a predominantly white, rural, low-income community as an opportunity to reach students who might not have the opportunity of learning through interaction with those of "different races, ethnicities, religions, and ways of thinking." He pursued his social studies teaching credential with the intent of preparing students to think critically and analytically as they studied history.

In summer 2020, Mr. Stewart was dismayed by what he considered administrators' "toxic optimism." Like Ms. Lehrer, Dr. Blum, and

Ms. Larsen, he was unhappy with his district's Return-to-Learn plans, describing them as "infuriating and scary."[6] Faced with the prospect of teaching fully in person with little assurance of adequate safety protocols, and disappointed by the union's timid response to the governor's insistence on in-person teaching, he took steps to speak up: "I've sent countless emails to admin and my union over the past few weeks just trying to make sure we have basic measures in place. For example, we have to go back for our professional development meetings tomorrow and originally those were scheduled face-to-face with all staff—hundreds of staff—in the district and it took countless emails to both the union and the administrators saying, 'Why are we doing this? OSHA still recommends distancing' " (August 2020).

Throughout, administrative communication felt disrespectful, sometimes even intentionally obfuscating. Mr. Stewart was demoralized by his efforts to uphold a school mask mandate that his principal mostly disdained by wearing his own mask below his nose. Particularly upsetting to him was the shift from remote to hybrid just one week before winter break, as COVID-19 cases were on the rise. The district justified the increased in-person instruction as both state-mandated and in students' best interests. Yet Mr. Stewart knew that a state waiver permitted the district to remain remote; he considered the sudden return to in-person teaching more political than principled.

At the same time, Mr. Stewart was grappling with the significance of Iowa's new law banning "divisive concepts" in the school curriculum.[7] His repeated requests for district guidance went unanswered and school-level leaders sidestepped questions about what he could and could not teach. As a social studies and history teacher, he feared this law could impede teaching, especially content related to race and racism. His fears were realized when he was advised by administrators that he should remain neutral on the question of whether slavery was wrong. With his teacher identity at stake, he decided, "I'm just going to do it anyway, meaning teach that systemic oppression is real through history." But then a local politician targeted Mr. Stewart in public forums, referring to him as "un-American" and rallying community members to call for his termination. Amid growing threats, intimidation, and even reports of violence against teachers, Mr. Stewart felt increasingly concerned for his own safety.

The complex and politically polarized experience of pandemic teaching challenged and stretched Mr. Stewart to the breaking point. He left teaching in 2022 because of his district's approach to the opening of schools during a pandemic, its unquestioning deference to the state's newly enacted censorship of school curriculum, and heightened controls over and threats to teachers and their work. He argued, "The lack of response to the pandemic seemed like one and the same with the complicity with this CRT [critical race theory] hysteria, this wanting to appease the loud and angry voices at the expense of supporting teachers and students." He did not leave because the work of teaching was challenging, the pandemic stressful, or the students difficult; rather, he left teaching because others questioned his expertise, undermined his professional judgment, and thwarted his commitments to his work and his students.

These six Leaver portraits—Natalie Lehrer, Sophie Blum, Rachel Larsen, Frances Carter, Emma Thorsen, and Sam Stewart—capture the general patterns and stories of the teacher Leavers. The earliest exits were motivated by safety concerns, negative assessment of public health decisions, and frustration over inattention to teacher voice and well-being. Later exits came only after those teachers worked to sustain their teaching commitments under difficult circumstances. But across the board, all who left found their working conditions unsustainable. Some, like Emma Thorsen cited exhaustion, disrespect, and problematic leadership. Others, like Sam Stewart, described disconnects among priorities, pressures, and supports.

As figure 3.3 shows, teachers earlier in their careers were more likely to leave teaching than mid-career or more veteran teachers. Yet teachers who left during the tumultuous first two years of the pandemic were all teachers who planned a career in teaching. They include teachers with impressive qualifications and deep commitments; most were in the early stages of their career and perhaps could be induced to return. Regardless, the reasons for their exit yield lessons for supporting teachers to teach in and through future crises.

Figure 3.3 Years of teaching experience of Leavers versus full sample

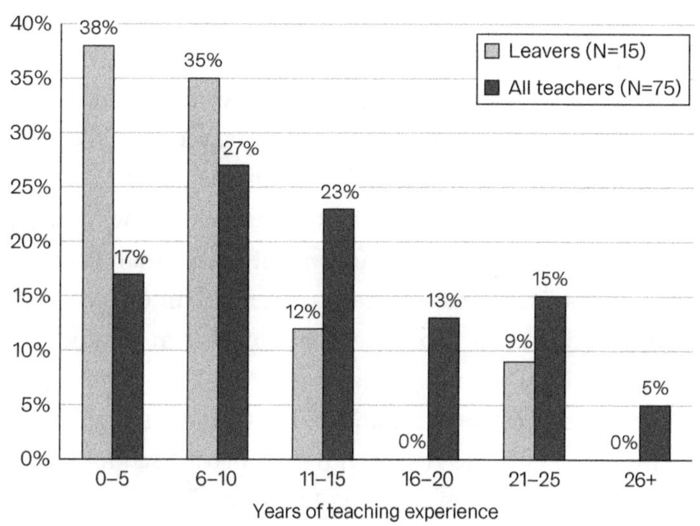

The Movers

Teachers have long shaped the contours of their careers by seeking grade levels, schools, and teaching assignments that suit their interests, preferences, and sense of a "good fit." At the school level, both Leavers and Movers constitute turnover, with significant organizational consequences. To the school, all teacher departures are exits regardless of where that teacher then goes. Teacher attrition results in fiscal costs, potential threats to community cohesion, and disruptions to student support.[8]

The pandemic heightened teachers' awareness of and sensitivity to those aspects of their work environment that fed or diminished their satisfaction with teaching. Nine project teachers moved voluntarily between summer 2020 and summer 2022, changing schools, districts, or even sectors (traditional public, public charter, private) in an effort to stay in teaching.[9] Movers expressed disappointment and frustration with the pandemic response and sought to escape conditions they found unduly burdensome, unsafe, or contentious. Some found themselves at odds with their school's or district's priorities, especially when those focused heavily on academic growth measured by testing and reflected less concern for students' social and emotional needs. All were bent on finding a school that offered more satisfactory working conditions, including a manageable workload, collaborative colleagues, effective leadership, community support, and a good fit with their values and goals as a teacher.

Although Leavers were concentrated among early-career teachers, Movers spanned the full range of the teaching career, with two in their first five years, five at mid-career, and two with more than twenty years in the classroom. Two teachers—an early-career urban elementary teacher in Texas and a mid-career suburban music teacher in Kentucky—moved from public to private schools. Nella Worth, the Texas teacher, sought to escape the renewed pressures around standardized testing: "I almost left teaching. Instead, I chose to try teaching at a private school where I don't think I'll feel the pressure of teaching to the test." Music teacher Rowan Finchley was chastised by her principal after conveying her safety concerns to school board members, leaving her feeling "vilified." She complained, "I feel like we are being asked to do the impossible every day and to potentially sacrifice our health and safety to resume in-person instruction as much as possible." She also worried about potential postpandemic budget cuts and the security of her job as a teacher of an "untested subject." Working with a career coach, she made the transition to a private school.

A wish to stay in public school teaching motivated Leanne Edwards's relocation from middle school to high school in her suburban Texas school district. A ten-year veteran, Ms. Edwards initially approached pandemic teaching optimistically. She embraced technology as a bridge to students, drew on her relationships with long-standing collaborators, and took on teacher leadership roles. But as time passed, her optimism waned, ground down by two and a half years of conflict, poor leadership, inadequate technology, and the high turnover of core colleagues. She navigated the 2021–2022 school year while considering an exit from teaching. A conversation with her husband shifted her thinking: "When he didn't like his job he switched. He didn't stop being a software engineer to something completely different. He changed companies." Ms. Edwards decided to try to change "companies" by moving from her middle school to a high school in the same district. "If it's still really bad I think I'm going to try to jump to a different district and see if it's just our district." She did not plan an indefinite search. Two years, two new places, two chances to find a place where she could stay. If not, Ms. Edwards was prepared to leave the profession. Yet even in summer 2022, knowing that her new department chair was a good friend, she anticipated, "I think it's going to be great."

Early-career Oregon high school teacher Noelle Cruz and veteran middle school teachers Leslie Spark in Florida and Francisco Vargas in California were also motivated to remain in public education but increasingly unhappy in their schools. Ms. Cruz had found herself isolated as a teacher of color and unheard by administrators, counselors, and fellow teachers. After an incident with a counselor that finally "broke the camel's back," she said, "I didn't feel like my voice was safe as a female of color." A move to a new community, district, and school was a "hard transition, and it was also exactly what I needed." Although Mr. Vargas respected the principal of his urban charter school, he found the priorities and practices established by the leadership of the parent CMO [charter management organization] deeply problematic—especially an increase in student testing starting in fall 2020 that he found blatantly insensitive to students' emotional capacity to focus on academics as they returned to school. Although his long-term career plans remained unchanged, he determined to change schools to find a place that shared and supported his student-centered teaching priorities. Ms. Spark, frustrated in fall 2020 with her principal's lack of leadership and missing a sense of connection to a meaningful "tribe" at her rural school, was "questioning myself daily about why am I going back." When a teacher she admired in another district reached out to tell her about a position at an elementary site, she decided to make the move. She sent a message to her principal to inform him of her plan, but "he never responded to it. And then I thought, that alone tells me why I left."

The Movers represent a group whose career satisfaction was eroded over time by their experience of pandemic teaching. Seven of the nine reported a change in long-term career plans, but all nine also hoped that a change of schools or districts would bring improved working conditions. Of course, moving schools or districts requires a gamble that the new environment will be better and will warrant the temporary dislocation and effort needed to adjust to a new school. Music teacher Rowan Finchley was uncertain, finding that she still struggled to assert the value of music and the arts in a school bent principally on core academics. But for Ms. Edwards, Mr. Vargas, Ms. Cruz, and Ms. Spark, the gamble paid off quickly. Ms. Edwards had anticipated that her move would "work out great," and in October 2022, she emailed, "I absolutely love it!" A more manageable workload was central to her satisfaction, alerting her to what she considered inequitable loads across elementary, middle, and high schools in the district. Mr. Vargas moved to another charter school where he felt heard and appreciated—and where he could teach in ways that felt core to who he was as a teacher. Ms. Cruz reported, "I came into a school that had a lot of the support for students that was missing at my old school, which took a huge amount of workload off me [and] I have a team. I didn't have a team before." Ms. Spark said she had been nervous about moving to a new district, new school, and new grade level, but she found exactly the kinds of connection with colleagues and supportive leadership she had been seeking. She enthused, "It's been one of the best years of my entire career. My kids flourished. I feel alive again. I feel like a teacher again. I feel like what I do matters."

The Dissatisfied Stayers

Reports of teacher labor market dynamics typically distinguish only among leavers, movers, and stayers. What the singular category of "stayer" obscures, however, is the distinction between satisfied teachers—those who are experiencing the rewards of the career and satisfied with life in the classroom—and those who are teaching but feel dissatisfied and disengaged. Of the seventy-five project teachers, eighteen of the stayers may be categorized as dissatisfied. All but two of those teachers indicated that their long-term career plans had changed, with plans to retire earlier or to otherwise leave teaching; we term them Outbound Stayers. Two teachers did not change their long-term plans but only because they felt financially constrained from leaving; we consider them Stuck Stayers. Surveyed in July 2022, nearly all of the outbound stayers and both of the stuck stayers listed overwork and exhaustion as a significant challenge; nearly all reported an increase in cynicism about teaching as a profession and a diminished sense of success as a teacher.

Outbound Stayers Movers left their schools in search of more supportive conditions, aspiring to remain in teaching. Outbound Stayers remained at their schools while making exit plans, some to retire early or otherwise just leave the profession. Some were more confident than others that their plans were realistic, but all of them expressed a strong interest in leaving the classroom.

Of the sixteen Outbound Stayers, six were veteran teachers adjusting their retirement timeline. After thirty years of teaching, suburban Oregon social studies teacher Victor Andrei wrote that teaching in the second full pandemic year was more stressful than the first: "I'm seriously considering early retirement. Instead of five years out, I'm planning on two years. This is due to overall increased stress and fatigue." In summer 2020, urban Florida high school history teacher Sarah Weaver avowed that teaching was "in my blood" and again in summer 2021 that "I am always going to be in the classroom." She even took on additional leadership responsibilities because she "saw the need." But by summer 2022, she was planning an early retirement, discouraged by a political climate that prompted widespread book banning and by new legislation that would dramatically constrain her as a history teacher. Claiming that COVID-19 had heightened the "absurdity" pervading public education, she added, "I just don't know if I can be a cog in the machine anymore when I can't teach reality and documented facts."

Florida teacher Janet Featherstone enthusiastically taught language arts in the same rural conservative community for twenty years. After consulting her district's human resources office in fall 2021 and learning she would need to teach eight more years to achieve a livable retirement income, she said, "I'm trapped by my own life. If I had a different retirement plan, I wouldn't be trapped."[10] In summer 2022 she was looking for a way out of the trap, exploring all the possible nonteaching jobs eligible for state-funded retirement that could get her out of the classroom sooner.[11] She added, "And it's sad, because no one was a more passionate teacher than me and no one loved it more than I did. But I'm done. And I worry about that because I had those teachers when I was in school who were done. Remember them? You had them, too. And I don't want to be like that in the classroom."[12]

Massachusetts teacher Carla Morrison, with only eight years in the classroom, was two years away from vesting in the state's teacher retirement plan.[13] Yet even in summer 2020, she had begun to think about leaving, worn down by parent criticism and a lack of community support. One-on-one, she said, parents were grateful for what teachers were doing, but when they assembled in groups "the pitchforks come out." Thinking about the timeline to retirement, she explained, "Even before all of this happened, I was thinking I can't do twenty years. I might be able to do fifteen. But now, I think I might be able to do two or three more years and then try something different." She added, "I love the teaching part. Everything else is pretty awful."

Early-career teachers often saw few costs associated with leaving teaching. Emily Kline, a fourth-year rural Massachusetts science teacher, was actively applying for government jobs in science, working with a career counselor, and planning to leave as soon as her daughter completed her senior year. The national rate of teacher exit is high among teachers in their first five years, so perhaps Ms. Kline would have left even without a pandemic. Nonetheless, she attributed her exit plans to her pandemic teaching experience, to the ways the response made evident that the system's priorities upon returning to school were not aligned with her own. At a time when students were struggling to readjust to school in person, "the whole drive from either our administration or from the state is: 'Push ahead, push ahead, push ahead. We've got standardized tests at the end of the year. Get everybody where they need to be.'"

Altogether, the Outbound Stayers tended to have personal or professional considerations delaying their exit: vesting in or maximizing pensions, waiting for children to complete a grade level, especially if the teacher taught at the same school, or even just ensuring a new job before resigning a current one. But the message was clear: they were staying temporarily and reluctantly.

Stuck Stayers For two project teachers, the absence of changes to long-term career plans reflected a lack of alternatives. Iowa teacher Ruth Cartwright, thirteen years into her career, felt well and truly stuck. Her motivation to teach arose out of her love of history and the pleasure she found in sharing that knowledge with students. "I like working with the students. I love learning history. I love all the new content. I mean, I'm always learning something, which is super fun, and I like interacting with the students." But over the course of the pandemic, she found she was increasingly dissatisfied with teaching, weighed down by the public disrespect for teachers and the lack of support for public education. Ms. Cartwright yearned to leave teaching because she was "sick of being the punching bag for everybody." She continued, "If there were another option, if there were another lifeboat available, I would jump into said lifeboat and I would do anything I could to get out of teaching." But single, dependent on her income, with an eye on her pension prospects, and without any other work experience, she made a pragmatic decision to stay. She concluded, "For me, it was just kind of the realization, well, this is probably what you're going to have to do and you're just going to have to make the best of it."

Financial considerations, including student debt, were also the determining factor for Oregon high school teacher Vivian Woods. Like Ms. Cartwright, Ms. Woods complained of a lack of public respect and recognition, but she also objected to what she considered a lack of student accountability as schools reopened, with teachers told not to give failing grades. She rejected the premise that students had all experienced trauma and she should be prepared to engage in "trauma-informed" practice and deal with students' mental health issues. "I don't want to be a social worker. I did not go to school to be a social worker. I don't like being forced to wear all these different hats." Ms. Woods wished she saw a viable way out. Like Ms. Cartwright, she made the pragmatic decision to stay. "I'm fourteen years in now and I'm at a place in the pay scale where you can't leave, like you're just stuck. Yeah, if I could find another job, and it was going to pay the same, I would. But I can't and I've looked."

Although there are only two project teachers clearly in the Stuck Stayer category, their presence and that of the Outbound Stayers remind us of the complexities in understanding career commitment and persistence. Not all teachers who persist are satisfied. Many disengage and want to leave, and yet they stay anyway. It reminds us that persistence, satisfaction, and engagement are not always packaged together.

Retaining teachers in times of calm and times of crisis is an important goal, but staying is not an unalloyed victory. As the experiences of outbound and stuck stayers demonstrate, staying does not necessarily signal engagement nor does it promise long term persistence.[14] It is important to differentiate among teachers who stay and are satisfied with the work and the working conditions from those who remain only while they plan their exit, or worse, stay because they see no way out. To put these teachers all into one stayer category is to obscure variation in teacher experience that has explanatory value in understanding teacher commitment and engagement.

The Satisfied Stayers

Satisfied Stayers chose to stay in teaching. That doesn't mean they never felt doubts nor does it mean they would stay under any circumstances. They may have deal breakers, things that could happen that would cause them to walk away. But as of summer 2022, after two and a half years of teaching through a pandemic and the related school tumult, these teachers were satisfied with teaching and they intended to stay. Their experiences are instructive in understanding what it takes to sustain teacher commitment.

New York City high school science teacher Jane Farley was a Satisfied Stayer. Teaching in an urban epicenter of the pandemic was undeniably challenging. In spring 2020, ambulance sirens broadcast the escalating rates of COVID-19 transmission and death. Her school served a primarily low-income community where students' families were particularly affected by the virus. Many of the students' parents were essential workers and while Ms. Farley did not have exact numbers, she knew that some of her students had family members sick and hospitalized. When schools suddenly shut, she and her colleagues scrambled to maintain connection with students. Ms. Farley found it helpful to think of what students needed from her as existing in two buckets: one bucket offered the comfort of routines and social emotional connections; the other bucket offered ongoing instruction, activities to build students' knowledge of chemistry and skills as science communicators. A big challenge of that spring was finding the right balance between those two buckets.

The 2020–2021 year was chaotic. The school's planned hybrid reopening was delayed and then disrupted all year by spiking COVID-19 case rates. Instructional modes changed seven times, shifting back and forth from remote to a parallel form of hybrid in which some students were fully in person and others completely online. The repeated changes added to Ms. Farley's workload and generated some anxiety, but her union worked hard to ensure that teachers did not have to contend with the added challenge of what we have termed blended hybrid, or teaching in-person and online students simultaneously. The full return to in-person teaching in 2021–2022 was stressful but in different ways, as teachers worked to support student well-being and readjustment to classrooms. And unlike many of the teachers whose career commitments were eroded by pandemic teaching, Ms. Farley was insulated from standardized test scores pressures as her college preparatory public school relied on practitioner-developed student assessments in lieu of state standardized tests.

Ms. Farley's sustained commitment to teaching was facilitated through structural support at the school level: strongly respectful and collaborative colleagues and school administrators, an established professional culture of teacher voice in school practice and professional development, and robust institutional support for classroom teachers in meeting student needs. She admitted to feeling demoralized by "polarizing conversations" in the broader community, but the "political climate around teaching" that "just makes me tired" was offset by the positive climate of her school.

"I'm in a really special school community" is how Ms. Farley describes her school. By special she meant that her school was committed to strong personal relationships, staffed by a stable and experienced faculty, led by strong collaborative teacher teams and a long-term capable principal, and represented by a union that negotiated successfully to provide safe and supportive conditions for teachers' work. During the pandemic, administrators made "respectful" demands on teachers, continued the established school practice of consulting teachers in school decision making, and did all they could to support teachers' work. As described in chapter 5, Ms. Farley benefited from an in-school supply of substitute teachers and from school social workers to whom teachers could confidently refer students struggling with social and emotional issues. "When students are struggling, we can refer them to counseling. I've heard the social workers say many times that the last year was just incredibly, incredibly hard and awful, and really, really hard. Again, it didn't feel like that was something that I was encountering."

The start of the pandemic coincided with Ms. Farley's sixth year teaching, a career about which she was unequivocally positive. Asked how she felt about teaching two years later, in summer 2022, Ms. Farley was staying the course; she was still very positive about teaching high school science: "Good! I know no one says that, but I do feel good. It continues to be a very hard job, but well worth it." She acknowledged that sometimes the work was hard and she had bad days, "but even on that bad day, I'm like, I want to go to work tomorrow. I will go to work tomorrow and tomorrow will be a better day and I'll get over it." She said, "At this point, I don't really think I would want to do something besides being a teacher in the classroom." Happy with teaching as a career, content in her school, she planned to concentrate on deepening her classroom practice.

Satisfied Stayers were found in every state, at each grade level, and in rural, urban, and suburban schools. Many, like Jane Farley, strongly identified as teachers. Veteran California urban teacher Henry Marquez was still committed to being a teacher after twenty-five years, saying, "This is part of my identity." Jennifer Donegal, an elementary school teacher in a small Florida town, also felt that teaching was a core part of who she is and was determined to not allow the pandemic effects on schooling to take that away from her. After eight years in the classroom, she said firmly, "I am a teacher. I am fully meant to be in the classroom. And if I'm not doing that, what am I then? It's my heart. If you take that from me, you're taking a part of me, pandemic or not."

Satisfied Stayers frequently referred to teaching as a calling. They invoked the intrinsic rewards of teaching, pride in a life of service, a sense of connection to the community, and relationships with students. Henry Marquez coupled his personal identity as a teacher to his belief that a teacher must be ready to commit to a life of service; teachers are "essential to society, public servants." He acknowledged and accepted the trade-off of smaller paychecks for personal fulfillment. "Of course, teaching is more than just our paychecks. Teaching is personal connections, community building. It's a critical thing." Rural Texas teacher Don Granger concurred, saying, "Teaching is a calling. Only go into it if you feel called."

For some who felt called, the pandemic further solidified their commitment to teaching. Mid-career teacher Julia Harper had been teaching elementary school in suburban Kentucky for nine years when the pandemic created a new level of stress for students and teachers. She felt the strain and she saw the needs of her students: "I can't walk away right now when it's the hardest, when I'm needed the most. I can't. I wouldn't turn—it's hard for me, it's stressful for me. But I can't imagine walking away from them, walking away from my kids, my students at this point and saying it's too hard. I'm not doing it. I'm going to keep fighting for them and I'm going to keep being emotionally drained because I'm passionate about it and I feel like it's my calling and that this is just part of my story" (July 2021).

The refrain of teaching as a "calling," with its deep emotional resonance, helps to explain the personal dimension of career choice for the Satisfied Stayers, while the experience of the Leavers and the Dissatisfied Stayers supplies a cautionary note: it is unreasonable to expect that the country could build a teacher workforce numbering in the millions on the premise of a calling reliant on teachers subsuming themselves to their work. It is incumbent upon us to determine what it takes to build a system that supports and sustains teachers in the work they do supporting and sustaining their students.

TO TEACH OR NOT TO TEACH

Like pebbles dropped into a pool, teachers' experiences during the pandemic have the potential to ripple out and inform the lives and decisions of those around them. Crucially at issue might well be the pandemic's residue with respect to the appeal of teaching as a profession. In summer 2022, we asked teachers to "imagine that a student who's just starting college asked you today if you would recommend a career in teaching. What would you tell them?"

There is a strong relationship between teachers' own pandemic-related career trajectories and the advice they would offer prospective teachers. Those who felt good about teaching tended to encourage others to join the profession, although they often added a cautionary note. Those whose engagement was most greatly diminished tended to warn others away. Conditional advice came with warnings of low pay, little respect, external pressures, and escalating controls, culminating in the advice to explore all other alternatives before pursuing a teaching career.

Outbound Stayer Janet Featherstone, who felt professionally trapped by the pension time clock, warned a junior colleague to get out while he still could. Ms. Featherstone described him as brilliant and passionate but also deeply troubled by the current state of the profession. She told him, "You need to get out. You need to go find a job where they will pay you what you're worth and respect you for what you do and help you grow. You are wasting yourself here. Don't get stuck." With only three years invested in teaching, he followed her advice and was actively looking for a job as a technical writer. Ms. Featherstone didn't always feel this way. "Four years ago, I would have cheered on anyone who wanted to be a teacher." But that was before the pandemic, before the Florida governor began attacking public education with an eye toward privatization, prayer in schools, and a whitewashed school curriculum. Another Florida Outbound Stayer concurred. Social studies teacher Sarah Weaver cited the state's content and curriculum censorship as the rationale for her definitive response to anyone considering a career in teaching: "Please don't."

Teachers whose career path held steady were much more likely to encourage the next generation of young people to also become teachers. "Go for it" was the refrain sounded by these teachers, both metaphorically and quite literally. Kentucky Satisfied Stayer Nancy Walsh advised, "If that's where their heart is then go for it. If that's what their passion is, then that's what they need to pursue because we need good teachers." And Jennifer Donegal, the Satisfied Stayer for whom teaching was a core part of her identity, said, "I would say that it is very rewarding and that they should go for it." Her advice included acknowledging that teaching is all encompassing. To be successful they would need to teach with their whole hearts while still sustaining themselves and their families.

Jane Farley, the science teacher staying the course in New York City, would recommend teaching as a career. She acknowledged that teaching is hard and it takes time to develop a "personal, moral, practical guide" to one's own teaching practice. There are a lot of contradictory messages about the purposes of public education that a teacher must navigate, tensions between external classroom control policies and teacher autonomy, and a balance of academic and social emotional goals. Ms. Farley would urge prospective teachers to consider their work environment and know that working conditions would influence how well they are able to navigate the conflicting goals, ideas, and philosophies teachers encounter. But as a Satisfied Stayer who has found a place where she flourishes as a teacher, she would recommend the teaching profession to others.

CONCLUSION

The pandemic profoundly affected the careers of many teachers, shaking the commitment of some and reinforcing that of others. It is not enough to ask who stayed, left, or moved. To grasp the significance of the pandemic crisis for teachers' careers requires that we understand the contexts that teachers inhabited as the pandemic struck as well as their experience of the pandemic response as it unfolded.

Under ordinary conditions, some teachers leave teaching every year. A certain level of teacher turnover—like turnover in other fields—must be considered normal. But the patterns of attrition and retention during the pandemic help to illuminate the contextual conditions of career commitment. The Leavers had no plans to leave until the pandemic revealed an unexpected level of public disrespect, intensified working conditions, and reduced professional supports for their work. The Satisfied Stayers and successful Movers also attest to the significance of teaching context, with the local context being especially salient. That said, political and policy-level messages beyond the local influenced career outcomes, especially for Leavers and those stayers who were stuck or outbound. Altogether, teachers' career perspectives and decisions were rooted in who they were as teachers, the contexts in which they worked, and the local and state responses they experienced.

Teachers' decisions to leave, move, or stay reflected a combination of individual circumstances and contextual conditions. Early Leavers Natalie Lehrer and Sophie Blum both had sufficient financial resources to tolerate a period of unemployment, while Stuck Stayers Ruth Cartwright and Vivian Woods felt financially trapped. High school teachers Claire Macalister and Emily Kline stayed at their schools but knew that their credentials as experienced chemistry teachers gave them the option to leave or to move. That is, teachers' family circumstances and professional qualifications position them differently to pursue alternative career paths.

However, the import of context becomes apparent when imagining some of these Leavers in different contexts. One might readily imagine different outcomes for Natalie Lehrer and Sophie Blum, the two early Leavers who objected to inadequate virus mitigation in fall 2020 return plans. Retaining these two science teachers would have been possible had they worked in states and districts that adopted an online modality or even just enacted mask mandates in schools. Similarly, Rachel Larsen was driven from teaching by a felt lack of respect for her well-being, professional commitment, and personal sacrifice. Different leadership decisions and projected attitudes may have kept her in her school. She wanted to stay.

Imagine Sam Stewart, self-professed activist teacher, in Jane Farley's New York City school. It seems likely Mr. Stewart would have found the strong and collaborative leadership there that was lacking in his Iowa school. He certainly would have been represented by a stronger union to buffer him against political calls for his removal. Similarly, it seems less likely Ms. Farley would have stayed the course in teaching if she had had to endure a conflict-ridden return to in-person schooling and confront restrictions on her curriculum and pedagogy.

Contextual factors loomed especially large in teachers' career decisions and form the basis of implications that lend themselves to postpandemic changes in policy and practice. The next three chapters look closely at the conditions and contexts of teachers' work during the pandemic, drawing out the importance of increasing collective capacity to create and sustain a robust teaching profession. Chapter 4 highlights the significance of large-scale system responses to the pandemic and efforts to restore pre-pandemic structures and practices, highlighting the emerging significance of state-level responses. Chapter 5 concentrates on the local working conditions that teachers encountered day by day, with an emphasis on the workload they shouldered, the workplace culture they inhabited, the professional learning opportunities they sought and found, and the quality of school and district leadership. Chapter 6 takes up the matter of teacher voice and influence in the context of a crisis that relied crucially on their effort and expertise.

Unlike the [illegible] expressed [illegible] in June [illegible] [illegible] seems likely [illegible] would have found [illegible] strong and collaborative leadership. In [illegible] would have been represented [illegible] political [illegible] novel. Similarly, it seems less [illegible] would have stayed the course [illegible] had [illegible] complete [illegible] return to [illegible] schooling and confront [illegible] curriculum and pedagogy.

[illegible] contextual factors [illegible] large [illegible] teachers' [illegible] the basis of implications that [illegible] policy and practice. The next three chapters look closely at the [illegible] and [illegible] during the [illegible] pandemic, drawing out the importance of [illegible] collective agency [illegible] a crisis. Chapter 4 highlights the significance of [illegible] system [illegible] efforts to [illegible] pandemic [illegible] and practices, including [illegible] experiences [illegible] teachers' working conditions [illegible] encountered daily, with [illegible] the workplace culture [illegible] opportunities [illegible] and the quality of [illegible] leadership. Chapter 6 [illegible] teacher voice and influence [illegible] in their

4

The Significance of System Responses

Effective responses to transboundary crises require coordinated decision-making by system-level actors—leaders and policy makers—that in turn enable and support on-the-ground action. Teachers' experience of teaching during the pandemic took shape in relation to system-level messaging and decision-making at multiple levels: national, state, district, and school. At each level, the pattern of leadership combined with the prevailing political climate and social context to shape the professional life of teachers through a period of crisis. This chapter examines these system-level patterns to consider how system responses amplified or mitigated the experience of crisis, with special emphasis on state and district-level messages and actions.

The chapter begins with a puzzle. How was it that every state governor ordered or recommended the closure of public schools within a seven-day period in mid-March 2020—regardless of the reported rate of COVID-19 infection in the state—but states and communities then varied widely in the nature, scope, and timing of school reopening in the following school year? Sorting out that puzzle, and its significance for teachers' experience, illuminates the role of leadership at every level as well as the power of the existing social and political contexts in which teachers worked and the pandemic unfolded.

To unpack the puzzle, the chapter first identifies the short-lived moment in mid-March 2020 when unified messaging at the federal level triggered executive actions by the governors of all fifty states, resulting in the abrupt closure of public schools everywhere and the adoption of "no harm" policies with respect to student attendance and performance. That unified stance soon fractured in the following weeks and months, with conflicting, confusing, or ambiguous pronouncements from federal officials. States emerged as principal system actors in the pandemic response but took markedly different positions with respect to the speed of school reopening, the form that reopening would take, and the decision-making latitude granted to local districts. States that pursued a rapid return to in-person schooling, exerted tight control over the form of reopening, and demanded compliance were also states where newly enacted state legislation placed restrictions on teachers with respect to curriculum and instruction. Those states presented a starkly different environment for teachers than states that pursued a more incremental and cautious timeline, offered guidance keenly attuned to public health recommendations, and placed decision-making discretion in the hands of local districts. The latter states were not immune from social and political controversies related to curriculum and instruction, but teachers were not subject to newly constraining legislation.

A caution is in order regarding the significance of state-level messages and actions. States have authority under the US Constitution to set education policy, but teachers' stories testify to the long tradition of local control over the working conditions that bear most directly on their satisfaction and commitment. States figured more prominently in teachers' narratives when the state acted in ways that teachers felt compromised their safety during the pandemic, stripped them of established autonomy on matters of curriculum and instruction, and impugned their professional judgment and integrity. And in all states, teacher experience was most powerfully shaped at the local level, as is taken up in chapter 5. That said, transboundary crises of substantial duration, like COVID-19, require action by large-scale system actors and thus compel attention to the national and state-level responses and the meaning they held for teachers.

A BRIEFLY UNIFIED RESPONSE IN THE FACE OF ESCALATING RISK

After originating in China in late 2019, the new virus spread widely and rapidly. On January 30, 2020, the World Health Organization (WHO) first signaled a "health emergency of international concern," echoed a day later in the United States by the message from the Centers for Disease Control (CDC) of a "national public health emergency." In the six weeks afterward, media coverage of the COVID-19 spread spiraled upward, and teachers, principals, superintendents, and school boards—like parents and other local citizens—were awash in news reports of multiplying cases, hospitalizations, and deaths. Some teachers fully expected that a shutdown was imminent. Elementary teacher Linnea Harris in California recalled, "We could all see it coming. We were reading the news." Florida high school teacher Janet Featherstone and her students had monitored the growing news coverage: "The day we were getting ready to leave for spring break, we had already been talking about COVID on and off for weeks. They knew that something was afoot and there was a possibility we might not come back to school. And so, we talked about making sure you know how to access these certain things online." Michael Donovan in Massachusetts typified the project's science teachers: "We all knew it was coming, especially the science teachers. I remember saying something to one of my colleagues (on March 12)—something big is about to happen."

Some teachers remained skeptical, especially in communities with low rates of reported infection. Lori Perenno, preparing to go on spring break in a large suburban district in Arizona, warned her colleagues to prepare, but they voiced doubts: "I had already told my teammates, you need to pack it up, take home what you need because we're not coming back. [They said] 'Why would they close schools? There's nothing going on here.' " Charlotte Adams, in a suburban school in Texas, said her district was likely to follow the lead of the state's big urban districts but "you had a lot of pushback from parents and community members saying, 'Why are we doing this when, you know, it's not even here.' " Rural Oregon middle school teacher Layla Karim was in touch with teacher friends elsewhere, including some in Europe, and said, "I saw it coming. But when I told my colleagues and my friends about it, even days before it happened, they kind of laughed at me. And then, three days later, the schools were closed."

In a move that took many by surprise, and despite wide variation in COVID-19 cases, all fifty states acted to order or recommend school closure within days of each other in mid-March. The nearly simultaneous state-level actions were triggered first by the WHO's declaration of a global pandemic on March 11 and a nationally televised address by President Trump the same day, followed closely by his official proclamation of a national public health emergency on March 13, 2020.[1] The president's address and proclamation propelled a result not achieved by the CDC announcement six weeks earlier, pointing to the symbolic significance of White House pronouncements even where other agencies were those in command of scientific expertise, relevant data, and formal authority to act.[2]

Even teachers who had been expecting such a decision remarked on its abruptness. Linnea Harris, who said, "We could all see it coming," nonetheless also said, "It was all very, very abrupt. I think we had only one day's notice." Rural Iowa chemistry teacher Natalie Lehrer, having seen the governor's press release on March 14 that stated, "At this time, school closures are not recommended," was then taken aback when the governor recommended closures the very next day. She said, "The announcement wasn't a surprise, but the timing was earlier than I expected." Middle school teacher Summer Diaz in California, recalling "that infamous Friday the 13th," said, "It happened really, really quick. We weren't prepared." Middle school teacher Layla Karim in Oregon had anticipated a possible closure but still recalled, "The entire school community, including myself, was caught off guard. The teachers didn't see it coming. I didn't see it coming. Parents and families didn't see it coming."

Scramble, Scramble, Scramble

Despite growing indications that a shutdown was likely, especially in communities with rapidly increasing rates of infection, there was little indication of advance contingency planning in states or districts. When state governors ordered or recommended school closures, local administrators were suddenly left to mobilize food distribution for families eligible for free or reduced-price meals and to get technology devices in the hands of students. In areas with limited internet access, teachers worked to prepare and distribute packets of paper materials. Simply contacting families became a priority, one achieved more readily in those places accustomed to overnight closures for "snow days," where automated phone systems were in place.

In a few instances, local administrators anticipated the closure and took steps to prepare. In New York City, Jane Farley's principal was one of those exceptions. As Ms. Farley tells it,

> My principal was like, "I am worried about what will happen when we do close, because there's no way we're not going to." And so that Friday, even though the DOE was insisting that we were not going to close, my principal sent word out to families and just said, "I want to get tech in every student's hands." And thank God we did, because lo and behold, two days later, that Sunday at 4:00 p.m., the mayor announced that schools were closing. It was really, really, really, really difficult for students and teachers in schools that did not do what my principal did. (August 2020)

In the absence of system-level preparations, it was more often individual teachers who sensed a looming shutdown and took steps on their own to supply students with materials to take home, including Chromebooks or tablets where that was a possibility. High school English teacher Sherry Lincoln, whose California district "waited and waited and waited" to act, joined her colleagues in organizing materials for students to take home. She recalled, "I think we all, at least at our site, kind of knew something was coming. And so, by Monday, Tuesday, people were trying to run off copies and check books out to kids and just trying to get ahead of the game a little bit." Kentucky elementary teacher Gail Miller described her school's "shock and disbelief" when the school suddenly closed, but she also said, "Because I kind of knew it was coming, I had already got all my students on their Chromebooks. I tried to get them prepared as best as possible. I had them take some of their textbooks home so that they could work on things. And I felt like we were in a pretty good place."

Teachers were alert to the signals around them: a canceled field trip or musical performance, or reports of school closures in other counties, states, or even countries. Leanne Edwards in Texas took her cue from a canceled field trip and put together a "remote-only skeleton plan." Clara French, also in Texas, saw her elementary principal dressed in a suit and heels to go to a district meeting on Wednesday, March 11, "and I was like, 'oh, OK.' So, I threw together these take-home packets and I sent home school supplies. And sure enough, we closed." California elementary teacher Amanda LaScala, working in a suburban district in southern California, was alerted by a friend that Los Angeles Unified was shutting and that San Diego would likely be next. "So I started pulling things from their desks that could go home and be their work for a couple of days or weeks or whatever. I think I sent them with as much as I could fit in their backpacks."

The abrupt shutdown experience was further complicated by the mid-March timing, coinciding in many places with spring break. High school teacher Rachel Larsen in Iowa was one of many teachers who learned of her school's closure while on spring break: "And then we kind of started scrambling for what services we were going to provide for schools, for students, for distance learning. We had problems because we had left for spring break. That was an issue we had to overcome." Elementary teacher Jennifer Donegal in Florida was set to return from spring break when she heard the news: "They pulled everybody [teachers] into the media center and they told us that we were going to be going virtual. And so, everything was kind of frantic. I ran into my room and I got as much as I could, as much as I thought I would need."

Districts' apparent reluctance to act, and the lack of communication regarding any contingency planning, left most teachers scrambling to assemble materials for themselves and students when closures were announced—especially when those announcements were made at the last minute, only a day or even hours before the closure itself. Sherry Lincoln, who had prepared packets in advance, still found that the official announcement late on Thursday, March 12, made for a frantic Friday the 13th, "scrambling, trying to gather things and communicate to families and try to hand off packets." High school teacher Casey Wright in California reported the same late-Thursday notice: "I got that email Thursday afternoon. It was like four p.m., and I started scrambling, trying to put a bunch of stuff together so that I could create two weeks' worth of learning for my students." Summer Diaz sounded a familiar refrain, noting a pattern of delayed decision-making and an absence of contingency planning and advance preparation: "And instead of preparing for the inevitable closure, it's like I feel everyone was just a deer in the headlights. And in retrospect, it makes it really frustrating because we could have prepared better for the disaster that we saw happening all around us but our leaders didn't prepare us for that" (August 2020).

The Widespread Embrace of "Do No Harm" Policies

As it became clear that school closures would extend until the end of the school year, system-level messages issued by states, districts, and schools fell under an umbrella of "do no harm." Those messages and a set of associated policies acknowledged big disparities, in all but the most affluent communities, in students' ability to access assigned work, get instructional help, and remain in contact with their teachers and classmates. The no-harm policies had a broad reach, including a relaxed requirement for attendance; an emphasis on review or enrichment rather than new academic content, especially in the first weeks of the shutdown; restrictions on grading; and a suspension of state and local standardized testing.

Teachers generally understood and accepted the rationale for the no-harm policies but also quickly came to see their unintended consequences as student participation in remote instruction plummeted. Over 80 percent of teachers reported a substantial drop in student participation following the shift to remote teaching. Natalie Lehrer traced the steady attrition of the ninety students in her chemistry classes—from seventy shortly after the shutdown to "maybe five or six" by the end of the spring term. California elementary teacher Jeff Stevens said, "We did the hold-harmless model. So there was no accountability for attendance or any of that." California middle school teacher Henry Marquez reported low levels of student participation even in an urban district with sufficient technology access—a loss he attributed to a no-harm grading policy: "We had a hold-harmless policy and I think, like most districts did, that a student's grade could not fall behind what it was on March 13. And with that hold-harmless, I had a lot of students tune out. I didn't have more than maybe 30, maybe 40 percent of the kids."

The widely adopted "do no harm" stance reflected a concern that students were differentially positioned to access new curriculum content and complete work successfully without the support supplied by classroom instruction. Yet the no-harm policies played out differently given local contexts and student groups. There were notable exceptions to the overall pattern of lowered student participation. Teachers in more affluent communities, in schools with a predominantly white student enrollment, and in technology-rich schools and communities were more likely to secure higher student participation. Teachers elsewhere expressed concern about those they considered systematically more disadvantaged by the school closures. Those included students with special needs, students categorized as English language learners, students from low-income families, and students in schools and communities with limited technology infrastructure.[3] Such differences underscored the stark prepandemic variation in school and community context made even more evident by pandemic conditions.

Reopening Schools: From "Do No Harm" to the Pursuit of Normal

Although some scholars, entrepreneurs, and educators sought to seize the moment of crisis as an opportunity for innovation and transformation, that moment passed quickly.[4] As reflected in chapter 2, teachers chronicled a policy decision-making arc from the rapid, widespread adoption of "no-harm" policies in spring 2020—accompanied by substantial flexibility and autonomy—to the equally rapid and widespread effort to restore prepandemic expectations, with renewed controls over teachers and teaching. The opening of the 2020–2021 school year saw a return to prepandemic expectations for student attendance and curriculum coverage, coupled with a renewal of grading and standardized testing. The nature and scope of those changes reflected a widespread policy-level impulse to restore the familiar structures and processes of schooling. Crisis interpretations had shifted, with public officials and health professionals raising alarms about children's "learning loss," mental health, and emotional well-being.[5] Yet the pandemic continued to surge in many places, and the term "hybrid" emerged as a common umbrella term for a range of pandemic-modified schooling configurations.[6]

Teachers returned to teaching in fall 2020, many still remotely, with renewed system-level expectations for curriculum coverage, student assessment, and preparation for state and local testing. Teachers generally lauded these policy turns—except for the return to standardized testing, which they almost uniformly disapproved of—as they enabled a return to what felt like real teaching. They once again taught classes with scheduled times where students' attendance was required and grades were assigned. By the time of the March 2021 survey, 90 percent of teachers reported that they could use at least some of their preferred instructional methods.

Yet teachers found themselves struggling to engage students and to cover the full curriculum. Their accounts illuminate the residual effects of the no-harm policies on students as well as the challenges associated with an attempted return to "normal." Student engagement remained an elusive goal, with 78 percent of teachers surveyed in November 2020 and more than 80 percent of those surveyed in March 2021 listing it as a major challenge. In the same numbers, teachers expressed concern about their most vulnerable students. Linnea Harris wrote, "I notice that my students with learning disabilities and other special needs are the ones who are having the hardest time accessing learning in this distance learning format."

Teachers' concerns and frustrations were exacerbated by renewed accountability expectations. Jennifer Donegal, responding to the return of state testing, reported new pressures: "So, there is a lot of pressure—we have pacing guides and there's a lot of pressure to keep up with the pacing guides because now my fourth graders are taking a state standardized test for the first time because they didn't take it last year." Such system-level expectations did not account for the daily realities that teachers were confronting. Texas elementary teacher Nella Worth complained in June 2022, "Focusing our instruction on getting students to pass the state test became the school's sole focus and as a teacher I felt incredibly unsupported in teaching authentically, focusing on social emotional learning or meeting the students where they were. Expectations for us as teachers to get the students to pass the state test put a huge amount of pressure and stress on me." Ms. Worth changed districts but also said, "I no longer am 100 percent sure I want to stay teaching long term."

The local pursuit of a prepandemic normal stretched fully over two school years in schools and districts in most of the study locales. In November 2020, 63 percent of teachers reported that they were still working fully remotely; 31 percent were teaching in some hybrid configuration.[7] Few teachers, only six percent, had returned fully to in-person schooling and even those teachers were often supporting quarantined students remotely. Teachers in stronger labor states like Oregon and California were more likely to be teaching fully remotely, while some level of in-person teaching was reported in the weaker labor states of Florida, Iowa, and Texas. By March 2021, teachers in every state except California had returned to some form of in-person instruction, with districts in California seeking to reopen in hybrid configurations by mid-April.

A SHIFT IN CRISIS INTERPRETATION AND THE FRACTURING OF SYSTEM-LEVEL RESPONSE

The closure of schools in March 2020 reflected a largely unified interpretation of COVID-19 as a public health threat, with the shutdown of schools aimed at limiting community spread. Federal and state actors aligned around a shared goal of minimizing public health risk by closing schools in a coordinated effort to "flatten the curve."[8] Yet over the four months following the school closures, even as the pandemic continued to surge, the crisis rhetoric began to shift, focusing first on the threat of school and business closures to the economy of states and communities and subsequently on the threat that sustained remote learning posed to children's learning and well-being.

The economic dimension of crisis took three forms: the short-term need for parents to return to work, restoring economic productivity; the long-term reduction in lifetime earnings potentially suffered by individual students whose academic development was compromised; and the long-term threat to a well-prepared and competitive workforce if a generation of young people was denied an adequate education. In one White House briefing, the president argued, "The education of children is more than an essential business—it's a top national priority to ensure America can continue to aggressively compete with the rest of the world."[9] Governors in all nine states took steps to reopen businesses at least partially within weeks following the school closures. In August, as many districts indicated a plan to continue remote schooling in the fall, a White House briefing warned that a failure to return to in-person schooling could "hinder our Nation's economic comeback."

The crisis purportedly facing children and adolescents centered not only on academic development but also on threats to students' social development and their emotional, mental, and physical well-being. In June 2020, the American Academy of Pediatrics (AAP) issued a statement urging that "all policy considerations for the coming school year should start with a goal of having students physically present in school."[10] Based on available evidence, the group concluded that "the academic, physical and mental upsides associated with reopening outweigh the risks." In a subsequent release in July, the AAP was joined by the American Federation of Teachers (AFT), National Education Association (NEA) and School Superintendents Association (AASA) in a statement that more explicitly addressed the need for a *safe* return.[11] That statement reiterated the compelling reasons for a return to in-person instruction but added to that message: "Local school leaders, public health experts, educators and parents must be at the center of decisions about how and when to reopen schools, taking into account the spread of COVID-19 in their communities and the capacities of school districts to adapt safety protocols to make in-person learning safe and feasible. . . . A one-size-fits-all approach is not appropriate for return to school decisions."[12]

Furthermore, the revised AAP statement specifically called for Congressional funds to maximize safety in school reopening, for local school decisions to be guided by public health agencies "based on evidence, not politics," and declared as "misguided" any threats to withhold funding from schools that did not open fully in person.[13] But as pressure mounted for a return to in-person schooling, deliberations over the nature and extent of risk prompted a question: are teachers essential workers?

A Debate: Are Teachers Essential Workers?

With shifts in crisis interpretation and the accelerating pursuit of normal schooling, debates ensued about whether to designate teachers as "essential workers." Three arguments dominated the essential worker debate in media outlets, press briefings, and public and political discourse. Two of the arguments—one focused on the economy and the second focused on learning loss and children's well-being—favored a rapid return to in-person schooling and the designation of teachers as essential workers. A third and opposing argument centered on the risk to teachers' health in the absence of vaccine protection.

Consistent with the crisis reframing described above, the economic perspective highlighted concerns about national and individual financial damage incurred by prolonged school closure. Proponents of this argument pointed to decreased earnings reports in the early months of the pandemic and to parents' need for childcare to resume economic productivity. The student-focused perspective held that the limited instruction and social isolation experienced in remote learning threatened students' academic development, emotional well-being, and physical and mental health. This perspective gained significant traction when the AAP issued its appeal for in-person schooling, contingent on appropriate safety measures.

Countering those two arguments and reflecting a continued focus on the pandemic crisis itself, teacher organizations at the national, state, and local levels insisted that public health risks of reopening schools outweighed economic and educational drawbacks of distance learning. This viewpoint held that schools should remain remote until sufficient safety measures could be achieved; until then, teachers could reasonably fulfill their responsibilities from a distance.

By mid-July 2020, articles and op-ed pieces in major news outlets made the case for defining teachers as essential workers. An article in the *Washington Post* on July 21 argued, "When schools reopen, teachers and school staff will become the new front line in our fight against the pandemic. For them to succeed, we must stop treating teachers as peripheral to this crisis. They are, in every sense, essential workers."[14] The article went on to acknowledge that treating teachers as essential workers would require involving them in planning and supplying them with access to COVID-19 testing, protective equipment, and priority access to vaccines when available. In mid-August 2020, the Department of Homeland Security released an advisory considering teachers to be "critical infrastructure workers," an advisory made widely public in a White House briefing and echoed by the CDC the following day. Under that designation, teachers would be expected to work even after exposure to a confirmed COVID-19 case, provided they were asymptomatic. The move was widely seen as part of the Trump administration's campaign to press for a return to in-person schooling. Four of the nine states—Arizona, Florida, Iowa, and Texas—all defined teachers as essential workers who could be obliged to work in person even if exposed to COVID-19 or otherwise at risk. A fifth state, Kentucky, defined teachers as essential workers whose work obligations could be met by working at home, as distinct from "frontline workers" who "must report to work, despite potential risk to their health."[15]

Teachers' own portrayals of the essential worker debate echoed each of the prominent arguments. Teachers highlighted the fundamental importance of education—and thus teachers—to society, recognizing that schools also functioned to support the economy. They nonetheless objected to any expectation that they work in person without sufficient safety protocols. Elementary teacher Imani Johnson in Oregon summed up the sentiment expressed by many: "As important as I think education is, it doesn't come at the sacrifice of health." Sam Stewart in Iowa, disappointed by the national, state, and local pandemic response, said in August 2021, "I think being labeled an essential worker means society wants me to feel obligated to work in unsafe conditions." Those who explicitly accepted the designation of "essential worker" did so with the proviso that adequate safety measures were in place. New York high school teacher Tom James opined, also in August 2021, "Teachers are civil servants, public servants. If we're asking so many on the margins of our economy to work, I think it's fair to ask teachers to work. And work with children in schools. I do so cautiously, but I feel an obligation to serve. I want every kid to be in school every day—with safety standards being honored." Teachers in some states and districts, like Mr. Stewart, were skeptical that those safety standards would be honored.

The essential worker debate illuminated the emerging divides over the role of schools and teachers in the unfolding pandemic response. What appeared briefly as a unified response to a national emergency, guided by the nation's leaders, quickly fractured as the CDC and the White House revealed conflicting positions with respect to risk and remedies. As the pandemic news coverage and rhetoric became increasingly polarized and politicized, pandemic responses evolved in multiple and disparate ways. Guidance regarding masks and masking emerged as a particularly salient fracture. Speaking from the White House on April 3, the president announced, "The CDC is advising the use of nonmedical cloth face covering as an additional voluntary public health measure. So, it's voluntary. You don't have to do it. . . . I don't think I'm going to be doing it."[16] In mid-August, as schools were preparing to reopen, the president again expressed ambivalence about masking: "We have urged Americans to wear masks, and I emphasized this is a patriotic thing to do. Maybe they're great, and maybe they're just good. Maybe they're not so good."[17]

Controversies and divisions over mask mandates surfaced in teachers' accounts as they recounted local plans and decisions, most prominently in states with weaker labor strength. Divisions over masking, as noted above, were apparent in states' position on the return to in-person schooling. Florida, Iowa, and Texas sought to prohibit mask mandates in schools, although some local districts defied the state. In contrast, Arizona directed that "districts shall develop a policy to require face coverings," California required masking for staff and for students in third grade and above, New

York required masks for students and staff, and Oregon required masks for students from kindergarten up.[18] In requiring masking for staff and for students in second grade and above, Massachusetts argued, "As the primary route of transmission for COVID-19 is respiratory, masks or face coverings are among the most critical components of risk reduction."[19]

The Emerging Significance of States

The impulse to seek a return to normal was widespread but manifested quite differently within and across states. In news accounts, on social media, in the official actions of governors and legislatures—and in teachers' own stories—states emerged as key system actors but with markedly different orientations and approaches. The stance of governors, agencies, and legislatures with respect to the nature and timing of in-person schooling, masking and other safety measures, and the designation of teachers as essential workers, distinguished some of our nine states from others. Whatever the stance taken, whether an aggressive push for in-person schooling or a more cautious and gradual approach, it conveyed a message about the value associated with teachers and teaching as well as the degree of risk that teachers should be prepared to take.

Speed, Control, Local Compliance In three of the nine states—Florida, Iowa, and Texas—governors and other state officials took an early stand on a rapid reopening of schools for in-person instruction. In a presentation early in June 2020, Florida's governor asserted, "Florida can only hit its economic stride if schools are open."[20] The state's Department of Education online archive of pandemic-related decisions and guidance declares, "The Florida Department of Education took bold steps to be the first state to reopen schools for in-person instruction five days a week during the 2020–21 school year."[21] In mid-July, Iowa's governor signed a proclamation that "in-person instruction is the presumed method of instruction" and that school districts "shall take all efforts to prepare to safely welcome back students and teachers to school in-person this fall."[22] When it became apparent that some districts had planned to open with remote instruction, responding to Iowa's situation as a COVID-19 hot spot, the governor established a requirement that all schools be open at least 50 percent for in-person instruction. Following the Texas governor's announcement to legislators in mid-June that students would be returning to public schools in person in the fall, the Texas Education Agency (TEA) issued a directive that districts were required to provide on-campus instruction, with the option of limiting access to buildings for up to eight weeks.[23]

Each of these states took steps to constrain local district decision-making. Guidance issued by the Florida Department of Education on June 11 maintained that "reopening is a locally driven decision," but the subsequent Executive Order 2020-EO-06 signed by the Commissioner of Education on July 6 stated that schools were expected to be open "at full capacity" for the traditional start of the school year in August.[24] Districts were required to submit plans to the department that were compliant with that expectation. Similarly, districts in Iowa were prohibited from providing instruction primarily through remote-learning venues unless authorized to do so by an official emergency proclamation by the state. Texas districts proposing to continue remote learning after eight weeks were required to seek approval from the TEA.

With those expectations and constraints in place, and with a pandemic still surging, how did those three states address the issue of safety? In Florida, officials adopted the metaphor of the "dimmer switch," a step-by-step approach to reopening—but still with the expectation that schools would be open "at full capacity" by mid-August.[25] Guidance provided in June advised social distancing and other mitigation strategies "where feasible," but an executive order signed by the Florida governor on July 30 (Executive Order 21-175) argued that "despite recent Centers for Disease Control and Prevention (CDC) guidance, forcing students to wear masks lacks a well-grounded scientific justification." That executive order, titled "Ensuring parents' freedom to choose—Masks in schools," cites a statement by the Florida surgeon general that mask wearing poses a "risk of adverse and unintended consequences." Although Florida presents an extreme example, guidance issued by the Iowa Department of Education advised that "requiring face coverings for all staff and students is not recommended," while the TEA referenced the AAP argument that

"COVID-19 risks must be balanced with the need for children to attend school in person."[26] The TEA guidance focused primarily on mitigation strategies centered on sanitizing and encouraged social distancing "where feasible without disrupting the educational experience."

In effect, teachers in Florida, Iowa, and Texas—all considered weak labor states—were afforded the fewest state-level assurances of and resources for a safe return. Yet some districts in each of these states acted in opposition to state expectations and restrictions. None of the three states issued a mask mandate, but one-third of Florida counties had reportedly established one by July 2020 and 60 percent of Iowa districts, principally those with active local union chapters, had adopted one by October 2020.[27] Rachel Larsen offered one picture of the within-state variations; her own children's school district was defying the governor, opening at less than 50 percent in-person and "working toward compliance," but the district in which she worked was going back "one hundred percent full time and in person."

Caution, Guidance, Local Discretion The remaining six states adopted a markedly different approach to school reopening, orienting toward caution and safety over speed, providing guidance rather than mandates, and deferring to local discretion.[28] Governors and education officials in those states underscored the importance of in-person learning but pursued a more cautious and incremental return, with an emphasis on returning safely. A statement jointly issued by the Oregon Department of Education and the Oregon Health Authority prefaced the state's comprehensive and detailed guidance with the statement: "Returning to in-person instruction is one of Oregon's highest priorities, and so is providing safety for our students and school staff. . . . Whether this schooling is provided in person, will depend on many factors. The most important factor is the spread of COVID-19 in our local communities. Schools cannot operate on-site until it is safe, and we cannot create an arbitrary timeline."[29] Oregon's stance was mirrored in the other states, all of which provided detailed guidance on safety measures and benchmarks and five of which issued statewide mask mandates.

Each of these six states relied on districts to make decisions that would enable a safe return. California offered districts the broadest scope for local decision-making, with the state's Department of Education stating that "school districts and county offices of education . . . will determine the most appropriate instructional model, taking into account the needs of their students and staff, and their available infrastructure. This guidance is not intended to prevent a school from adopting a distance learning, hybrid, or mixed-delivery instructional model to ensure safety."[30] In Arizona, districts were asked to submit learning plans to the Department of Education but were also trusted to make decisions about a physical return "based on health data, the needs of the community and capacity to return with sufficient mitigation strategies."[31] Oregon required districts and schools to develop an Operational Blueprint for Reentry in consultation with public health officials and local stakeholders, a blueprint "tailored to this local context and informed by local needs. . . . Every school, under the direction of the district, determines whether they teach all students on-site, teach all students through comprehensive distance learning, or utilize a hybrid model."[32] In Massachusetts, the Department of Elementary and Secondary Education released guidance in late June, requiring districts to develop plans for remote and hybrid alternatives to in-person teaching "should those alternatives be needed" but left the details to local districts.

State Stance, Vaccine Access, and the Return to In-Person Schooling

A vaccine for COVID-19 became available in December 2020 and brought with it debates about access and distribution priorities. Many urged that teachers be prioritized quickly to facilitate a safe return to in-person schooling, but teachers were not widely prioritized until March 2021, even in places where they were categorized as essential workers and already teaching in person. Figure 4.1 displays the incidence of in-person schooling in each state in relation to vaccine availability. The vertical black line marks the date the vaccine became nationally available to all teachers, authorized by a decree from President Biden, and the dotted black plot line charts the US mean of in-person schooling.[33] All four states that

Figure 4.1 Return to in-person schooling by state in relation to vaccine access*

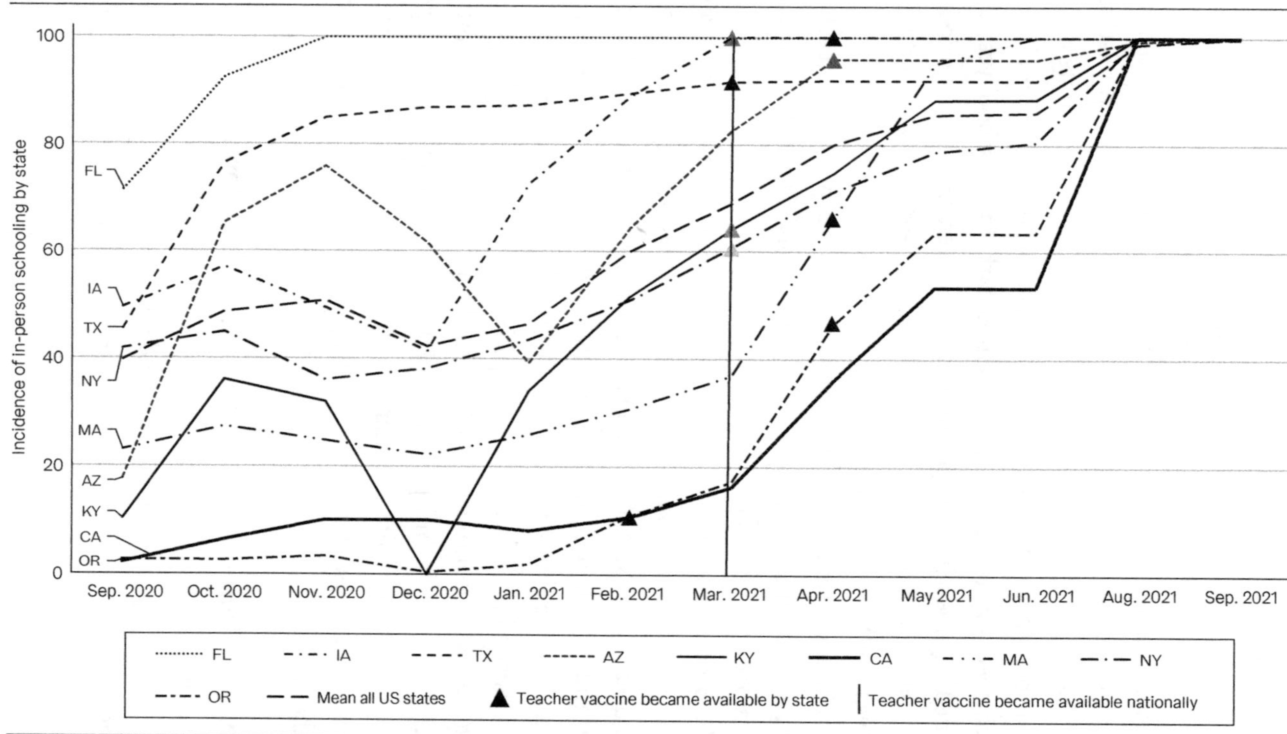

* Data is based on Burbio K–12 School Opening Tracker: On March 8, 2021, teachers became eligible nationwide to receive the vaccine under the Federal Retail Pharmacy Program; however, some states continued to provide vaccinations at their state-run sites based on their own roll out plans, under which some teachers were not yet eligible.

categorized teachers as essential workers, Florida, Iowa, Texas, and Arizona, resumed in-person schooling faster than the national average.

The contrast in states' orientation played out in the timeline on which schools returned to in-person instruction and the degree to which that timeline was affected by the availability of vaccines to teachers. The three states with *speed, control, and local compliance* orientations and relatively weak teacher labor contexts moved rapidly in fall 2020 to institute a high level of in-person instruction, prior to vaccine availability. Florida and Texas achieved a nearly complete reopening early in the school year and maintained high levels of in-person schooling even through a period of pandemic surge in the late fall. Iowa moved somewhat more slowly, but schools were fully open in person by the time vaccines became available. Once vaccines were available, none of the three states prioritized teachers in the first or even second round of distributions, despite categorizing teachers as essential workers.

At the other extreme, districts in stronger labor states that were oriented toward *caution, guidance, and local discretion*—California, Oregon, Massachusetts, and New York—relied more fully on remote teaching in fall 2020 and ramped up in-person instruction only after vaccines became available. In November 2020, the Massachusetts Department of Elementary and Secondary Education urged districts to prioritize in-person learning statewide, contingent on COVID-19 data in local communities; nonetheless, as shown in figure 4.1, the level of in-person schooling in Massachusetts did not increase markedly until vaccines became available. New York, which hewed closely to COVID-19 metrics, prioritized teachers for the vaccine prior to the national authorization.[34]

The Complication of Curriculum Controversies and Culture Wars

While a fracturing of system-level pandemic response was evident and enduring, and while teachers encountered community-level divisions over pandemic responses in all the states, some teachers also found themselves embroiled in controversies that centered directly on the curriculum they were authorized to teach and the instructional methods they were entitled to use. The orientation to schools and teachers during the pandemic was thus further shaped by the existing and evolving social and political context at the state and local level, including the rise of social justice activism and the competing furor of the "culture wars."[35] Divisions over social values and controversies related to race and gender predated the pandemic but played out during the pandemic in legislative efforts to control curriculum and instruction. State laws and regulations broadly described as "educational gag orders" emerged in seven of our nine states.[36] Four states (Florida, Iowa, Texas, and Kentucky) passed legislation placing curricular and instructional restrictions on teachers; in Kentucky, legislators overrode a governor's veto to do so. Three states (Arizona, New York, Oregon) saw legislation introduced that ultimately failed. Only two states (California and Massachusetts) experienced no state-level legislative efforts.

Varied state COVID-19 policies thus coincided with public positions on social and political issues. Sam Stewart, already frustrated by Iowa's pandemic response, ultimately resigned when the state's "divisive concepts" law (House File 802, June 2021) made it impossible for him to teach concepts and information he considered central to his expertise and commitments as a teacher of history. Sarah Weaver in Florida, also a history teacher, would now dissuade young people from entering teaching: "Especially in the state of Florida right now, with content and curriculum, our hands are tied." Although she had once enjoyed encouragement and support from her district for her practices of culturally responsive teaching and her selection of books addressing racism, that district encouragement and support withered with the passage of Florida's "Stop WOKE" legislation. Ms. Weaver was told by district administrators, "If you're doing this, stop," instructing her specifically to remove Ibram Kendi's book *Stamped from the Beginning* from her classroom. Texas science teacher Claire Macalister objected to legislation that she said placed parents in control of the curriculum, demonstrating a lack of respect for teachers' professionalism and leaving "educated professionals in science" concerned about asking fundamental questions on examinations: "The idea that facts aren't facts anymore is very scary."

In a vivid contrast, teachers in Oregon were teaching in a state that explicitly advanced curricula, instruction, and professional development aimed at enabling educators to pursue equity goals. Among the four principles guiding its *Ready Schools, Safe Learners* document, Oregon included "Center Equity: Apply an equity-informed, anti-racist, and anti-oppressive lens to promote culturally sustaining and revitalizing educational systems that support every child." In the section of the document devoted to this principle, the Department of Education recommended that educators "provide counter narratives to biased representations of race, culture, gender, abilities, and poverty; . . . invest in professional learning for all staff in culturally responsive-sustaining instruction, anti-bias and anti-racist teaching, and trauma-informed, healing processes; . . . and develop capacity to speak up against racism and xenophobia."[37]

SYSTEM RESPONSES AND TEACHERS' CAREER PERSPECTIVES

Teachers' thoughts and decisions regarding their own careers, as well as their perspectives on teaching as a career, reflect a range of personal and professional circumstances. Accepting the caveat about the power of state-level influence, there is yet some indication that the messages conveyed and the actions taken by some states during the COVID-19 pandemic played a significant part in teachers' thinking. More than half of all project teachers reported a change in career plans as a result of their pandemic teaching experience, but teachers were more likely to do so in the three states that pushed hard for an early return to in-person teaching, limited local discretion to adaptively respond, took a less than firm stance on safety measures, or enacted legislation restricting teachers' autonomy with respect to curriculum and instruction. Table 4.1 shows that nearly two-thirds of teachers in those states (64 percent) changed career plans compared to just over half (53 percent) in states that took a more incremental approach that emphasized a safe return.

State-level differences present themselves most clearly in the incidence of leaving. Seven of the thirteen project teachers who left the profession

Table 4.1 State policy stance and teacher career outcomes (N=75)

State stance	Leavers N=13	Movers N=9	Satisfied Stayers N=25	Dissatisfied Stayers N=18	Other N=10
Speed, control, compliance (N=22)	7 (32%)	4 (18%)	6 (27%)	3 (14%)	2 (9%)
Weaker labor states					
*Florida (N=8)	1	1	2	2	2
*Iowa (N=7)	5	0	1	1	0
*Texas (N=7)	1	3	3	0	0
Caution, guidance, discretion (N=53)	6 (11%)	5 (9%)	19 (36%)	15 (28%)	8 (15%)
Weaker labor states					
Arizona (N=7)	1	1	4	1	0
*Kentucky (N=9)	3	1	2	1	2
Stronger labor states					
California (N=9)	0	2	5	1	1
Massachusetts (N=10)	0	0	1	6	3
New York (N=8)	1	0	3	2	2
Oregon (N=10)	1	1	4	4	0

* Passed education gag laws.

for COVID-19–related reasons worked in the three states that adopted a "speed, control, and compliance" stance—approximately one-third of the project teachers in those states. Florida teacher Sophie Blum left her position as a science teacher "to protest the bullying of teachers into working in unsafe conditions" in fall 2020. Fellow science teacher Natalie Lehrer in Iowa also quit in fall 2020 when her district, following the governor's lead, insisted on a return in person and prohibited teachers from requiring masks in their classrooms. Rachel Larsen said, "I thought for a long time that this was my calling [but] I feel that my desire . . . has significantly changed because this year I felt very powerless. I don't want to be put in a position where I have so little say over the direction of my career." Sam Stewart expressed a "lack of trust and confidence in my state" and objected to what he saw as "bullying from politicians toward our admin during

COVID [that] made them so fearful they were no longer able to support teachers if our curriculum was anti-racist. And so, I felt obliged to resign."

System-level pandemic responses, together with other aspects of the social and political climate, also played a part in whether teachers would now recommend teaching as a career. Among the thirty-three teachers who addressed this topic in interviews, only one-third offered a definitive "yes," underscoring the rewards of classroom teaching. Yet even those teachers tended to add cautionary notes: that the lack of investment in public education, external pressures, and lack of respect from policy makers and the public could make it challenging to sustain the "passion" that those teachers thought essential to teaching. As veteran teacher Francisco Vargas in California put it, "It's still the best job in the world. There's still nothing like being in a classroom full of kids. But there are so many things outside the classroom that, I think, for a lot of beginning teachers, would spoil it."

Some teachers in every state would still recommend teaching as a career, and some teachers in every state would dissuade newcomers from teaching. Yet state context mattered. For teachers in some states, the pandemic experience and the turn toward legislative controls on curriculum and instruction eroded what had been a deep enthusiasm for teaching. Teachers who would previously have urged young people to pursue teaching as a career found themselves discouraging young people or advising caution. Nancy Walsh in Kentucky, Lori Perenno in Arizona, Sam Stewart and Ruth Cartwright in Iowa, Janet Featherstone, Sarah Weaver, and Leslie Spark in Florida, and Robin Beach in Texas all cited the political climate in their states as reasons to seek careers other than teaching. Ms. Spark critiqued Florida's easing of teacher licensure requirements to address staffing shortages when she said, "I think my answer would have been different before they did this rollover on teachers. We are so disrespected." Ms. Cartwright exclaimed, "Hell, no!" when asked whether she would recommend teaching but noted that before the pandemic and before the changing political climate in Iowa, "I'm not sure I would be so vehement. I think COVID just accelerated and exacerbated all the issues in education." For her and for others, a public health crisis, and the response made by states and districts, only served to expose more fully the precarious state of public education and the teaching profession that predated the pandemic.

CONCLUSION

The interpretations of crisis and the system responses at multiple levels have the potential to bolster the fortunes of the teaching profession, making it a more respected and trusted workforce, or to further erode the profession's standing and appeal. In this chapter, we have focused on the variations that emerged in the messaging and decision-making across nine states and the significance of those variations for teachers' pandemic teaching experience.

In the face of a national public health crisis, states initially took their cues from the federal response. Yet a confused and conflicted federal response contributed to fractured responses at the state level. A public health crisis became politicized and polarized. After the nearly uniform response by states following a federal proclamation of emergency, prepandemic social and political contexts quickly proved powerful in shaping state and local decision-making. The uneven effectiveness of system-level responses, and the significance of those responses for teachers' work and commitment, yielded four lessons that could be the point of departure for planning and preparation in advance of any future crisis—especially a transboundary crisis of substantial duration.

Lesson 1: The need for contingency planning.

The experience that teachers, students, administrators, and families endured in the school closures of March 2020 underscores the importance of emergency contingency planning at the state and local level. The very abrupt shutdown, after weeks of media coverage, hampered the ability of teachers, students, and principals to manage a smooth transition to remote instruction. The tumult of school closures was further complicated where it coincided—as it did in many places—with spring break (rather like the complicating factor of the August vacation culture in the 2003 Paris heat wave crisis).[38] Decision-makers at both the state and district level might have done more to anticipate and prepare for a closure scenario.[39]

Lesson 2: The value of a communication and technology infrastructure.

The decision to close schools placed a premium on a well-developed communication and technology infrastructure that could be mobilized rapidly in a crisis. Those schools and districts with well-established communication routines (such as those employed for the announcement of "snow days" in some locales) were better able to reach teachers and families quickly and consistently. Districts and schools with well-developed technology capacity were better able to help teachers and students pivot to remote instruction. Such capacity included existing learning management systems, Chromebooks and other devices for all students, digital tools for instruction, assistance offered by technology specialists, access to timely professional development, and adequate internet connectivity. A recurrent theme in teachers' accounts centered on the marked improvement in the technology capacity of individuals and systems over the course of the pandemic—likely a resource in future crises—but teachers were less likely to point to comparable improvement in communication routines and resources.

Lesson 3: The unanticipated costs of "do no harm" policies.

The short-term policy response of "do no harm," while deemed mostly sensible by teachers at the time, proved to have unanticipated costs and drawbacks. As detailed in chapter 2, student participation declined precipitously, and student motivation and engagement waned. Teachers were reluctant to focus solely on the review of content already taught. The requirements of the no-harm policies—relaxed expectations for attendance, a focus on review, restrictions on grading—and the ways in which they were implemented were determined primarily by districts but might have benefited from consultation with teachers in the context of contingency planning.

Lesson 4: The power of public messaging.

The messages conveyed to and about teachers by state governors, legislatures, education agencies, local politicians, school boards, and superintendents were potent signals of the regard in which teachers were held, the obligations they were expected to meet, and the conditions in which they were asked to work. Chapter 3 demonstrated how those messages had immediate import for practicing teachers—teachers who left, moved, or stayed—but also suggested the potential for longer term and more widespread consequences for the appeal and satisfactions of the teaching profession. In chapter 5, we turn attention to the local working conditions that supplied a crucial context for teachers as they encountered, interpreted, and responded to system-level messages and decisions.

5

The Power of the Local

As states and school systems forged an arc from early crisis response to the pursuit of a prepandemic or a new normal, teachers threaded their own narratives with details of the local: what it meant to traverse that arc with these colleagues, this principal, or that superintendent or school board. The immediacy of teachers' local working environment—the workload, professional culture, learning supports, and leadership—figured prominently in the vivid portraits of our study's leavers, movers, and stayers.[1] Jane Farley, the urban New York science teacher, sustained her commitment to teaching in the context of strong collegial ties and a supportive veteran principal—a "really special school community." Sam Stewart, the Iowa middle school teacher who resigned in 2022, spoke of his repeated but failed efforts to secure support from school and district leaders for COVID-19 safety protocols and for his social studies curriculum. And Leslie Spark, a Florida math teacher, found her enthusiasm for teaching restored after moving to a new district where she found close colleagues and supportive leadership: "There's nothing worse than being an island, and that's what I felt like at the other school."

This chapter shifts the focus from system-level policy responses to the local working conditions that supported or frustrated teachers' efforts to grapple successfully with the pandemic teaching experience. Teachers' experiences during the pandemic recall the lessons of prior research but also illuminate aspects of teachers' professional lives that emerged with special salience during the pandemic, including the heightened role of professional networks in supplying teachers with instructional and social support and the urgency attached to teacher voice and influence in local decision-making.

A recurrent theme in school workplace research is that schools vary widely with respect to a collaborative professional culture, supportive and effective leadership, and a collective capacity for improvement and adaptation to change. Such variations were much in evidence in teachers' interview and survey accounts. In this chapter, we explore teacher experiences as arising, in part, from the degree to which their schools embraced the norms, practices, and policies associated with a thriving teacher workplace.[2]

FOUR ELEMENTS OF WORKPLACE LIFE

We focus here on four elements of the workplace context that affected teachers' capacity to teach through and beyond the pandemic: workload demands and sustainability; professional culture and collaboration; timely and relevant professional learning opportunities; and effective school and district leadership. Each of these factors proved significant for teachers as districts and schools adopted a range of instructional modalities for the 2020–2021 school year and then returned largely in person the following year. Teachers weighed these factors seriously—especially the quality of school and district leadership—in their decisions to leave, stay, or move.

A Sustainable Workload

In the short-term turmoil of initial school closures and throughout the ensuing two years, teachers found themselves working longer hours and taking on additional responsibilities. For some, heightened workload demands were mitigated by workplace supports; for others, including those who left teaching and those who moved schools or districts, the workload demands fueled teachers' dissatisfaction and disengagement.

It is hardly surprising that teachers experienced exhaustion in the early stages of the pandemic; 76 percent rated overwork a significant challenge in fall 2020 as they coped with new modes of instruction, a steep decline in student engagement, and renewed accountability requirements. Yet even at the end of the 2021–2022 school year, two-thirds of teachers continued to complain of overwork and exhaustion.

Nonetheless, the single term "overwork" fails adequately to capture the range of workload demands conveyed by teachers through their interview accounts and open-ended survey responses. Three conditions affected not only the time that teachers devoted to their work but also the relationships they were able to establish with their students and the satisfactions they were able to derive from teaching: hybrid instructional configurations; added classroom coverage in the face of a substitute shortage; and system expectations misaligned with teachers' own values and priorities.

As detailed in chapter 2, hybrid instructional arrangements placed new and unfamiliar demands on teachers, especially when teachers were responsible for both in-person and remote students. Schools and districts significantly reduced the demands of hybrid teaching when they did not require teachers to take on responsibility for both in-person and remote students. Claire Macalister, a National Board–certified science teacher in a rural Texas high school, found blended hybrid a "nightmare," but the nightmare was not prolonged; in the face of teachers' complaints of overwork and a high incidence of failure among students learning remotely, her school adjusted quickly to eliminate the blended hybrid arrangement and Ms. Macalister did not include overwork among the challenges she faced. Middle school math teacher Leslie Spark also found relief from the burdens of blended hybrid teaching when a new superintendent, driven by teacher complaints and student failure rates, shifted the district to a parallel hybrid model that did not entail teaching of both remote and in-person students: "All online kids will come back to class or they will go on independent study through our school. But we no longer have to do both at once, which was exhausting." In the blended mode of December 2020, Ms. Spark had cited overwork and exhaustion as significant challenges, but in the parallel mode of March 2021 those were no longer an issue.

A shortage of substitute teachers compounded the demands placed on teachers in many schools and districts. Looking back at the 2021–2022 school year, three-quarters of the teachers reported that a lack of substitutes presented a significant challenge for their schools. Often the challenge of substitute coverage fell directly on full-time classroom teachers, demonstrably adding to their workload in ways they found exhausting. Elementary teacher Gail Miller in Kentucky, who left teaching in June 2022, wrote, "My colleagues and I tired quickly of being used as substitutes often. We always dreaded the daily text coming from admin for coverage." Massachusetts high school science teacher Emily Kline, looking to exit by summer 2022, summed up the reality that we heard from others: "*No one* wanted to be a sub this past year (2021–2022) in our district, so it left teachers constantly covering for other teachers. This led to lots of teacher burnout and overwork and exhaustion because those 55 minutes that teachers would typically have to themselves was eliminated, and you were running all over the school covering classes while exhausted" (July 2022).

In some cases, school administrators found ways to manage classroom coverage in ways that protected teachers' planning and preparation time. Imani Johnson, the Oregon elementary teacher who remained a committed stayer, credited her principal's efforts to recruit and retain a pool of substitutes: "Our admin did a beautiful job of getting ahead of [class coverage]. She was personally calling subs in the fall: 'Can you? Will you? Can you help us?' And the first time someone subbed in our building, our administrators were checking on them: 'How can I help you? What do you need? Let me fix it.' So, if it was your first day, I mean, she was like, 'We can't do this without you' " (August 2022).

While that Oregon principal's approach might prove less feasible in large districts or for most secondary schools, teachers in a few of those settings also spoke about administrators' efforts to limit the burden on their full-time classroom teachers. High school teacher Noelle Cruz praised school administrators who "really stepped up and filled those gaps. If spots weren't filled, admin jumped in and filled those spots. And I know that as a building, we worked really hard to make sure our subs felt safe and welcome." Michael Donovan in Massachusetts and Jane Farley in New York benefited from the permanent substitutes employed by their schools and the assurance of extra compensation for others who agreed to sub as needed. Two elementary teachers in large urban districts, Vicky Bauer in New York and Nancy Walsh in Kentucky, described the use of retired teachers or specialists to cover classes; both noted that these efforts, while appreciated, entailed trade-offs. Ms. Walsh wrote, "We are lucky that we have four retired teachers on staff who usually provide academic interventions. They are not providing those interventions this year (unfortunately), but they are available to sub in needed classrooms." Similarly, Ms. Bauer reported, "The reading teacher, math push-in teacher, and ELL teacher were often pulled from their regular schedules to cover for other classes, so my students did not get the support they should have received." Despite the trade-offs in direct student support, these teachers were largely free from requests to cover others' classes.

More than three decades of research on workplace stress and burnout suggests that workers are more likely to engage actively in their work when their own work-related values and priorities are congruent with those of the organization.[3] As instruction resumed in fall 2020, teachers were acutely attuned to the expectations they encountered regarding students' attendance, behavior, and academic progress. Emily Kline spoke favorably of the expectations that her principal conveyed to teachers and families as her high school reopened for hybrid instruction in fall 2020:

> It's been really, really good, with high expectations. Right from the get-go, our principal sent an email out to teachers: "Look, this is not the spring. We are doing as normal a school as possible in this weird (hybrid) format." [And to families]: "So your child is expected to show up to meet when they're asked to. They're expected to turn in work when they're asked to, they're expected to communicate with their teachers if they need extra time in any way, shape, or form. And I'm going to be supporting the teachers on this because I think our kids need it, too." (December 2020)

Ms. Kline found the principal's clearly stated expectation—that "you can set the bar high and you can expect people to meet it"—to be "a huge relief for us as teachers because we felt like we could actually now expect more from the students and that they would rise to that occasion. Which they have."

Yet in March 2021, four out of five teachers reported student engagement to be a significant challenge. As districts pursued a path "back to normal," some teachers considered administrative priorities to be misplaced, especially if those priorities failed to acknowledge the range of students' social, emotional, and academic needs. Teachers generally rejected the policy and media narrative of "learning loss" and the push toward "accelerated" instruction. Elementary teacher Carl Graham in Oregon, a committed stayer, voiced a perspective widely shared by others:

> I started to hear about this idea of "acceleration" [but] education doesn't work like that. What students need is stability. They're going to catch up. They're going to be fine. My concern is that you've got somebody saying, "Run, run, run, run, run, run." That's not how learning works. We're going to create a safe learning environment. We're going to get this momentum back and it's going to be good. But if we try to do a weird acceleration thing, students who are struggling are really going to feel overwhelmed, they are going to feel left behind, and that will be very bad. So you can't do that. (August 2021)

Teachers almost uniformly disapproved of the return to standardized testing in the 2020–2021 school year, especially in light of the emotional, social, and behavioral difficulties that students displayed. California math teacher Francisco Vargas wrote of his charter organization, "The organization leadership has actually *increased* the number of tests compared to previous years. I find it cruel to students and evidence of a complete lack of awareness of the inequities of distance learning. This is one of several reasons why I am leaving [the school] after this year." California teacher Summer Diaz was considering leaving, exasperated in part by her district's test-driven decision to return in person in April 2021: "You really want to send us back in person just to test the kids? Wow, what happened to social emotional learning as the most important thing right now?" For the many teachers who disapproved of the rapid resumption of standardized testing, the decision signaled a misalignment of values and left them with a sense that their priorities were being undermined.

Teachers were especially attuned to both the nature and the extent of workload demands as they navigated the uncertainties of the pandemic. Iowa teacher Taylor Brennan, who left teaching in June 2022, said, "COVID was a wake-up call to the dismal conditions teachers face. It prompted me to look outside of the teaching profession. I'm glad I got out, but it also breaks my heart." Yet in times of crisis, as in more ordinary times, three aspects of workplace life—where they existed—made those demands more manageable: a collaborative workplace culture; timely and relevant professional learning opportunities; and effective and supportive school and district leadership.

A Collaborative Workplace Culture

As teachers confronted teaching from a distance during school building closures and then teaching under an array of remote and hybrid arrangements, most turned to fellow teachers for problem-solving, information, ideas, and emotional support. When surveyed in March 2021, more than 70 percent of the teachers singled out subject-matter or grade-level colleagues as their most useful source of support. Without a blueprint for pandemic teaching, teachers supported each other in multiple ways. They introduced each other to new technology, shared resources, planned lessons together, divided the lesson-planning load, and helped one another reach out to students and families.

Many examples of collaborative support took the form of short-term arrangements focused on instrumental tasks, such as the division of labor described by Linnea Harris as she and her fifth-grade colleagues divided up responsibility for planning online lessons in reading, writing, and math. Such arrangements, aided by technology and driven by the immediate and unexpected demands of the pandemic, enabled cooperation and coordination responsive to the moment, but they did not always signal the existence of more deeply collaborative professional relationships. In some instances, the pandemic generated a newfound awareness of the support to be found among colleagues. Michael Donovan had previously enjoyed his connections to fellow high school teachers, especially fellow science teachers, but the pandemic shifted that experience from being "frosting on the cake" to a lifeline, or "blood," as he termed it.

Teachers who felt especially well supported during the school closures and through the tumult of school reopening were those who could count on a prepandemic workplace culture marked by shared goals and values, strong collaborative relationships, and structures that enabled a nimble and organized response to crisis.[4] Arizona elementary teacher Lori Perenno confided, "I will tell you that in the spring, if I did not have a teaching team that I adored, I would have just walked away. We walked through and planned out everything together." When things got especially stressful, she could count on one of them to "talk me off the ledge." Nancy Walsh in Kentucky spoke of the strong schoolwide culture in her elementary school, especially the "good grade-level teams." Imani Johnson in Oregon was already immersed in a "very collaborative team" when the crisis struck, and she credited that team with being "one hundred percent, my strongest support." Massachusetts teacher Carla Morrison praised her fourth-grade colleagues as "rock stars," saying "I do have a really amazing team that I'm on. And we all just share the work. There are no egos." Jane Farley cited her school's "incredible coordinated teams," while science teacher Michelle Yang was able to count on her "tight-knit department" and "a lot of collaboration," adding, "We are each other's second family."

Teachers who could attest to a strong prepandemic collaborative culture typically described a set of structural supports. Carla Morrison and the fourth-grade colleagues she considered "rock stars" were able to plan and create instructional materials together because their physical proximity and common schedules enabled them to do so: "Our classrooms are all on the same hallway, we're all next to each other. Our schedules are the same, we have snack at the same time, we have recess at the same time. So we get to talk every day." In elementary schools, relatively small size and common instructional responsibilities both enabled and inspired collaboration. At the secondary level, those knowledgeable and supportive colleagues were often found at the department level. Don Granger, a high school teacher in Texas, described a department whose prepandemic collaborations were aided by the physical layout of his large school: "Within our [English] department we were very close and worked well collaborating together. The way the school is set up, we're on one floor of one building, and we have our own faculty lounge there." He added, "That's a departmental expectation, that we work together," pointing to the kind of organizational norm characteristic of the strongest cases of collaborative culture found in the research literature.

In the strongest instances of prepandemic collaborative culture, teachers also spoke of a shared philosophy and practices. Francisco Vargas described the "incredible close bond between the five of us [ninth-grade teachers], four content area teachers and a special ed specialist, all veteran educators, remarkably aligned in terms of ways of thinking about kids." The teachers' shared commitment to students' academic, social, and emotional well-being, and their common pedagogical orientation to student collaboration and sensemaking in the classroom, infused the meetings they held each morning. "We schedule a half hour meeting before advisory starts, just to check in with each other. It makes us very close and lets us tackle all sorts of questions and issues." Similarly, Imani Johnson's collaborations were rooted in her school's adoption of the International Baccalaureate Primary Years Program: "You can't do IB without collaborating. In fact, it's built into the program. You have to be collaborative. So, I don't know how to teach otherwise and I'm grateful. I wouldn't teach any other way."

In contrast, teachers who struggled most were those who felt the least workplace support from colleagues, administrators, or other specialists; some described a workplace that was "toxic," "cliquey," "harmful," or "dysfunctional." Texas high school teacher Claire Macalister lamented, "Our teachers don't collaborate and it's very unhealthy." Iowa high school teacher Ruth Cartwright, asked about any support she experienced, exclaimed, "Support? I have a worthless PLC [professional learning community]!" Imani Johnson, the elementary teacher who has "always had really collaborative relationships," expressed gratitude for those relationships in part because "I talk to colleagues around the district who are not part of collaborative teams, and they're sinking, I mean, they're just drowning."

Timely, Relevant Professional Learning Opportunities

Teachers were dependent largely on their own initiative and resources to navigate the steep learning curve presented by remote and hybrid teaching. They did so by turning to colleagues, as described above, but also by participating in organized professional development (PD) activities and by exploring a wide range of online venues. A recurrent theme in surveys and interviews centered on teachers' desire for PD opportunities that were timely, responsive to teachers' expressed needs and interests, and sensitive to differences in their experience and expertise. Sarah Weaver's previous experience with her designated social studies PLC had been a largely perfunctory response to administrative directives, but that changed with the pandemic as the teachers took charge of identifying and responding to their own learning needs: "In years past it was just kind of 'let's check the box.' But now it seemed like we actually had a lot to talk about and a lot to learn from each other instead of jumping through the hoops. Administration was so busy they couldn't dictate to us, you have to do this, you have to do that. So we were able to chart our own course and it was successful. It really was" (August 2021).

Learning New Technology Platforms and Tools The abrupt pivot to teaching from a distance entailed, for nearly all, reliance on technology platforms and tools to establish contact with students and families and to manage instruction. Some teachers—although a minority—entered the early weeks and months of the pandemic with substantial experience using Google Classroom or other online platforms. Some were accustomed to using digital tools like SeeSaw, Nearpod, Jamboard, or Desmos to enhance classroom learning. However, even those teachers had not used such systems and tools to teach entirely from a distance or to manage hybrid instruction. Middle school teacher Henry Marquez characterized himself as "a very online teacher" and "very adept with the computer" in a district with good technology PD and tech specialist support and in a school where "most of us use Google Classroom. We've been using it for years." This prior experience positioned him and his colleagues well to communicate with students and families. But familiarity with Google

Classroom did not prepare Mr. Marquez for the experience of teaching entirely online, which he initially found "very static."

Unlike Mr. Marquez, most teachers scrambled to familiarize themselves with new technology. Describing her experience as "a lot like being a first-year teacher again," preK teacher Liz Darcie, in her tenth year of teaching, said, "You know, we kind of got thrown into it. There was nothing. We had no training. I didn't even know what Zoom was on March 16 last year." A year later, she believed she had "come a long way."

More than three-quarters of the teachers found PD useful in learning the technical features of new online platforms and tools, but only half found it helpful in learning to create or adapt interactive lessons for online spaces. Even fewer found formal PD offerings useful for creating online lessons that would boost student participation and engagement, build classroom community, enable assessment of student learning, or support special-needs students or English language learners. In addition, the rapid proliferation of platforms and tools was sometimes overwhelming for teachers, students, and parents. Florida high school teacher Janet Featherstone recalled that when schools first shut down, "part of the confusion and the difficulty was everyone was using something different," leaving students frustrated. She characterized the situation as "like the Wild West." Liz Darcie, who had "come a long way," still complained, "They've thrown so many different learning apps at us to use, I can't figure half of them out." In summer 2022, high school English teacher Don Granger suggested that he and his colleagues would have benefited from a more measured, selective, and targeted adoption of technology: "I think if we had strategically gone through finding tools that were useful across the curriculum that were somewhat easy for teachers to master, and maybe introduce one or two at a time as opposed to 'Here's a list of things you can use. And you must use this one and this one and this one and this one whether it really fits your class or not' " (July 2022).

Mr. Granger's observation found echoes in the experience of other teachers who were pleased to have developed a new awareness of the affordances of technology and new facility with technology platforms and tools but who also wanted technology to be meaningfully integrated with their pedagogy.

The Uneven Capacity of Schools and Districts The sudden onset of remote teaching and the uncertainties that accompanied hybrid instruction exposed substantial variation in the capacity of schools and districts to provide timely, responsive professional development. Henry Marquez praised his urban district's rapid and coordinated approach to technology-related PD: "They offered us just hundreds of different workshops. I mean, there were so many digital or online tools to be able to communicate with students and instruct online." As a teacher already familiar with classroom technology, he added his appreciation for the latitude to choose PD suited to his needs: "People were at different levels so they could pick and choose which workshops worked best for them." Having responded to the early demand for technology-related PD, but sensitive as well to the upheavals spawned in the wake of the George Floyd killing in May 2020, the district also developed offerings related to social justice and anti-racist teaching, resulting in what Mr. Marquez termed "robust conversations" among teachers. "When we came back at the end of August, we had weeks of professional development on strategies to engage students [remotely]. We had a lot of workshops on equity. So that was a lot of preparation." He benefited from an urban district with well-developed PD infrastructure. Teachers in small or rural districts were more likely to find themselves largely on their own.

District staff who organized professional development after schools reopened in fall 2020 were often seen by teachers as out of touch with teachers' needs. Carl Graham, an elementary teacher in Oregon, criticized his district for relying on "canned programs" that he found insulting to veteran teachers. He expressed his preference for PD that was more consistently differentiated and led by individuals with a deep understanding of classroom teaching. Mr. Graham was not alone in objecting to a district's reliance on packaged, one-size-fits-all programs, where the presenters knew little of the local classroom context and failed to acknowledge differences in teacher experience, knowledge, and skill. Sam Stewart, the Iowa middle school social studies teacher who resigned in 2022, was disappointed by his district's embrace of "canned, recycled things from the '80s business world." Mr. Stewart would have welcomed meaningful professional development that focused on effective remote teaching and that equipped him to contend with students traumatized by the pandemic. Similarly, Iowa high school teacher Ruth Cartwright envisioned the kind of PD with an instructional coach that would have helped her adapt prepandemic lessons to a virtual platform instead of content that wasn't aligned with pandemic-related learning needs: "We didn't spend any of our professional development time talking about what it means to teach during COVID."

Teachers' comments focused on whether the focus, amount, and timing of PD constituted support or a burden. Jennifer Donegal in Florida criticized her district for requiring teachers to attend a half-day training on the platform Canvas several months after the teachers had figured it out on their own. In her view, "the district had a hard time keeping up with what we actually needed." Unlike Henry Marquez, who was given the latitude to choose among an array of options for technology-related PD, high school science teacher Amy Locke worked in a district where "they want us to try all the things available online and they want us to be certified in everything and they want us to do all the PD available all the time." In her case and others, the district approach to PD simply added to teachers' work overload. Kentucky elementary teacher Emma Thorsen, who ultimately left teaching, wrote, "Professional developments were conducted almost weekly. Overall, PDs felt rushed, they lacked substance, and they were cumbersome when our time was already spread thin."

Teacher-centered and teacher-led professional development stood in stark contrast, in most cases, to the formal professional development offered (or required) by schools and districts. Iowa middle school teacher Judy Aldrich appreciated the autonomy granted to her sixth-grade team to identify their own learning priorities and to spend their monthly PD meeting focused on their chosen priority. Jennifer Donegal also credited her administration with recognizing teachers' wish for "appropriate professional development" and, more specifically, professional development led by teachers and rooted in their practical experience and expertise. She elaborated on her experience:

> One Tuesday a month, they seek out two or three teachers who are willing to do a short thirty-minute PD on some area that the teacher has a strength in. Then the rest of the staff get to choose which PD they want to go to. And I think that's really powerful because when you're asked to do the PD, you take pride in that, realizing that you're acknowledged. And then, I feel like it is also a sign of respect that they're letting us choose what we think would be an area of our own growth, an area of our own interest, and that we're able to seek that out, too, instead of just telling us to sit down and listen to this outsider. (August 2022)

Regardless of whether they found meaningful professional development in their local schools and districts, teachers extended their reach beyond the local, seeking information, ideas, and insight in teacher networks accessible online.

The Significance of Networks Teachers' responses to pandemic teaching conditions illuminate the role of existing and new teacher networks outside the school in helping teachers navigate a steep learning curve. A growing body of research has employed social network analysis to examine teachers' informal ties within and across schools and districts, with a focus especially on how those networks provide support for teachers' professional development and the pursuit of curriculum reform and instructional improvement. In recent years, research has expanded to include a focus on networks formed through social media platforms like Facebook and Twitter.[5] As teachers turned to fellow teachers for support via social networks, including networks formed through social media, they were engaging in a well-known process of emergent network formation that is characteristic of effective crisis response.[6]

More than three-quarters of teachers surveyed in March 2021 pointed to existing teacher networks as significant sources of instructional support, and two-thirds sought out new Facebook groups, Twitter groups, professional organizations like the National Writing Project, or other networks. Amy Locke in Arizona belonged to multiple online science teacher groups and declared that "social media is my go-to" for professional learning opportunities. Emily Kline, already a member of a Facebook group for teachers of Advanced Placement science courses, said, "I've never used the group more than I have this year." Jane Farley reported that district PD was rather "hit or miss," but "teacher Facebook groups were really helpful." Experienced high school science teacher Claire Macalister declared her external networks, including those formed through state and national science teacher organizations, to be "the best PLC I get," adding, "The chemistry community is amazing."

For some teachers, like Ms. Farley and Ms. Locke, external networks complemented strong school-based relationships; for those without such relationships, like Mr. Stewart, networks formed a crucial lifeline. In the absence of local PD that met his needs or interests, he turned to outside groups and organizations as his primary source of learning and support, saying, "I leaned really hard on my personal and professional networks this year and was and am so grateful to have them."

Individually and collectively, teachers were generally more flexible, nimble, and adaptive during the pandemic crisis than school or district systems. Meaningful, relevant, just-in-time learning opportunities have multiplied in a digitally connected world, suggesting that schools and districts could think more strategically about how to help connect teachers more systematically to those opportunities and resources. And yet teachers also continue to value learning opportunities constructed close to the classroom. For example, Jane Farley benefited substantially from her long-term ties to a national network of mathematics and science teachers but also said she would have welcomed opportunities for feedback based on observation of her classroom.

While the pandemic gave new urgency to the availability of professional learning resources, both local and online, teachers' experiences underscored the value they placed on high quality, timely, and relevant professional development opportunities in which they have significant individual or collective choice. In this regard, as with respect to issues of workload, teachers rely on the enabling decisions and practices of leaders at multiple levels.

Supportive, Responsive, and Effective School and District Leadership

Of the four aspects of workplace context highlighted here, school and district leadership emerged as the most crucial to the level of support teachers experienced, the satisfaction they expressed, and the career plans they made or contemplated. Leaders' perspectives and practices convey their conception of the teacher's role, reflecting a professional orientation rooted in trust or a bureaucratic conception tied to hierarchy and control.[7] Their decisions bear directly on the crucial working conditions of workload, workplace culture, and teachers' professional development options.

Leaders Under Pressure Teachers acknowledged that district and school leaders were confronted with rapid but complicated decision-making in the wake of school closures and in the short period available to plan for reopening. News accounts, school board meetings, and Facebook postings conveyed divisions within communities and signaled the kinds of challenges faced by district and school administrators. Parent groups—not always in agreement with each other—mounted public campaigns around the scale, timing, and form of school reopening. Janet Featherstone observed, "Our principal was under a tremendous amount of pressure. The pressure I felt is probably nothing compared to what this man went through this year." Jane Farley reported that she and her colleagues were "shielded from this (turmoil) as much as possible" by the school administration but that her very experienced principal said, "This is the hardest year I've ever dealt with." Other teachers noted that administrators were doing the best they could in the face of continued uncertainty.[8] Yet the actions taken by local leaders, first when schools closed and then over the following two years, played a part in sustaining or weakening teachers' engagement with teaching and their career commitment.

Leadership That Sustained Engagement In the face of the pressures and uncertainties created by the pandemic, some leaders rose to the challenge in skillful and strategic ways. Effective and supportive leadership played a large role in teachers' ability to remain positive and engaged despite the challenges posed by pandemic teaching. By the end of the second year, more than half (55 percent) of focal teachers, when interviewed, had credited school or district leaders with meaningful support and prudent decision-making. Arizona elementary teacher Lori Perenno was emphatic: "My principal, I don't even know what I could do to ever repay her for what she's done to keep everybody calm and moving forward. She's an amazing leader. And she knows what stress we're under." Ms. Perenno's decision to remain teaching despite her objection to her state's mistrustful stance toward teachers can be attributed to the local support she received, especially from a principal who actively worked to relieve stress. Florida high school teacher Sarah Weaver admired her urban district's administration and school board for defending mask mandates in the face of the governor's threat to withhold pay: "I applaud them. They stuck to their guns and they did not drop the mask mandate." Henry Marquez enthused, "The support of my administrators was enormous. We have a very accessible administrative team and that's positive." He added, "I think that they have really been equitable in listening to teachers and also to the community."

As we explore more fully in chapter 6, focused on teacher voice, leaders' disposition and ability to listen earned them the respect of teachers, even when the voices in the room might prove contentious and when leaders' capacity to respond was constrained. Julia Harper, an elementary teacher in Kentucky, said, "I felt respected. That didn't mean that it always went the way I wanted it to when their hands were tied. They can only do so much [but] we were respected enough to know they considered how we felt."

Teachers praised administrators who took steps to mitigate the added workload demands associated with complicated instructional arrangements and COVID-related safety protocols. In summer 2021, looking back over the school year, Massachusetts high school teacher Emily Kline reported, "Our principal was pretty good at regular communication. He'd send out an email every single morning with any sort of information, any new things. So, I never felt totally disconnected or thrown to the wolves."

Supportive administrators were a visible presence in classrooms and hallways, helping to establish a sense of order and responding to problems.

Arizona high school teacher Amy Locke credited a new principal and nearly total administrative turnover with restoring order—and her commitment to staying—after the prior "horrendous" year: "They're catching attendance issues, and they're catching dress code issues, and they're catching tardy students. So, a lot of that stress we had last year, we're not seeing it in the classroom because it's already being handled before it gets to the classroom." Claire Macalister underlined the moral support she derived from a principal who was visibly working hard ("I know she's working just as hard as I am and that makes a huge difference"), coupled with the more instrumental boost she got when a new superintendent restructured the workday: "We were teaching seven periods out of eight, which meant I had no break other than lunch, and now he's giving us PLC time every day. That's another big change for this year is that we actually have time to team."

Like Ms. Macalister's superintendent, principals took concrete steps to create a manageable workload. They structured time for teacher planning and collaboration while reducing the number of required meetings. Noelle Cruz in Oregon said, "I have two incredible administrators who are constantly asking, 'What do you need, what do you need?' And adjusting. We've been given a lot of time back. 'Do we need to meet for that?' Nobody's wasting anybody's time. And that is a gift."

Leadership That Produced Stress and Weakened Engagement Teachers highlighted the value they attached to good leadership and their disappointment when that leadership fell short. As New York high school teacher Tom James voiced in summer 2021, "I think any time there's a crisis you look to the person above you and you look to leadership to be a vanguard of whatever change is happening and to communicate those changes." Those who expressed disappointment or frustration with local leaders cited both deficiencies—steps not taken or actions that were problematic—and missed opportunities, including failures to capitalize on teacher expertise, experience, and motivation.

The most prominent teacher complaint centered on unclear or untimely communication, especially in the weeks leading up to the return to school in fall 2020. High school teacher Eve Nowak in New York was not alone in complaining that "we were always finding things out after the fact." Teachers struggled to make sense of confusing guidance or mixed messages. Oregon high school teacher Vivian Woods sounded a common refrain: "The amount of confusing messages, and the amount that seems to just be open to interpretation is part of what makes it so hard." A lack of clear and timely communication regarding district-level decisions affected teachers' ability to plan and prepare.

Amid this uncertainty, and contributing to it, teachers experienced little of what they would term authentic consultation and voice, a condition we examine more fully in chapter 6. In one example, Lori Perenno reported in summer 2021 that she had been included in a committee focused on a safe return to school but found it "very obvious they already had a plan. So, I don't know how much our voice was truly used in the decision-making process."

Teachers who were critical of local leadership also felt their professional expertise, experience, and judgment to be underestimated and undervalued. Surveyed in June 2021, more than 80 percent of the project teachers felt professionally respected by their school principal and 57 percent felt respected by their district. However, fewer were convinced that decision-making was informed by teachers' experience, judgment, and perspective at either the school (49 percent) or district (33 percent) level. In failing to capitalize on teachers' professional knowledge and motivation, and especially on what teachers learned during the pandemic, leaders missed opportunities to strengthen the capacity of schools and districts to weather future crises. At the end of the 2020–2021 school year, a high school teacher in Florida expressed frustration with administrators' control orientation. Sarah Weaver recalled, "I thought there would be more autonomy and trusting our professional judgment, but there was a lot of micro-management." As elementary teacher Carla Morrison in Massachusetts put it, "The most frustrating part has been dealing with administration throughout this—I think they underestimate us a lot. I look at my colleagues and these are incredibly accomplished, educated, thoughtful, reflective people who deeply care about the development of children and teaching and doing their best. But we're always underestimated" (September 2020).

Where it was evident, the combination of disappointing leadership actions and a propensity to underestimate teachers' expertise and motivation eroded teachers' enthusiasm for their work. Both deficiencies and missed opportunities were sometimes compounded by leaders' inexperience or lack of skill, suggesting implications for leadership preparation, support, and supervision. Yet as described above, there were also plentiful examples of leadership that bolstered that enthusiasm and helped sustain teachers' commitment to teaching.

Leadership Turnover and Transition The significance of leaders' stance and competence to teachers' satisfaction and commitment invests leadership turnover and transition with particular importance. At least one-third of the focal teachers experienced a change of principal or other school-level leaders; four described a change in superintendent.[9] Leadership turnover inevitably spawns uncertainty and anxiety, especially when those departing are admired and well respected; a crisis magnifies the uncertainties and intensifies the sense of urgency about the quality of incoming leaders. Interviews vividly conveyed teachers' relief or excitement over successful transitions—some of which represented a pronounced improvement—and their dismay over changes for the worse. Their accounts underscored the importance of administrators' dispositions, skill, and practice to teachers' satisfaction and engagement in ordinary times and especially in periods of crisis and change.

High school teacher Sarah Weaver in Florida expressed the staff's palpable relief at the departure of a principal who had flailed in the face of crisis: "We have a new principal now who's amazing. The previous principal was a 'put fires out' type of person and she just reacted. It seemed like she could never get ahead of the curve. There was a lot of just panic, panic, panic, panic all the time. So, it was not the best place to be. The kids could feel it. The teachers could feel it because it came from the top." Similarly, Leanne Edwards in Texas reported that she and her high school colleagues were "not disappointed" to see their principal leave amid a rash of disciplinary problems and parent conflicts. According to Ms. Edwards, the new principal announced upon arrival, "This is not going to be the way this works anymore [and] boom, fixed 80 percent of what we had been complaining about almost instantly." Emily Kline in Massachusetts was disappointed when the principal of her high school, whom she had praised for his leadership during the early stages of the pandemic and for the high expectations he conveyed upon the return to school, left suddenly in the middle of the 2021–2022 school year. His replacement—a former elementary school principal—was ill-equipped to lead the high school, and Ms. Kline lamented, "Ever since they've done that, I feel like our culture is starting to go downhill."

Despite the disruption that leadership turnover may produce, most of the teachers' descriptions of leadership turnover had a certain opaque character. Departures often took teachers by surprise, sometimes in midyear, as in Ms. Kline's case. With a few exceptions—for example, an assistant superintendent's conferring with the staff of an elementary school about their leadership priorities following the principal's sudden resignation—new appointments were made without teachers' input.

"Transitions are hard, and new leadership can be hard and tricky when you're trying to navigate expectations on both sides," observed Oregon elementary teacher Imani Johnson. In an exception to the more common turnover stories provided by the teachers, Ms. Johnson had the good fortune to experience a planned transition from a long-term administrator who "will always be a mentor" to an incoming principal who was "driven to understand culture." She explained further: "[The new principal] has brilliant questions, her doors have been open all summer, and she's made it very accessible—in-person, group settings, one-on-ones, online—with all the same questions out to people, bringing lots of folks in for interviews, and having [their] voice involved. [She is] meeting with all the grade levels in a week-and-a-half just for quick grade level check-ins. What do we want it to be like? What do we want to bring back? What don't we? She was asking great questions about all of that" (August 2022).

Teachers' experience during more than two years of pandemic-related teaching was shaped in significant ways by the words and actions of school and district leaders, reinforcing the insights derived from decades of research on the role of leaders in the relative success or failure of schools and school systems. In times of calm and in times of crisis, school leaders can best support teachers' work through words and actions respectful of teachers' professional expertise, judgment, and motivation.

WORKING CONDITIONS AND CAREER COMMITMENT

Teachers elect to leave or stay in teaching, or move from one school or district to another, for a variety of personal and professional reasons. However, in a crisis of long duration like the pandemic, personal considerations take on more complexity and urgency while key elements of the work environment become magnified in importance.

Figure 5.1 displays the pattern of career decisions or orientations among thirty-five focal teachers as of summer 2022 in relation to their expressed engagement with teaching and their reported working conditions.[10] Teachers were considered highly engaged when they expressed a firm identity as a teacher and found reward in classroom teaching and in their relationships with students; engagement might also be reflected in teachers' connections with professional activity beyond the classroom through teacher networks or teacher leadership roles. Teachers signaled low engagement when they reported diminished satisfaction with classroom teaching and pronounced cynicism or pessimism about teaching as a profession. Working conditions were considered strong when teachers described strong collaborative ties with colleagues, a supportive leadership, and access to good professional learning opportunities; strong working conditions were further cemented where teachers enjoyed the respect of parents and community and where they found avenues for voice and influence. In contrast, teachers suffering from weak working conditions tended to be isolated from colleagues and to voice disappointment in school and district leadership; some suffered parent criticism or community divisiveness.

As portrayed in chapter 3, teachers' assessments of their working conditions figured prominently in their reported engagement with teaching as an occupation and in the career plans they expressed or carried out.

The dominant pattern in Figure 5.1 suggests a strong relationship between working conditions and teachers' decisions to stay, leave, or move. Cases are concentrated in one of two quadrants. Quadrant 1, representing high engagement and strong working conditions, is populated almost entirely by teachers considered Satisfied Stayers or Movers. Of the twenty teachers in Quadrant 1, seventeen were Satisfied Stayers or Movers.[11] Quadrant 3, associated with low engagement and weak working conditions, is represented by teachers who had left, were seeking to exit, were waiting out retirement, or were trapped by financial considerations. Of the thirteen teachers in Quadrant 3, four left teaching, four were actively seeking to exit, three were looking to retire sooner than originally planned, and two were unhappily stuck. Of the three teachers in Quadrant 2, one left at the end of the 2021–2022 school year. Two have remained in teaching despite weak working conditions; one is looking to retire sooner than planned, while the other cited her strong ties to her local rural community as a reason to stay.

Figure 5.1 Focal teachers' career position in relation to engagement and workplace conditions

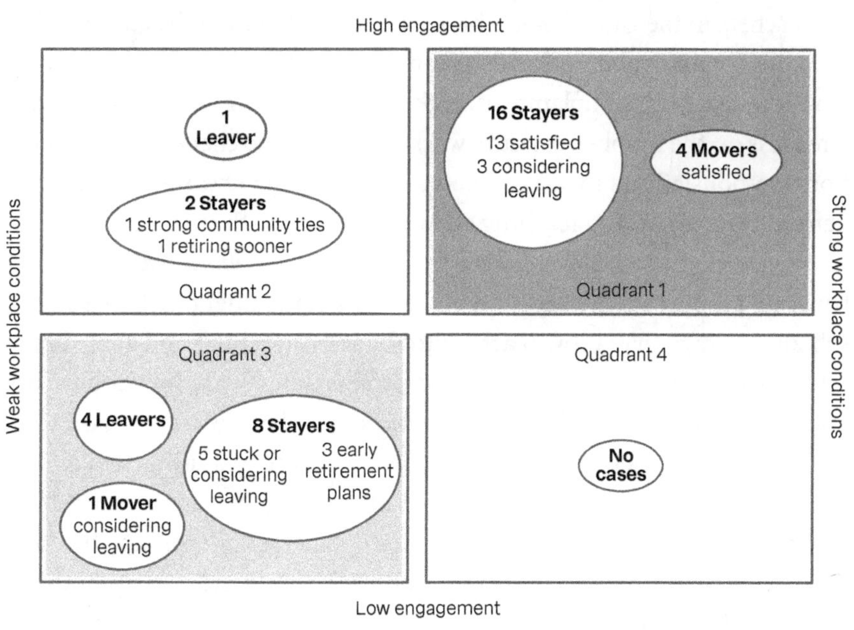

Overall, teachers who were Satisfied Stayers or who were satisfied after having moved schools or districts were more likely to describe favorable working conditions in the form of strong collegial ties, responsive and effective leadership, useful local or network-centered professional development, and professional respect.

CONCLUSION

The findings presented in this chapter underscore the significance of workload and the role of school workplace culture, including the strength or weakness of collegial ties, the nature of professional learning opportunities, and the quality of school and district leadership, in differentiating teachers' experience of teaching during an extended pandemic. They reinforce the working conditions teachers need to thrive in schools during ordinary times while pointing to the conditions required to adapt in times of extreme challenge and disruption. The findings support five lessons for policy and practice, described briefly below.

Lesson 1: Mitigating work overload and enabling work-life balance.

Teachers in the United States have long worked beyond the contract day, spending evenings and weekends grading student work or planning lessons. However, teachers' complaints of work overload during the pandemic centered less on the number of hours worked than on the challenges and additional responsibilities that combined to diminish the rewards that teachers derived from classroom teaching and relationships with students.[12]

Remedies that would ensure a more sustainable workload in normal times and moderate the urgent demands of a crisis might include staffing schools in ways that allow teachers to focus on teaching and that supply relevant supports from other trained professionals including counselors and social workers; modifying the ratio of in-class to out-of-class time during the contract workday to allow for more planning, collaboration, and professional learning time; building a stable supply of substitute teachers; and ensuring during times of emergency (perhaps through union contracts) that teachers need not teach simultaneously in both in-person and remote modes.

Lesson 2: Preparing a teacher workforce with the dispositions and skills for productive collaboration.

The pandemic experience underscored the advantage that accrued to teachers accustomed to frequent and productive interaction with their teacher colleagues and other school-based professionals. Teachers who were immersed in close collaborative relationships had a markedly different pandemic experience than teachers with weak ties to colleagues or, in extreme cases, what could be considered a toxic workplace. However, fewer than one-third of the project teachers described a robust prepandemic workplace culture. This has implications for teacher preparation and mentorship, the preparation and support of school administrators, and the organization of the professional workday, workweek, and work year.

Preservice teacher preparation presents the first opportunity to equip newcomers to the profession with the dispositions and skills of collaboration that enable steady improvement in normal times and that supply a crucial resource for effective response in times of crisis. Such preparation would likely be built around cohorts who work together throughout their preparation. It would entail student teaching placements that encompass not only classroom experience but also experience as a novice member of a school, participating in grade-level or department meetings and attending whole-school faculty meetings. Teacher preparation that remains highly individualistic and that provides novice teachers only with classroom experience is unlikely to equip them well to work effectively as a member of a team. At its best, teacher preparation might also include opportunities to learn alongside those preparing to be school counselors, school psychologists, or school social workers so that each group understands what they might expect from fellow professionals.[13]

Lesson 3: Investing in teacher learning and teacher leadership.

Teachers demonstrated impressive initiative, expertise, and adaptability as they navigated more than two years of pandemic-era teaching. They navigated a steep learning curve, sometimes with the aid of structured professional development offerings and nearly everywhere with the help of teacher colleagues. Their experience highlights the value of high-quality, timely, and relevant PD—and the infrastructure to support it—as well as the power of teacher-to-teacher learning.

A meaningful investment in teacher learning would entail structuring the workday and workweek to enable professional learning time, with learning agendas and activities more often determined by teachers themselves than by administrators or outside consultants; differentiating PD to respond to teachers' experience, expertise, and expressed needs and interests; establishing meaningful roles and resources for teacher leaders; and enabling teachers' individual and collective participation in conferences and other external learning opportunities through funding and the availability of substitute teachers.

Lesson 4: Building the capacity for effective, responsive administrative leadership at the school and district level.

The quality of school and district leadership emerged as a significant and consequential factor in teachers' satisfaction with teaching prior to the pandemic and in their pandemic teaching experience. The findings highlight the importance of a district-level stance that favors professional trust and judgment over a reliance on bureaucratic control, a stance reflected in decision-making structures and processes that function well in normal times but can also enable a rapid and effective response to crisis. Similarly, the findings point to the importance of recruiting and supporting school-level administrators who are adept at cultivating collaborative and improvement-oriented workplace cultures that engage both teachers and students. Such administrators encourage and model collaboration and inquiry; they promote shared goals and values conducive to improvement; they structure time and space for teachers to work together; and they provide teachers with the autonomy to structure the use of that time, avoiding what has been termed "contrived collegiality."[14]

Lesson 5: Establishing structures, processes, and norms that provide teachers with the opportunity to exercise voice and influence in school- and district-level decision-making.

Previous studies have demonstrated a relationship between teachers' involvement in decision-making and their organizational and professional commitment.[15] In interviews, teachers expressed appreciation when they felt respected and heard, but more often—especially in states or districts with a weak organized labor presence—complained of enduring crisis-related decision-making with little or no teacher voice. In chapter 6, we delve more fully into the nature and extent of teacher voice and influence, and the conditions that bolster or impede them.

6

The Value of Teacher Voice

Teacher voice matters. It matters in times of crisis, making possible nimble on-the-ground responsiveness. It matters in school management, improving school-level decision-making in times of crisis and calm. And it matters in terms of teacher career satisfaction, as acknowledging teacher expertise and respecting teacher knowledge increases career commitment and engagement. If readers take only one thing from this book, let it be this: authentically including teachers' voice in the daily work and directional decision-making of schools is essential to sustaining professional teachers in their work.

By voice, we mean that teachers themselves see their professional expertise as respected and influential in organizational decision-making. Feeling respected as a professional includes an awareness that your professional knowledge is valued. Conversely, seeking the input of someone in decision-making is a form of professional respect. Given the systemic disruption of the pandemic and the implications for district and school level modifications, the exploration of voice here attends primarily to school- and district-level respect and influence as assessed and reported by teachers. This conceptualization of voice is informed by three related strands of research: sociological work on professionalism and the framing of respect and influence in determinations of teacher professional status; organizational conditions of work in relation to teacher job satisfaction, commitment, and retention; and the political economic framing of voice and exit in organizational behavior and the provision of public goods.

In chapter 1, we noted the long-standing body of literature demonstrating that teachers' perceived voice and influence in decision-making are associated with career satisfaction. This chapter draws further upon the framing of the noted economist Albert Hirschman, who situated *exit, voice, and loyalty* as interdependent and sometimes mutually exclusive responses that employees and other group members face when confronting dissatisfactory conditions. In his seminal 1970 book, he argued that expanded avenues for employees to affect change—or assert voice—decrease the likelihood of employee exit. Hirschman was concerned with what he saw as an inevitable decline in public service provisions if people left the public sector and took their voices with them. The framework acknowledges that people are differentially positioned to exit, and that those left behind are often poorly positioned to speak up. Later refinements to the framework differentiated between types of exit: internal exit and complete exit. Internal exit in teaching is captured by those we call Movers, who leave one school for another but remain schoolteachers; complete exit is the departure of teachers from the field—the Leavers. In this way, both teacher leaving and moving can be a response to insufficient voice. Further refinements differentiated between individual voice (speaking up for oneself), and collective voice (joining together in a shared expression, campaign, or action), which are both ways teachers seek to improve dissatisfactory situations that could otherwise lead them toward exit.[1]

During pandemic-modified schooling, teacher voice was a decisive factor dividing those who stayed the course, teaching through and beyond the crisis, from those who quit teaching or who now want to quit teaching. Of all the teachers we followed, Satisfied Stayers had more voice in schools' pandemic navigation. As a group, they reported higher levels of consultation and representation at every stage of the response—from the fall 2020 return planning through the myriad decisions that needed to be made as schools everywhere charted a challenge-filled course through two full academic years. Notably, teachers in strong teacher union states reported the highest levels of voice. Most Satisfied Stayers in strong union states felt school leaders included them in planning for COVID-19 safety measures and the pandemic-modified instructional shifts needed to return to schooling in fall 2020. In summer 2021, Satisfied Stayers in strong union states felt the most respected by school leaders and the most likely to report that teacher expertise and perspective was included in school and district decision-making.

In contrast, Outbound Stayers—those teachers still in the classroom but with an eye on the exit door—and Leavers reported the lowest levels of consultation and representation. At every turn, they felt unheard at best and were often completely disregarded. Rarely consulted on fall 2020 reopening plans, Leavers and Outbound Stayers expressed low levels of influence in vital school decision-making. Teachers who experienced a diminished professional commitment were also the teachers who felt the least respected by their school leaders. They felt on the outside of school decisions that were important to classroom practice, student success, and school safety. Teacher union strength was a factor for these teachers, with most Leavers in places where the union was weaker.

While teachers in stronger labor states were more likely to feel respected and have influence on organizational decision-making than teachers in weaker labor states, it is also true that there were Satisfied Stayers, Leavers, and Outbound Stayers in all states. Teachers' experiences of pandemic teaching indicate that many find influence and representation through the collective voice of their unions. This is evident in the overall patterns reflected in teacher surveys but also in the detailed accounts of teacher experience. There are, however, other avenues to voice. Satisfied Stayers in weak union states also felt more respected and consulted than Leavers, Outbound Stayers, and the overall sample. And the presence of Leavers and Outbound Stayers who felt voiceless in both weak and strong labor states puts to rest any notion of a simplistic equation between state-level union strength and teacher commitment. It remains, however, that feeling respected for one's professional knowledge, as evidenced by school and district inclusion of teacher expertise, is a powerful force in teacher career commitment.

What follows is an analysis of teachers' perceived professional respect and influence in school and district decision-making at various moments in the thirty months of pandemic-modified schooling and the relationship to teachers' career trajectories. A sense of voice is not static, and feelings of respect and influence can and do fluctuate across a week and certainly across thirty months of pandemic teaching. Situating teacher experience of voice entails building an understanding of motivations, preferences, and experience over time and in context. Tracing fluctuations in teachers' feelings and perception affords insights into individual experience in relation to contextual change and organizational affordances for teacher voice. The patterns and accounts of teacher voice capture its importance in teacher career paths and illuminate several options for ensuring teachers experience professional respect and influence in school decision-making: union affordances of collective voice, effective local grassroots organizing, and organizational affordances for teacher voice.[2]

PATTERNS OF TEACHER VOICE

A Dominant Pattern: Insufficient Voice

Throughout the pandemic schooling response, teachers struggled to have their expertise, judgment, and knowledge included in school and district decision-making. While some teachers had more influence than others, in general, teachers felt excluded from organizational decision-making. Teachers consistently reported insufficient opportunities to contribute their knowledge, priorities, and hard-earned pandemic teaching expertise to pandemic response planning. By and large, teachers felt organizationally sidelined and unheard at every step of the process.

Summer 2020 was a time of planning for the much-anticipated fall return, including discussions about what form that return could and would take and debates about metrics and priorities to guide decision-making. In interviews that summer, teachers detailed their school return plans and the degree of teacher involvement in developing them, including how teacher input was solicited. Of sixty-nine teachers, forty-four (66 percent) felt teacher input was minimal to nonexistent. Teachers dismissed as "performative" organizational practices that might be considered consultative, including opinion surveys and teacher representation on a task force.

Criticisms included examples of survey requests that followed on the heels of fall plan announcements and task force committees that met only once in the early summer and had no real influence.

Opportunities to inform district- and school-level decision-making remained scarce throughout the 2020–2021 school year. In summer 2021, most teachers again expressed that district- and school-level decision-making excluded teacher voice. This was more pronounced at the district level than the school level. Two-thirds of teachers felt district decisions were made in the absence of teacher experience, knowledge, and perspective, whereas just more than half felt school-level decisions lacked teacher input. Teachers were frustrated by district-level decisions that did not account for their safety concerns. As vaccine availability grew and transmission and death rates declined, teachers felt safer—but many also carried lingering resentment for disregarded safety concerns and ongoing frustration that their instructional knowledge was rarely tapped as districts and schools worked to modify school practice. Teachers felt their professional knowledge and classroom practice, combined with the specific skills and expertise they developed through spring 2020 responsive innovations, uniquely positioned them to inform systems-level decisions.[3]

Leanne Edwards, a Texas teacher who moved schools in an effort to find working conditions that would allow her to stay in teaching, characterizes the arc of teacher influence from strong in spring 2020, to a rapid decline in fall 2021, to the complete exclusion of teacher voice: "We felt we had a lot of voice at the beginning and then we didn't. When we shut down, we had a lot of voice on how that (process) worked. Then when we started back up . . . midway through that year the state came out with all their mandates, and we were done. There was no more (teacher) voice to be had—they took that away" (Summer 2022).

Florida elementary school teacher Jennifer Donegal, who loves teaching but struggles with the lack of voice she is afforded as a professional, invokes the specialized knowledge and preparation of teachers that qualify them as professionals who are well positioned to inform decision-making at all school levels: "I have my master's in this. It's what I do. I have my certification. I've gotten all of the endorsements: my reading, my ESOL, my gifted. I'm constantly learning and growing and researching. . . . It's a specialized field. There's so much science behind it and so much learning that you have to do. . . . It's not a job. It's a profession" (Summer 2022).

Ms. Donegal expresses the views of many teachers when she asserts the need to center teachers' voice and classroom knowledge in navigating school planning and crisis response because of their professional expertise and their location close to student learning: "I think that we should be at the forefront. I think that we should be considered at every turn because what happens in the classroom, nobody knows that except for the people in the classroom" (Summer 2022).

Most of the teachers we followed agree with Ms. Donegal's assessment that teacher knowledge and professional expertise is undervalued as a school leadership resource and that improving schooling capacity and effectiveness, in times of crisis and calm, requires more teachers at the table where decisions are made.

Pathways to Voice

Amid the upheaval of the pandemic, some teachers reported considerable voice in organizational response, ranging from the modality of schooling to COVID-19 safety precautions. Three distinct sources and systems of voice were evident in teachers' pandemic teaching experiences:

1. *Teacher unions*: First, teachers experienced collective voice through their unions. Unions advocated for educators' voices at the bargaining table and organized collective action to influence district and statewide decisions.
2. *Grassroots unionism*: Second, even in the absence of strong formal unions, some teachers found collective voice through grassroots organizing efforts. These teachers drew upon preexisting networks of solidarity to apply pressure on decision-makers in conjunction with and outside of formal union channels.
3. *Organizational affordances*: Third, teachers experienced voice at the school level through strong organizational culture and leadership that intentionally included teacher knowledge and perspectives in

decision-making. These sources of voice are evident in the Satisfied Stayers' experiences of voice at the state, district, and school level.

The Collective Voice of Teachers' Unions

Teachers in stronger union contexts were more readily able to engage with and inform policies across multiple dimensions including school reopening plans, instructional modalities, and pedagogical practices. Unions solicited teacher input, provided protections to otherwise vulnerable teachers, and served as a mechanism for influencing policy decisions. As Massachusetts teacher Michael Donovan put it, "The union helps because we're a voice at the table." Teachers in New York, California, Oregon, and Massachusetts experienced stronger unions at the state level, while those in Texas, Florida, Iowa, and Kentucky faced a more hostile statewide labor environment. Yet even in weaker union states, some teachers experienced and built union power at the local level.

Unions amplified teacher voice, seeking teacher input and advocating for teachers' priorities. Henry Marquez, a California Satisfied Stayer in a strong state union context, captured this process: "The union was very proactive. . . . Our union (reps) communicated with us consistently, and I would say successfully, to share plans that needed teacher input and then to relay that teacher feedback back up to the union (leadership) and to the district." Similarly, Oregon Satisfied Stayer Imani Johnson's union gathered teachers' feedback on school reopening plans and then, "just very loudly reflected teacher concerns. And those concerns were health and safety and logistics. . . . And so now the union is bargaining . . . at the table having really hard conversations." Ms. Johnson trusted her union's bargaining team to have those hard conversations on her behalf, confident that the union spoke for her and her colleagues.

Even teachers in weaker union states sometimes found voice in strong local union activity. Despite her union's weakness at the statewide level, Janet Featherstone, one of the Florida Satisfied Stayers, said, "Our [local] union is fighting to move online. Our teachers are fighting. There are demonstrations and rallies and picketing outside the school board office." Sarah Weaver, another Florida Satisfied Stayer, also credited her local union with meeting the moment by taking on more than it had in the past: "Our [local union] was very involved—because normally our unions are very weak, but they really stepped into the fray this time and they really, really fought. So that was nice to see. . . . They did a really, really good job." Both of these teachers were surprised and heartened by their local unions' willingness to fight despite a hostile statewide labor climate.

That state and local unions helped facilitate teacher voice is evident in Satisfied Stayers' career decisions. The stories of two teachers, in particular, underline the role of unions in amplifying teachers' collective voice: urban elementary school teacher Carl Graham expressed his voice and sustained career commitment in Oregon, a state noted for the strength of its teachers' union. Meanwhile, suburban elementary school teacher Nancy Walsh found her voice through her local union despite the weaker Kentucky state union context.

Carl Graham: A Case of a Strong Local in a Strong State Union Context Carl Graham characterized his teachers' union as "exceptional" and declared in summer 2020, "I am so grateful for our union. . . . They really fight for us." As a union building representative at his school site for several years, Mr. Graham remained active during the pandemic. His local union is bolstered by the Oregon Education Association's relative influence at the statewide level, as illustrated by a report that ranked Oregon second in overall teacher union strength and third in perceived influence over state policies. Oregon is one of just thirteen states that allows teacher strikes and requires or permits collective bargaining over a wide range of topics, from classroom curriculum to terms and conditions of teacher employment.[4]

During the pandemic, Mr. Graham's union represented teacher priorities and perspectives in key areas of organizational decision-making, including pedagogical concerns and workforce considerations. Teaching modality was a major focus for the union in the 2020–2021 school year. The school year began in a remote learning mode but soon after the district announced a planned shift to hybrid schooling. The district proposed a blended hybrid model—the version of hybrid that teachers found most challenging to deliver and the least suited to serve students well without substantial, but notably absent, additional support. Teachers across all nine states were adamantly opposed to this model as it required educators to juggle teaching remotely and in-person simultaneously. Texas teacher Claire Macalister put it this way: "The teacher can't be doing both [teaching in person and remotely]. . . . You're going to burn them out. And I'm not talking a little burnt out. I'm talking quitting, never coming back." Mr. Graham and his colleagues felt the same concerns and opposition to the blended hybrid model. In December 2020, he shared, "One of the [questions] in a recent union survey was, would you support a ban on teachers having to teach online and in person (at the same time)? And of course, members were like, yeah, we don't want to do that."

The reopening plan was subject to a bargaining agreement, which provided teachers with a mechanism to reshape the hybrid model. Right away, the bargaining team raised opposition to the blended hybrid modality, arguing that it would erode the quality of education. In a February 2021 communication, the union president stated, "At this time, we are unsure how [our] members will have the time or ability to create lessons that work equally well in an online format and in an in-person class [simultaneously]." They continued, "When asked what districts they are drawing their inspiration from or where such a model is working well to serve students, no one on the district's bargaining team could reference a single example." The union's steadfast objection to the blended teaching modality swayed the district: in a March 2021 bargaining session, the district announced that they wished to "break the logjam" of the disagreement regarding the instructional model and proposed a revised hybrid model that still offered students remote and in person options, still reduced numbers in school, but did not involve blended hybrid teaching.

This successful instructional mode negotiation is especially notable given the struggles teachers and schools experienced with blended hybrid. As a model, blended hybrid was more prevalent in weak labor contexts, associated with lower rates of teacher commitment, and eventually recognized in some places as damaging to effective instruction. Ten of the twelve teachers assigned a blended hybrid modality worked in weaker labor states. These teachers, like Carl Graham and his colleagues, expressed their opposition to the blended hybrid model on the grounds of both pedagogical and student engagement challenges. However, these teachers lacked the same channels for asserting voice as those in Mr. Graham's district did. Their career outcomes capture the ramifications: of the twelve teachers who taught in a blended hybrid model, only three were Satisfied Stayers in summer 2022. And of those three, two were in Texas districts that quickly abandoned the experience of blended hybrid schooling once the negative effects on student learning became apparent.

The advocacy of Mr. Graham's union contributed crucially to his career satisfaction and the confidence he felt in the spring 2021 resumption of in-person schooling. In summer 2020, he was one of the few teachers who had input in his school's fall reopening plan and that played a pivotal role in his complete satisfaction with the plan. In summer 2021, he felt influential in organizational decision-making and highly respected by both his principal and school district leaders. He reflected, "I'm fortunate to be in a district where we have a really strong union representation and there was a ton of dialogue . . . [so] I didn't feel there was any problem going back. . . . I was eager to get back and I was much happier teaching in the spring, even with having to teach a quarter of my students online in the afternoons." Mr. Graham knew his voice mattered, as he saw his knowledge and perspective reflected in school and district plans, and he credited his union with ensuring teacher voice was an integral part of organizational decision-making.

Nancy Walsh: A Case of a Strong Local in a Weak State Union Context Nancy Walsh, an elementary teacher in Kentucky, found voice through her local union. Yet for Ms. Walsh, the strength of her local union stood in stark contrast with both state union strength and that of other locals in her state. She explained, "[Our district] is a little bit different, because we have a strong union but the rest of the state does not. . . . I think we had more voice [during the pandemic] than the rest of the state."

Kentucky has a long history of labor organizing alongside statewide labor repression, encapsulated by the infamous 1931 and 1973 Harlan County mine worker strikes.[5] Kentucky teachers have historically engaged in sustained collective action: in 1970, over seventeen thousand Kentucky teachers led a strike to demand greater funding from the state legislature; this strike was followed by a 1976 work stoppage in the state's largest school district and again in 1988 when Kentucky teachers shut down over half of schools across the state. In 2018, Kentucky teachers joined the Red for Ed movement and shut down dozens of school districts to protest a controversial pension reform bill. In 2019, teachers again staged a series of sickouts to oppose further changes to teacher pensions. Yet the state's teacher unions have steadily been demobilized, illustrated by falling membership rates over the past several decades. The contested and constrained state-level union influence makes notable the oppositional organizing in Ms. Walsh's district. In 2019, teachers in her district led the way in the statewide protests—one of just a handful of districts to successfully shut down schools to oppose the pension reform bill. During the pandemic, her local union again amplified teachers' concerns by pushing for a reopening plan aligned with teachers' instructional priorities and bargaining for sustainable workloads during remote learning.

Like many places in summer 2020, there was little clarity in Kentucky schools regarding fall reopening. Ms. Walsh characterized the confusion: "It's been like, 'What are we doing?'" as the plans shifted and changed. And yet, she still felt included in the local deliberations and ended up satisfied with the reopening plan, in large part because of the back-and-forth between her local union and the district. Initially, her district announced plans to return in person with social distancing protocols. When it became clear that COVID-19 safety precautions were not feasible, teachers worked through the union to push back against this in-person model: "The union was fighting against that because it's going to be close to impossible to socially distance that many kids." Ms. Walsh was eager to return to in-person schooling in fall 2020 but she supported prioritizing safety and well-being. She remarked, "As much as I want to be in the classroom, I know right now the way our cases are spiking that they're not going down [for a while]."

In September 2020, only one in ten Kentucky students was attending schooling in person; in October 2020 that number rose to three in ten. Ms. Walsh's district, however, remained remote in fall 2020 even while the number of Kentucky districts operating in person increased. Her local union maintained that remote learning in her district was necessary due to COVID-19 transmission rates. All Kentucky districts then shifted into remote schooling from mid-November through December 2020 when Governor Beshear shut down schools for all Kentucky students. Upon lifting these statewide restrictions, a third of Kentucky's students again returned to in-person schooling in January 2021, but Ms. Walsh's local union continued to advocate for remote schooling prior to teacher vaccine availability. In December 2020, she reported, "[The union] is still advocating for staying virtual to keep the teachers and the staff and the students safe." Her district maintained virtual learning through spring 2021 and timed student return to coincide with teacher vaccination access.[6]

All along, Ms. Walsh explained, "I feel like our [local] union . . . had a pretty good pulse on my [school] building to see what we want." Despite union weakness at the state level, the local union represented her well. She reflected, "We have a big voice, and [policy-makers] kind of listen." In summer 2021, Ms. Walsh felt a strong sense of respect from school and district leadership and knew that they considered her priorities in organizational decision-making. Her sense of being heard contributed to her career satisfaction. Unlike other teachers who felt unheard and disregarded, Ms. Walsh planned to teach until retirement. She acknowledged that she felt exhausted, but she also maintained, "I just want to say I still love my job. Even though it's very challenging, I still love my job."

For Mr. Graham, Ms. Walsh, and other teachers in strong state or local union contexts, their unions served as vehicles for teacher voice and contributed to their career satisfaction. Of the twenty-five Satisfied Stayers, sixteen worked in strong union contexts: thirteen in strong labor states and three in strong local unions inside weaker union states. The remaining nine teachers had alternative ways to express collective voice, including grassroots organizing and working in schools with inclusively consultative leadership practices.

Grassroots Unionism: Amplifying Teacher Voice

In the absence of strong unions, some teachers worked through grassroots networks to apply pressure on decision-makers and influence decisions at the local and statewide level. These grassroots organizing efforts operated both in conjunction with and separately from formal union channels in places with highly restrictive labor environments. While some teachers launched fledgling coalitions, others drew on preexisting infrastructures within established networks. The Red for Ed movement, in which a surge of teachers in Arizona and other traditionally conservative states led statewide strikes in 2018, proved to be an important foundation for teachers' grassroots organizing, affording movement veterans with networks that positioned them well in mobilizing and amplifying teacher voice during the pandemic. Not all teachers had these networks to draw on. Teachers in contexts without preexisting organizing networks also sought to organize to influence decision-making and planning, yet these educators found fewer and less effective avenues for voice.[7]

The power and limits of grassroots unionism in weak labor contexts are evident in the experiences of Satisfied Stayer Lori Perenno as contrasted with those of Leaver Sam Stewart. Both teachers expressed serious concerns about the decisions and plans initially crafted by their states and districts, but each was differentially positioned in the response options available to them. Ms. Perenno, an Arizona teacher deeply involved with the Red for Ed movement, navigated the pandemic as an experienced organizer with close ties and established trust with both local and statewide teacher networks that shared her commitments and labor organizing knowledge. Sam Stewart taught in a context with few established collaborators and no recent legacy of teacher organizing, and he struggled to organize teachers locally in sufficiently powerful numbers to have an influential voice. Their stories demonstrate the power and limitations of grassroot organizing and demonstrate that just as political and labor landscapes shape the scope of collective voice for teachers, teacher movements shape political and labor landscapes in return.

Lori Perenno: Organizing from an Established Foundation Arizona elementary teacher Lori Perenno is a proud "product of the public school system" who characterizes herself as a "loudmouth" who "will advocate for students and schools." Ms. Perenno works in a suburban K–8 community school she described as "very much a family . . . [where] teachers definitely look out for each other." This sense of "looking out for one another" was formalized and expanded during the 2018 Red for Ed Movement. Ms. Perenno was working as a long-term substitute when teachers began planning for the statewide walkouts. She shared, "I could not help but support that. How could I not support the teachers and the finances that need to be taken care of in our school districts?" She became a school site liaison through Arizona Educators United, a statewide grassroots teacher organization that developed in 2018 out of the creation of a Facebook group. It led 2018 statewide strike activity in partnership with, but remained distinct from, the union. Her participation in the 2018 strike shaped her orientation to organizing during the pandemic: "I think that being involved with Red for Ed and the walkouts have empowered me to be very vocal."

The 2018 teacher strikes in Arizona took onlookers by surprise given the state's hostile labor climate and minimal history of teacher strike activity. In 2012, Arizona was ranked weakest of all the states in teacher union strength due to its "right to work laws," prohibitions against public sector strikes, and absence of strong collective bargaining mechanisms. However, the Red for Ed strike changed teachers' sense of what was possible and introduced teachers to new oppositional organizing strategies. Ms. Perenno was one of over two thousand school site liaisons affiliated with Arizona Educators United, who took on leadership roles at their schools and facilitated walkouts that ultimately shut down schools for 75 percent of Arizona students in 2018. This network of site liaisons formed a core part of the organizing structures that carried over to the pandemic and facilitated coordinated action among Arizona teachers.[8]

In summer 2020, Ms. Perenno was not actively consulted as a teacher by her district and school leadership and yet, ultimately, she was satisfied with the reopening plan. This was largely due to the labor organizing efforts of Ms. Perenno and her colleagues. As school districts were preparing reopening plans for the 2020–2021 school year, Ms. Perenno and other activist teachers were collaborating statewide to resist an unsafe return to in-person schooling. "I started speaking up in July . . . about my concerns about going back to school." She continued, "I actually started, as I call it, *the resistance.*" She attended a virtual Arizona teachers' town hall organized by Arizona Educators United. At that meeting, educators were encouraged to share COVID-19 rates in their area, knowledge of their districts' plans for fall 2020, and information about their rights as educators. The outpouring of teacher concerns at the meeting galvanized Ms. Perenno to steward a plan for action across districts: "I heard a lot of people concerned . . . but there were no answers as to what we could do. We're at the mercy of the districts. And so during that meeting, I kind of lost my patience and spoke up and I said we have to do something." She pointed out that many of the seventy thousand Arizona teachers who participated in the Red for Ed movement had concerns now about school reopening and were ready to be remobilized. She put out a call to other educators at the meeting who had interest in developing a plan for statewide action and ten teachers agreed to start planning.

Ms. Perenno and these ten teachers began planning for "Motor Marches" where car caravans of educators transformed into moving billboards calling for COVID-19 safety as a priority in school reopening. Ms. Perenno recalled, "We went on a wing and a prayer and planned out . . . how we could make it work." In mid-July, an educator's Motor March encircled the Arizona state capitol and governor's office. By the end of the summer, these marches extended throughout Arizona and beyond to other states, including Florida and South Carolina, whose educators held similar concerns about school reopening.

In some Arizona districts, teachers also organized sickouts to increase pressure on school boards to keep schools closed while COVID-19 cases peaked. By spring 2021, teachers had organized six sickouts in five school districts. Ms. Perenno reflected in August 2020, "I feel like we've made inroads and we've made districts change their plans. We do know that. . . . There were a couple districts that changed." Ms. Perenno's own school board voted to wait until October 2020 to return to in-person schooling. She noted, "Other schools went back face-to-face today, and some schools didn't go back because there was a group of teachers in [another district] who called for a sickout so their schools couldn't go back. So, it's been a mixed bag here in Arizona."[9]

Her school district's decision to postpone in-person instruction in response to collective teacher advocacy was central to Ms. Perenno's decision to continue teaching during the 2020–2021 school year. She stated in relation to the fall 2020 first day of school, "If I would have had to go back to school on Monday in person, I would have quit." Crying, she continued, "I'm sorry but I'm emotional about that." Ms. Perenno sees teaching as her calling but secondary to keeping herself and her children safe. "I love teaching. I love the work that I do. It is the hardest work in the world and I don't want to give that up, but I am prepared, if I have to, to walk away from it if I'm forced to go back before I feel it's safe." For Ms. Perenno, this was not an individual sentiment but rather a collective stance alongside her coworkers. She told her union president, "There will be a group of teachers that speak up . . . and we will walk away because there are many that have talked about it." As a result of their organizing efforts, Ms. Perenno and her colleagues avoided the last resort of walking away from teaching.

Notably, these grassroots organizing efforts that began in 2018 and carried over to the pandemic lent strength to the statewide union, Arizona Education Association (AEA), an affiliate of the National Education Association (NEA). Prior to the 2018 walkouts, the union represented just 25 percent of Arizona teachers; following the upsurge in strike activity, teacher union membership had climbed by 10.3 percent. This fluid relationship between grassroots unionism and formal unionism was illustrated by Ms. Perenno's involvement with her local union. In summer 2022 she reflected, "Over the past couple of months, I've gotten much more involved with our union. . . . [It] started with Red for Ed." Teachers' collective action was not bound by formal union channels, but their grassroots efforts did strengthen and reinforce teacher unionism throughout the pandemic.[10]

Thanks to teachers' labor organizing, Ms. Perenno's school reopening plan aligned with her priorities and allowed her to stay in a profession that she loved. She always felt personally respected by local educational leaders but also acknowledged that respect never extended to include teachers in organizational decision-making. Her school and district leaders did not willingly incorporate teacher expertise and priorities in bigger picture planning. It was only through teachers' collective action, which drew upon infrastructures of former teacher movements, that she and other educators were able to bring about the working conditions they sought.

Sam Stewart: Seeking Solidarity Without Preexisting Networks While Lori Perenno was organizing Arizona Motor Marches, Iowa teacher Sam Stewart poured himself into efforts to harness collective teacher voice. Locally and at the state level, he endeavored to organize other teachers to collectively influence policies for a safe school reopening. At a local level, he struggled to find like-minded teachers willing to take the political risk of challenging the status quo. Mr. Stewart and his colleagues lacked the organizing legacy of the Red for Ed states that had established networks of solidarity and introduced teachers to collective organizing strategies. Mr. Stewart further sought solidarity across the nation in his efforts to resist what he saw as censorial efforts to control subject content and teaching. He publicly added his voice to national calls for change—calls that increased local scrutiny of him professionally, highlighted his vulnerability, and contributed to his decision to leave teaching.

Though Iowa was categorized as a state with medium teacher union strength in 2012, it is now more aptly characterized as a weaker union state. In recent years, public sector workers have faced mounting attacks and restrictions to labor rights and actions. The 2018 teacher strike movement never cohered in Iowa, resulting in fewer preexisting networks of solidarity among teachers. The union's weakness at the statewide level only further demobilized teachers. Mr. Stewart observed, "In Iowa, we're still very constrained as far as how much power our union might have." In 2017, revisions to Iowa's public sector labor law severely hampered public sector unions' structural capacity. This legislation specified wages as the only mandatory bargaining topic, required recertification elections every two years for already established unions, limited contracts to two years, and reversed the dues-checkoff policy. Mr. Stewart described the effect of one aspect of this legislation, the membership number requirement, as a threat to the viability of his local union chapter:[11] "[We] have to maintain a certain number of members for the union to be viable, which we are dangerously close to going under, as many rural districts are in the state. And so, were we to lose members, which we do seem to have kind of a steady decline, then our union would more or less disband and would not have any power, which is very scary to think about" (Summer 2021).

In June 2020, Iowa announced school districts had the authority to create their own "Return to Learn" fall reopening plans. Yet when several districts put forth plans that involved fully remote learning, "[our governor] reneged on that, saying that districts now must be at least 50 percent face-to-face. That's the law, she says." The statewide union put out a statement opposing the state's plan but did not organize any further action. In August 2020, Sam Stewart bemoaned, "There's been a lot of [union] urging and strong rhetoric followed by little action." He and other teachers described a general sense that the union was largely absent throughout the pandemic. He concluded in summer 2020, "There doesn't seem to be the political will or the union boldness" to challenge the state's refusal to prioritize health and safety.

Mr. Stewart helped organize a Drive for Lives teacher protest in July 2020 that involved thousands of teachers—even though, as he characterized, "teachers are not known in Iowa for being outspoken politically." The protest amplified teachers' demands for science-based decisions to guide school reopening plans; however, it did not alter the state's or his local district's course of action. In fall 2020, despite ongoing safety concerns, Mr. Stewart was assigned to teach from his classroom in a blended hybrid format five days a week. He was deeply dissatisfied with the plan and felt completely disregarded by his principal and district leadership.

Additionally, Sam Stewart struggled to counter the rise of encroaching state policies limiting the content of history and social studies classes. In June 2021, Iowa passed a "divisive concepts" bill that banned Iowa K–12 schools from teaching any indication that moral character is determined by race or sex or that the United States or Iowa are "fundamentally, institutionally, or systemically" racist. The Iowa State Education Association responded, "We are seeing in our classrooms—since this legislation has passed—a chilling effect on our educators and the way they go about teaching our students." In an effort to draw attention to what he saw as a threat on ethical teaching, Mr. Stewart signed on to statements and petitions by national organizing groups objecting to these policies. His lack of local collaborators, however, left him vulnerable to backlash. Mr. Stewart found himself singled out by local politicians who identified his name on the national petitions and called him out as an un-American threat. Without strong local solidarity, Sam Stewart's efforts to be heard cost him more than he gained in terms of leverage and voice.[12]

Taken together, Ms. Perenno's and Mr. Stewart's stories reveal both the possibilities and vulnerabilities of grassroots unionism in weaker union contexts. Ms. Perenno and her colleagues mounted an effective challenge to unsafe school reopening plans by building upon organizing networks that developed during the Red for Ed movement. Those organizing efforts began as a grassroots mobilization that was distinct from formal union channels but went on to lend strength to the statewide AEA. In contrast, without formal or informal solidarity networks, Mr. Stewart felt that he was out of options. In summer 2021 his overall assessment of school leaders' respect for him and his professional knowledge was the lowest of all the teachers we followed. Feeling demoralized over his inability to have his voice heard, he reflected, "If I were in a district with a stronger union presence, I'd be able to do a lot more. My tentative plan is to leave this district and find one where there's a stronger union and teachers who are more interested in and advocating for public education and students." One year later, he instead exited the K–12 teaching profession altogether.

Organizational Affordances for Teacher Voice

In some places, schools and districts intentionally included teacher voice in deliberations and decision-making regardless of the relative union strength or grassroots organizing. These consultation and inclusion practices, a hallmark of strong leadership, increased teacher experience of influence and respect. Julia Harper, a Satisfied Stayer from Kentucky, reflected, "We were respected enough to know that [school leadership] considered how we felt. . . . At the state level, no." Ms. Harper extolled the ways teacher priorities were both solicited and listened to at her school. She shared, "I felt respected. . . . I felt like throughout the whole process we were checked in on." When teachers expressed that they wanted to be back in person because they felt that students were suffering in remote learning, her school administrators "respected it and they fought for it." Arizona high school teacher Fred Marino, also a Satisfied Stayer, taught in a charter school network and appreciated how his school leaders valued teacher voice enough to fight for it at the organizational level. When the charter management organization (CMO) proposed a reopening plan that sidestepped teacher input, his administration challenged the CMO leadership, arguing, "You're doing this, but you're not really consulting with the teachers at all. And the plan that you semi-rolled out is just not going to work." Both of these Satisfied Stayers found the lack of teacher input at state and district levels was counteracted by a school-level orientation to teacher expertise and priorities.

Other teachers moved schools or districts in search of greater voice. Leslie Spark, a middle school math teacher in Florida, saw no potential for substantive teacher input within her school as the pandemic progressed. She recalled, "We didn't feel like we were being heard at all. Absolutely not heard at all." Teachers' concerns were met with tone-deaf encouragement from school administrators. "[They would say] 'Oh no, you guys are just doing a great job. . . . We think you're doing wonderful.' We're like, 'No, we're not. You're going to be losing teachers.'" Her frustrations were compounded by teachers' lack of leverage at the statewide level. She explained, "We're in a right to work state. We can't [strike]. . . . So, we hold very little power." In summer 2021, Leslie Spark did feel somewhat respected by local educational leaders—she had worked with them for fourteen years—and yet she also felt excluded by them from organizational decision-making. This lack of voice was a major frustration for her professionally.

In fall 2021, Ms. Spark left her school in pursuit of a teaching environment that sought out teacher knowledge in decision-making and planning. By summer 2022, she enthused, "I feel like I have a voice again. I can come to the table and say, "Okay. This is what we think and this is why we think it." Ms. Spark compared her current teaching position to her prior one: "It didn't feel that way before. No. It was like, 'You know what? Go in. Do your job. Go home. That's all we want from you.' And now, it definitely feels like we (teachers) have a voice at the table." Ms. Spark still contended with limited channels for voice at the state level, but her new school's organizational culture provided teachers with a say over the conditions of their work and put her on the course of a Satisfied Stayer. She moved in search of conditions where her voice could be heard. As a Mover, her exit internal to the profession was a response to a lack of and a search for voice. Now she had found it, she thought she would stay.

VOICE AND CAREER TRAJECTORY

Variations in voice are reflected in career trajectories. By summer 2022, the career directions of the seventy-five teachers had diverged through a nested series of decisions. A nearly uniform sense of career commitment early in the pandemic gradually gave way to differentiated pathways as teachers experienced different working conditions. Teachers who reported higher levels of respect from educational leaders and more teacher involvement in school and district planning, were also the teachers whose careers were most likely to continue through and beyond the pandemic. In comparison, teachers whose career plans had changed during the pandemic were those who felt less respected and had less school and district influence in decision-making. Looking back over the two plus school years of pandemic-modified schooling, these differences in teacher voice and influence predate career change variations. As early as summer 2020, teachers whose career plans would eventually change were already reporting lower levels of input in school planning. And in summer 2021, a time by which some teachers had already left teaching, those who would remain as Satisfied Stayers felt higher levels of respect and influence.[13]

This does not assign all the responsibility to teachers' experience of respect and influence nor claim a direct causal relationship between early reports of voice and teacher career outcomes. Career decisions are complex and informed by myriad professional and personal factors. And there are enough exceptions to disrupt a claim of causality: a notable example being the presence of teachers with low levels of influence among the Satisfied Stayers. For some teachers, feeling respected holds more weight than decision-making influence, and vice versa. Still, considering the experiences of the seventy-five teachers through two and a half years of pandemic-era teaching makes the connections between voice and career path clearer and compels attention to the patterns. Understanding these patterns is the start of a road map toward improving overall teacher career persistence and satisfaction.

Satisfied Stayers: Respect Was Strong and Influence Highest

After the disruptive spring 2020 shutdown, followed by two full academic years of pandemic teaching, only one in three teachers expressed both satisfaction with their work and an intent to remain a teacher. These 2022 Satisfied Stayers are the group positioned to offer the most insight into what it takes to sustain teachers in schools, even during the worst of times. Looking back over the thirty-month journey, the twenty-five Satisfied Stayers consistently stand out for the comparative respect they felt as professionals and the influence and input they had in organizational decision-making.

There is a clear relationship between voice and satisfaction. Teachers with a voice in reopening plans were more satisfied with those plans (see table 6.1). Overall, in summer 2020, 71 percent of all (sixty-nine) teachers were satisfied with their school's fall 2020 reopening plans. But the twenty-five teachers who felt they had a voice in the planning were almost universally satisfied, with only one expressing dissatisfaction with the reopening plan. In retrospect, the satisfaction of those teachers we came to call Satisfied Stayers was evident early on. In summer 2020, 92 percent of them (all but two of the twenty-four) were satisfied with school plans for the fall return.[14] Of course, most teachers felt some anxiety about safety and stress around adapting their instructional style, but half of Satisfied Stayers felt their experience and knowledge gained teaching in spring 2020, and their priorities and concerns around safety and student needs, were a considered part of the back-to-school planning. In contrast, only about a third of the whole sample (36 percent) and less than a quarter (23 percent) of Leavers shared this experience of teacher voice in reopening plans.

Admittedly, these numbers are small and as such could be framed as coincidental—except the pattern continued. In year two, summer 2021, the highest estimates of respect and influence in decision-making were,

Table 6.1 2020 dis/satisfaction and voice in reopening plan by 2022 career outcomes

2022 career outcomes	Voice in reopening plan	Satisfied with reopening plan	Satisfied and had voice in reopening plan	Dissatisfied and had voice in reopening plan
All (69)*	36% (25 of 69)	71% (49 of 69)	35% (24 of 69)	1% (1 of 69)
Satisfied Stayers (24)**	46% (11 of 24)	88% (21 of 24)	46% (11 of 24)	0% (0 of 24)
Outbound Stayers (16)	25% (4 of 16)	63% (10 of 16)	18% (3 of 16)	6% (1 of 16)
Leavers (13)	23% (3 of 13)	46% (6 of 13)	23% (3 of 13)	0% (0 of 13)

* Table does not include subgroup details of Movers, Stuck Stayers, and others (N=17).
** One Satisfied Stayer was excluded because they began teaching at their school in fall 2020 and were not able to comment on the degree of voice or satisfaction with the reopening plan.

once again, reported by the Satisfied Stayers of summer 2022. Replying to closed-ended survey questions about professional respect and influence in school and district decision-making, Satisfied Stayers reported feeling more respected by school leaders and more included in decision-making than the 2022 Leavers or Outbound Stayers. Figure 6.1 summarizes teachers' 2021 experience of professional respect and influence on decision-making by all responding teachers and by 2022 career outcomes. The overall lack of influence in school and district decision-making is evident,

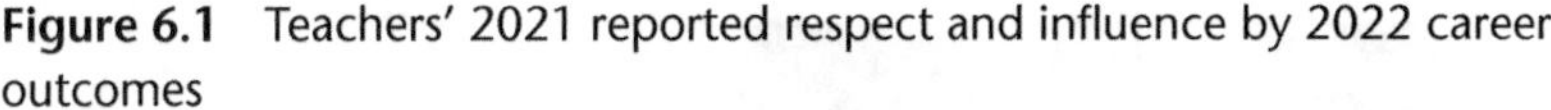
Figure 6.1 Teachers' 2021 reported respect and influence by 2022 career outcomes

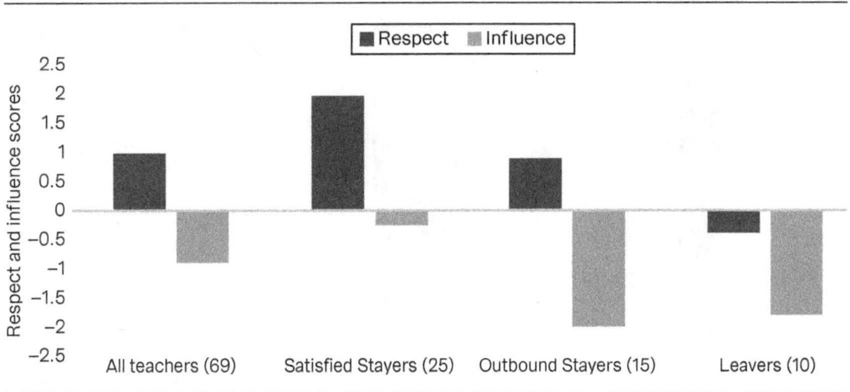

with no group of teachers reporting a positive level of influence. But in a world of insufficient teacher influence, the Satisfied Stayers were more likely to have influence.[15]

In 2021, Satisfied Stayers also reported the highest levels of respect with 72 percent indicating they felt respected as professionals by both their principal and district leadership (see figure 6.2). Of the seven Satisfied Stayers who experienced professional disrespect in summer 2021, most reported a mixed experience where disrespect at one level was balanced by respect at another. Four who felt disrespected by district leaders felt respected by principals, and two felt disrespected by their principal but not by district leaders. Only one Satisfied Stayer reported disrespect across the board from school and district level leadership.

In contrast, only 40 percent (10 of 25) of 2022 Leavers (4 of 10) and Outbound Stayers (6 of 15) felt respected by both school and district leadership. Of the 60 percent (15 of 25) who reported feeling disrespected, six felt disrespected across the board by both principals and school district leaders. Outbound Stayers were more likely than Leavers to feel respected by their principals. Only two Outbound Stayers felt disrespected by their principals, and they are the two who also felt disrespected by district leadership.

Figure 6.2 Sense of respect among Satisfied Stayers (25) and Leavers and Outbound Stayers (26)

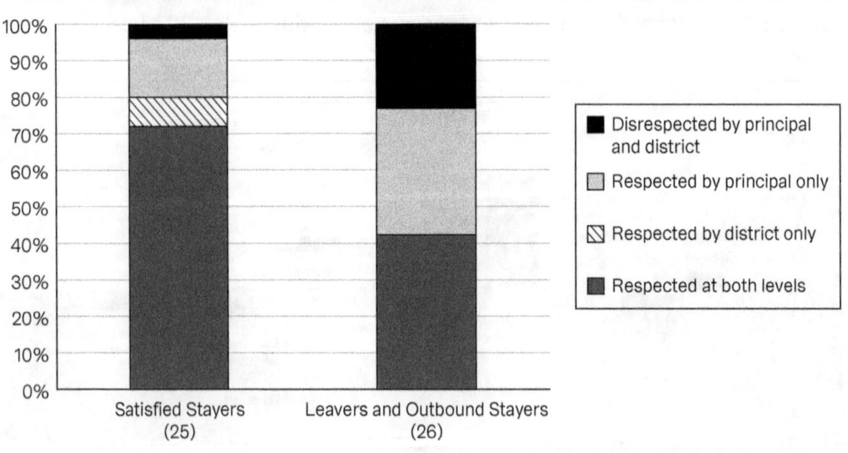

The Satisfied Stayers of 2022 had more voice throughout their experience of pandemic-modified schooling than the rest of the teachers we followed. In 2020, Satisfied Stayers were consulted on school reopening plans at higher rates and were the most likely to express satisfaction with those plans. In 2021, Satisfied Stayers felt the highest level of professional respect from school leaders and the greatest influence in organizational-level decision-making. This heightened experience of voice throughout, as evidenced in respect and influence, is a distinguishing feature of the teachers who stayed the course through and beyond the pandemic. All of this strongly suggests that feeling heard, having a say in school decision-making, and knowing that your professional expertise is valued increases teacher capacity to stay teaching in schools, even in times of crisis. As Claire Macalister put it, after her school district made changes to the schedule in response to teacher concerns, changes that helped her decide to not move to a new school district, "That's the thing about voice. . . . It does make a difference."

CONCLUSION

Teachers responded to the crisis by drawing on their individual and collective knowledge, skill, and judgment. Yet when it came to decisions on school reopening plans, pedagogical practices, and instructional modalities, teachers found few avenues through which to bring their insights to bear. Their experiences reveal the essential role of teacher voice and the consequences when that voice is stifled.

Unions proved to be the fundamental vehicle for teacher voice. Teachers in strong state and local union contexts were better able to inform policies and influence decisions informing their working conditions and their students' learning conditions. Unions solicited teacher input, provided protections to otherwise vulnerable teachers, and served as a mechanism for influencing decisions. For Carl Graham, his union's advocacy led his district to avoid a burdensome teaching modality; Nancy Walsh's union's opposition to an unsafe return to schooling contributed to her continuing career commitment.

Yet even in weaker union contexts, teachers engaged in grassroots unionism—especially where teachers were able to build on a history of such activity prior to the pandemic. Their organizing successes within hostile labor climates offer key lessons for building organizing infrastructures moving forward. Teachers demonstrated how labor landscapes are not static but respond to teachers' collective action.

Finally, at the local level, as noted in chapter 5, teachers lauded district and (especially) school leaders who demonstrated respect for teachers and who created inclusive structures and processes for decision-making. When teachers did not find themselves consulted or respected, some set out to find new school communities in which they could assert their voice.

Ultimately, the experience of voice and influence—being respected, heard, and taken seriously—held profound implications for career commitments. Teachers whose career plans had changed during the pandemic felt less respected and reported less involvement in decisions. Teachers who reported more influence in school and district decision-making were those whose teaching careers were most likely to continue through and beyond the pandemic, offering insights into what it takes to sustain educators in their work.

7

The Great Realization

"This Is Water" is an oft-quoted speech and essay by the novelist David Foster Wallace. It is premised on a parable of two young fish swimming along when they are greeted cheerfully by an older fish with a "Morning, boys! How's the water?" The two young fish turn to one another and wonder aloud, "What is water?" as they continue their swim. "The point of the fish story," Wallace interprets, "is merely that the most obvious, important realities are often the ones that are hardest to see and talk about."[1]

For many teachers, pandemic teaching was a perspective-shifting experience, opening their eyes to important realities of their working conditions, the status of their profession, and the current policy priorities in American public schooling. Long before the first school closure, US teachers were already working in a profession characterized by a half-century low in status, respect, compensation, and satisfaction—but not all of them were fully aware of the water. As Texas teacher Charlotte Adams described the insights that led her to leave her school district, "COVID seemed to shed light on issues that would have been more difficult to detect otherwise." This new way of seeing was echoed in Arizona teacher Lori Perenno's sense that the pandemic revealed the preexisting flaws in public schooling and teachers' work: "This year I feel that the cracks in public education are showing more than ever before. COVID has eroded the foundation and I feel that political pressure has taken advantage of that."

As a transboundary crisis, the COVID-19 pandemic disrupted every system within and across communities—including work, school, family life, institutional supports, and neighborhood connections—challenging the conventions and boundaries that traditionally characterized and differentiated these spaces. This mass disruption functioned like travel beyond our home communities has done for centuries, presenting the traveler with a set of alternative ways of being to those they had previously presumed to be taken-for-granted norms. This new view created an opportunity for people everywhere to reframe and reassess the world order and their own life decisions, giving rise to significant social change in the priorities attached to work as evidenced in the "great resignation" and "quiet quitting" of workers and their shift away from commuting and centralized work settings.[2]

For teachers specifically, the disruptions brought an increased sense of occupational risk combined with political and public debates about school and teacher priorities. Hot button topics like masking, the designation of essential workers, and whether and how to reopen schools put teachers at center stage of pandemic-response policy and conflicts. At the same time, disruptions to the traditional forms of schooling catapulted teachers into early pandemic leadership response roles that brought to the forefront values of innovation, collaboration, community relationships, and care of students. In the spirit of on-the-ground emergent crisis responders everywhere, teachers dedicated long hours to rapidly developing new skills and systems as they worked together to adapt to the needs of the pandemic response and their particular local contexts. They continued to reflect and adapt for over two years of pandemic-modified schooling in a climate of increased scrutiny, criticism, and intensified pressure.

Some teachers looked at the teaching profession—with eyes informed by the intensity of pandemic experience—and found it lacking. This change in perspective manifested in the nearly 60 percent of the Suddenly Distant Research Project teachers whose career plans changed between March 2020 and summer 2022. Career changes included leaving teaching, moving schools in search of better working conditions, seeking jobs outside the classroom, and retiring early. Other teachers found their working waters conducive to support, satisfaction, and success. Of the 40 percent of teachers whose career plans remained unchanged, the vast majority expressed satisfaction with their work and workplaces and intended to remain in the profession. The difference between the two groups of teachers was located largely in their working contexts rather than in individual teachers' characteristics or personal circumstances. Teachers stayed the course when they worked in supportive environments where they were treated with respect, included in planning, and felt aligned with the priorities of the school. Teachers struggled when those conditions were lacking.

For many teachers, their great realization of the COVID-19 pandemic was the recognition of the imbalance between professional rewards and costs. These teachers came face-to-face with policies and practices that highlighted the low status of the teaching profession, disregarded their safety concerns, and undermined their ability to live up to their ethical and professional commitments. Teachers responded in different ways consistent with Hirschman's exit, voice, and loyalty framing introduced in chapter 6.[3] Some gave voice to their concerns, with differing degrees of success. Individually and collectively, teachers identified and sought ways to address the organizational constraints that limited their capacity to meet student needs and that framed them as less than professional experts in teaching and learning. Others exited but often only after sustained effort to effect change through voice. And some teachers neither left nor voiced concerns. Hirschman's exit, voice and loyalty frame tells us that when commitment is high, exit is lower and voiced engagement more likely. An exception occurs when neither exit nor voice is a viable possibility; then, staying is neither an actual choice nor a guaranteed sign of commitment. It is in the relationship among exit, voice, and loyalty that patterns of teacher engagement are revealed. Sometimes teachers stayed out of a sense that they lacked real alternatives; other times they stayed because their voiced concerns resulted in improved conditions for teaching and learning.

EXIT, VOICE, AND LOYALTY

In this study of seventy-five teachers across nine US states, the patterns of exit, voice, and loyalty are consistent with Hirschman's model. Teacher commitment was lower and dissatisfaction higher when teacher voice was marginalized. When exit was possible, dissatisfied teachers without influence left teaching. When exit was not possible, or even just less possible, and voice limited, teachers stayed in teaching but at a price to their engagement and well-being. This framing makes more visible the decline of project teacher commitment and engagement.

States Where the System Response Centralized Control and Limited Local Discretion

As detailed in chapter 4, a third of project teachers in the *speed, control, and compliance* states left teaching in contrast to only 11 percent of Leavers in the *caution, guidance, and discretion* states; the latter states favored a cautious model that provided state-level guidance but preserved local level discretion. And of the twenty-five Satisfied Stayers, nineteen were in caution, guidance, and discretion contexts (see table 4.1). Chapter 4 explored the relevance of this system-response orientation for teachers, including the pronounced effect when state mandates disregarded teachers' safety concerns or were compounded by new legislative efforts to control content and curriculum.

Local Conditions That Did Not Support Teachers' Work

Teachers' capacity to sustain their commitment to teaching was negatively affected in schools and districts where teachers lacked supportive local working conditions, as detailed in chapter 5, specifically where the workload was excessive, professional development fell short, collaborative colleagues were scarce, and school and district leadership was disappointing. Of the focal teachers, the Leavers worked in schools characterized by weak workplace conditions while nearly all Satisfied Stayers worked in schools that offered strongly supportive workplace conditions (see figure 5.1). For some teachers, a strongly supportive workplace context could counter, or at least mediate, the stressors of a speed, control, and compliance state-level system response.

Where Teachers' Voices Were Marginalized in School Planning and Decision-Making

In places where teachers lacked voice (see chapter 6), they felt less respected and were more likely to experience a decline in their work satisfaction and commitment. Leavers consistently reported lower levels of respect and professional inclusion in decision-making than Satisfied Stayers, who reported the highest level of voice and professional influence. That pattern held true from the reopening planning for fall 2020 through the next two academic years into summer 2022 (see table 6.1, figure 6.1, and figure 6.2). Teachers were more likely to have voice in places with strong teachers' unions, but grassroots organizing and workplace conditions also afforded increased voice.

The experiences and career outcomes of the project's Iowa teachers encapsulate important variations of exit, voice, and loyalty patterns. All worked in a top-down system context with constraints limiting collective voice. Iowa took a speed, control, and compliance approach to the pandemic response, mandating in-person schooling prior to vaccine availability, constraining school agency over modality, and attempting to limit local discretion to require masking. In 2021, Iowa passed new laws limiting classroom content. In this weaker labor state, teachers' unions had limited scope for amplifying teacher voice. Still, some teachers voiced concerns and called for change they felt was essential, though to little effect. Teachers with lower commitment thresholds, to the community or to the work, left with little or no attempt at voice. And those who didn't view exit as an option stayed regardless of the effect on their engagement and satisfaction.

No voice. Exit. High loyalty: Natalie Lehrer took a one-woman stand, issuing her school principal and superintendent an ultimatum: ensure a masking mandate or she would resign. Rachel Larsen tried to work with her disempowered local union to be heard. And Sam Stewart spoke up individually and worked to organize a teacher coalition. Their voice efforts are a testament to their commitment to teaching—what Hirschman calls their loyalty—but the ineffectiveness of their advocacy efforts resulted in their exit.

No voice. No exit. High loyalty: A lack of exit even in the absence of voice or satisfaction, Hirschman contends, is a form of loyalty. An inability to exit kept Ruth Cartwright and Judy Aldrich in teaching. For Ruth Cartwright, the material cost of exit made her feel professionally stuck with fifteen years' seniority, pension expectations, and concern that her skills were not transferable to another field. Lacking a sense of exit as a viable option, coupled with deep dissatisfaction with how the state and schools navigated the pandemic response, galvanized Ms. Cartwright to move into an active union role. Stating she didn't have anything to lose and indicating her realistic understanding of the current limits of Iowa's teachers' union, she nonetheless chose to speak up in an effort to change the influence of teachers' voice in Iowa's schools.

Sometimes there is no way to fully exit, and this is especially true in the consideration of a public good. In those cases, individual choice can be constrained by a moral sense of commitment to occupation or community, and a sense that exit would be incomplete and leave the organization worse off. Judy Aldrich lived in a rural community on the farm her husband grew up on, taught at the same school she attended as a child and her own children also attended—and that her grandchildren would attend. She had concerns about the school's pandemic response and the overall organizational support for her work, but there was no real way for her to completely exit the school community, a small community with multigenerational ties and strong relationships. She could resign her teaching post, but her family members would continue to attend the school and the school would continue to educate her community. She shows up as a Satisfied Stayer because her loyalty to her teaching job was also loyalty to her community, a community she described as family.

Voice: There are other possible combinations of exit, voice, and loyalty. Most notably, where there is voice and loyalty there is a pattern of reduced exit. Members of an organization whose influence is integral to decision-making are less likely to exit—a situation that is evident in the experiences of Satisfied Stayers.

Hirshman highlights the tensions among the three elements: easy availability of exit makes the recourse to voice less likely, but the effectiveness of the voice mechanism is strengthened by the possibility of exit.[4] The ability to boycott or threaten exit, through individual exit or collective striking, is a key source of leverage in places where voice is not invited. Loyalty is a force that postpones exit and strengthens voice, mobilizing actions to elicit change. But "it is possible for loyalty to overshoot the mark and thus to produce an exit-voice mix in which the exit option is unduly neglected."[5]

The exit, voice, and loyalty frame complicates assumptions about the meaning of exit as a simple measure of discontent and, conversely, the degree to which a lack of exit signals satisfaction. Simultaneously, it raises awareness of the role voice plays in deepening and sustaining engagement and commitment, especially in times of dissonance resulting from a disruption to business as usual. The pandemic was such a disruption, resulting in dissonance, which affected the way teachers viewed the realities of their work and world. Loyalty to the profession and work of educating children led many teachers to take action: for some that led to deepened commitment and for others it eroded commitment.

CANARIES IN THE COAL MINE

Burnout scholars Christina Maslach and Michael Leiter offer the vivid metaphor of the canary in the coal mine to consider the relationship between people and their jobs. For decades, canaries were used to signal dangerous air quality in the coal mines. If the canary was unwell—or died—the miners knew to get out quickly. The system was designed to identify problematic working conditions, not troubled workers, and no one ever suggested the solution was more resilient birds. Burnout, Maslach and Leiter persuasively argue, is the canary in the coal mine of workplaces in that it manifests in the workers but is caused by the working conditions. The solution, then, is to remedy the workplace and conditions of labor, not create more resilient workers.[6]

Scholars and policy makers have noted the potential canaries amid the pandemic that may signal a larger crisis within the teacher workforce. Some watched for evidence of increased teacher exit as an indication of problems. Teacher exit is indeed one important canary, and teacher attrition definitively increased during the pandemic (see figure 7.1 and table 7.1). Statewide teacher turnover data revealed a substantial rise in the percentage of teacher attrition in 2021 and a smaller but still increasing rate in 2022.[7] Five

Figure 7.1 Percentage change in teacher turnover by state*

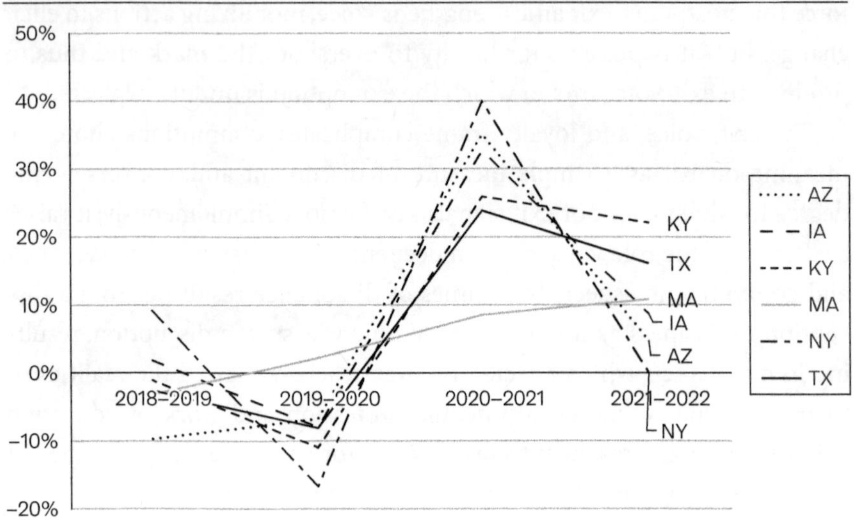

* Arizona rates are based on data from https://www.azed.gov/teach/classroom-teacher-attrition-and-retention-dashboard; Kentucky rates are based on data from https://www.kyschoolreportcard.com/organization/20/school_overview/faculty_staff_community/faculty_profile?year=2023; Texas rates are based on data from https://tea.texas.gov/reports-and-data/educator-data/employed-teacher-attrition-and-new-hires.pdf; Massachusetts rates are based on data from https://profiles.doe.mass.edu/statereport/staffingRetentionRates.aspx; New York rates are based on data from https://data.nysed.gov/studenteducator.php?year=2022&state=yes; Iowa rates are based on dataset provided by the Iowa Department of Education, Bureau of Information and Analysis Services, Basic Educational Data Survey (BEDS), Staff Files.

of the six states included in the study where attrition data are publicly available saw teacher turnover rates from 2020 to 2021 increase by more than 24 percent. These statewide patterns mirror national data, as RAND reported an increase in US teacher turnover from 6 percent in 2019 to 10 percent in 2022.[8] And yet, teacher exit provides an incomplete warning system.[9]

As potential crisis canaries, teacher turnover and shortage data measure occupational exit and absence but fail to account for those teachers still present—*loyal* according to Hirschman, *stayers* in the workforce vernacular—but laboring under the burden of exhaustion, feelings of cynicism, and sense of ineffectiveness characteristic of burnout. A true teacher workforce canary must encompass data on both leavers and career stayers whose commitment and satisfaction has diminished—those who want to exit, make active plans to exit, and yet remain in the classroom. In one

Table 7.1 Percentage change in teacher turnover by state

	Teacher attrition 2017–2018	Teacher attrition 2018–2019	% change from 2017–2018 to 2018–2019	Teacher attrition 2019–2020	% change from 2018–2019 to 2019–2020	Teacher attrition 2020–2021	% change from 2019–2020 to 2020–2021	Teacher attrition 2021–2022	% change from 2019–2020 to 2021–2022
Arizona	15.51%	14.00%	–9.74%	13.06%	–6.7%	17.65%	35.1%	18.49%	4.8%
Iowa	11.10%	11.30%	1.8%	10.40%	–8.0%	13.80%	32.7%	15.00%	8.7%
Kentucky	18.40%	18.20%	–1.1%	16.20%	–11.0%	20.40%	25.9%	24.90%	22.1%
Texas	10.43%	10.16%	–2.6%	9.34%	–8.1%	11.57%	23.9%	13.44%	16.2%
Massachusetts	9.50%	9.20%	–3.2%	9.40%	2.2%	10.20%	8.5%	11.30%	10.8%
New York	11.00%	12.00%	9.1%	10.00%	–16.7%	14.00%	40.0%	14.00%	0.0%

snapshot of these dissatisfied stayers, a 2022 report by the National Education Association found that 55 percent of educators were considering leaving teaching earlier than they had planned. It is these dissatisfied stayers whose stories are left out of the debates.[10]

Teacher commitment and satisfaction were affected by realizations gained through the experience of pandemic teaching—realizations that shifted teachers' occupational perspectives and made them more aware of their working context, the flaws in the system, and their professional priorities and nonnegotiables. The pandemic raised the heat and in the process revealed and exacerbated the cracks in the structure and framing of the teaching profession in these most notable ways: 1) the professional disrespect and low status endured by teachers and, 2) the misalignment between teachers' educational priorities and the priorities manifest in schooling structures and policies, which, in turn, 3) led many teachers to a new cost-benefit analysis of teaching as a career. The rest of this chapter details, as David Wallace calls upon us to do with his story of the awareness of water, the "most obvious, important realities" that emerged, the realities that "are often the ones that are hardest to see and talk about." In naming these important realities of the teaching profession during a time of crisis, we draw important lessons for change.

REALIZATION 1: DISRESPECT AND LOW STATUS

The pandemic crisis response made disrespect more apparent to teachers. Some of that disrespect was present before the pandemic in the form of low pay, low status, and constrained professional autonomy, which all contributed to the conditions that put the teaching profession at a fifty-year low in 2019. More disrespect, though, was revealed by the handling of the pandemic in increased public scrutiny of teacher practice and in the marginalization of teachers' expertise and health concerns in planning for reopening.

Fundamental assumptions about teachers' motivations and goals pervade the waters teachers navigate. Public perception, policy frames, and structural conditions of teachers' work are shaped by how others understand teachers' work and teachers' orientations to that work. Those who assume teachers are motivated by supposedly easy work with an abbreviated work year (summers off) are more likely to enact a managerialist and directive approach to teachers. Such an assumption—that teachers will likely be lax regarding their obligations to students unless coerced—gives rise to policies that purport to gauge teacher performance and effectiveness on the basis of standardized student test scores. In contrast, those who assume teachers are intrinsically motivated by a commitment to student learning and an ethic of professional efficacy are more likely to enact a support and resource approach to teachers. The assumption of intrinsic motivation is the foundation of policies that center on teacher voice, collaborative practice, and professionally controlled practice.

The London School of Economics scholar Julian Le Grand has memorably characterized variations in public service delivery models as arising from assumptions that cast public service workers as either knights or knaves. Knights are motivated by professional ethics and primarily concerned with the well-being and interests of those they serve. Knaves are driven by self-interest, attending to their own concerns rather than the concerns and interests of the wider community and the specific purpose of their role. Le Grand contends that trust determines how public service workers are perceived, with mistrust giving rise to command-and-control policies intended to coerce knaves.[11]

In spring 2020, project teachers were seen as knights. They generally felt recognized for their leadership, long hours, and creative adaptations in identifying and meeting the needs of their students. Their achievements were made all the more notable by the pervasiveness of the transboundary crisis. Teachers were not simply attending to student needs; they were often sidelining their own needs in their dedicated service to their school and students. This celebration of teachers' dedication and sacrifice was ubiquitous. In May 2020, *Teen Vogue* ran an article entitled "National Teacher Appreciation Day: Educators Are Standing by Students During Coronavirus" and subtitled "Teachers are doing *the most*."[12] The *New York Post* celebrated a "hero" teacher who taught her special-needs students remotely even as she and her family struggled with the virus.[13] In Florida, kindergarten teachers' first day of online school was featured as a newsworthy event.[14] Meanwhile, Jimmy Fallon, *Tonight Show* host and parent of two school-age children suddenly learning from home, broadcast his song "They Should Make a Billion Dollars," recognizing teacher dedication to student learning during the pandemic.[15] Families hosted teacher appreciation car parades and posted yard signs declaring their thanks.

Parents and the public celebrated teachers in part because the everyday realities of teaching work became more visible during remote schooling and because teachers shouldered more during the pandemic response. The transboundary crisis disrupted the tight managerial control that has characterized teachers' work in recent decades, with effective response necessitating that teachers act as emergent on-the-ground responders. Teachers acted both individually—from rural mailbox material deliveries in Texas to Zoom classes broadcast from walk-in closets in Manhattan to late night Google Classroom sessions with working students in Florida—and in concert through newly created and established teacher networks to determine student needs and the methods to meet them. Teachers were knights and recognized as such.

However, as pandemic risks persisted and a return to in-person schooling was delayed, conflict grew and teachers were widely painted as knaves who were "according to some, lazy, whiny, cowardly adults who can't figure out how to get these darn kids back in school face to face."[16] The *New York Times* reported that teachers were "fearful and angry" over pressure to return to in-person schooling while parents protested mask mandates.[17] Teachers' health concerns were pitted against student needs even as national polls indicated parents and teachers were aligned in their concerns about reopening and shared a majority preference for remote instruction.[18] On one side there were assertions of safety by the US Department of Education Secretary: "There's nothing in the data that suggests that kids being in school is in any way dangerous."[19] And yet live-streamed school board meetings, where student needs were pitted against virus risks, took place all over the country in debates that often left teachers feeling their safety was not a consideration. Sometimes the dismissal of teacher safety concerns extended to pronounced disdain for teachers themselves, as when a Pennsylvania father in a February 2021 school board meeting declared,

"Our children are more important than teachers' lives. . . . Our children are failing and being left behind. . . . That is more important than if a teacher were to contract COVID and pass away. . . . Get the children back into school where they belong. . . . The children are more important than teachers. End of story."[20]

This parent's statement is unquestionably an extreme expression of prioritizing in-person schooling over teachers' health concerns, but teachers felt this disregard even when it was not stated as baldly. Teachers' voices countered such blatant disregard with sentiments like those expressed in a July 2020 *New York Times* op-ed by Washington State public school teacher Rebecca Martinson, "I Won't Return to the Classroom, and You Shouldn't Ask Me To": "Every day when I walk into work as a public-school teacher, I am prepared to take a bullet to save a child. In the age of school shootings, that's what the job requires. But asking me to return to the classroom amid a pandemic and expose myself and my family to COVID-19 is like asking me to take that bullet home to my own family. I won't do it, and you shouldn't want me to."[21]

The shift from hero to villain, knight to knave, was deeply felt by teachers as disrespect for their safety, their commitment to students, and their professional expertise.[22] It drove Texas middle school teacher Leanne Edwards out of local community social media groups. She knew she could not read the vitriol that parents wrote there about teachers and still sustain herself in teaching. And it drove Iowa teacher Rachel Larsen out of teaching altogether after she went to great lengths to teach in person, throughout fall 2020, only to hear her school board disregard CDC guidelines and teachers' health concerns during a virus spike. Framing these concerns as frivolous, Ms. Larsen's school board justified its decision to stay fully in person by implicating teachers as more motivated by time off than by health concerns. At the same time, connections to and feeling valued by parents and communities were also in short supply, adding to relational loss and driving up the high cost of being a teacher.

These individual moments of disrespect—seen in a Facebook group, heard at a school board meeting, or read in the newspaper—accumulated. Collectively, they revealed to teachers the lack of regard for the teaching profession and themselves as teachers. The cumulative effect of this vilification, this presumed knavery, is seen in the overwhelmingly negative career outcomes of the project teachers in places that institutionalized the disregard for teachers' lives. Specifically, Leavers, Movers, and Outbound Stayers were concentrated in places that mandated prevaccine teacher returns to in-person teaching, resisted shifting modes in response to virus spikes, excluded teachers from decision-making, and compounded stress with new policies that increased scrutiny and control over content.

REALIZATION 2: MISALIGNMENT IN VALUES AND PRIORITIES

The ultimate manifestation of framing teachers as knaves lies in the four-decades-long rise of the standards and accountability school reform movement: a movement premised on the notion that teachers must be externally controlled to ensure they attend to the work of teaching students well.[23] In developing a command-and-control system, establishing goals for learning was centralized and politicized, multiple-choice exams adopted as evidence of learning, and managerial control of teachers' work expanded. This simultaneously narrowed the scope of teaching practice and intensified the conditions of teachers' work.[24] Discussions about content shifted from school rooms to legislative halls and determinations of student learning from teachers to standardized test results. Through this process emerged a policy and organizational conception of a "good teacher" as one who is aligned with state educational mandates, demonstrates fidelity to centrally adopted curricula, coaches students to attain high standardized tests scores, and willingly works beyond contract hours.[25]

This framing of teachers as followers, implementers of a curriculum created by others, contributed to the decline of teacher satisfaction and status that characterized the prepandemic teaching profession's fifty-year low. But the pandemic shook things up with tangible changes, including the suspension of standardized accountability measures, new flexibility in expectations, and prioritization of engagement and connection over grading and assessment. While there were many challenges to and limitations of the "do no harm" era of the pandemic response, the disruption and resumption of *normal* schooling clarified educational policy priorities and highlighted misaligned values. This misalignment was notable for teachers in system-level decisions to resume standardized testing and accountability systems and in the discourse premised on concerns about *learning loss.*

As schools resumed regular operations in the wake of pandemic modifications, some teachers resisted a narrow system focus on testable student knowledge, a focus they considered insufficient, misdirected, and damaging to student learning. Standardized testing, suspended for the 2019–2020 school year, was reinstated for essentially all project teachers' schools in spring 2021 despite teachers' overwhelming concerns.[26] Teachers saw the rapid return to testing as harmful to students, impeding their efforts to address students' learning needs. Leavers and Movers almost universally disapproved.[27] Kentucky Leaver Gail Miller saw testing as a misguided distraction: "The results of these tests do nothing to provide the social-emotional support students currently need." Another Leaver, Iowa teacher Taylor Brennan, mourned the "waste of precious instructional time" given to testing. Outbound Stayer Sarah Weaver in Florida called the testing resumption "ridiculous" given students were barely surviving, sharing that she had four students hospitalized involuntarily for mental health treatment.[28] As Kentucky Mover Rowan Finchley put it, "Why spend billions of dollars on standardized tests to tell us students did not grow normally this year, when we already know that?" Instead, she argued, those funds should be channeled into supporting student learning given the trauma and need to attend to students' social-emotional well-being.

Testing orientation drove a discourse of *learning loss*, fanning public and parental anxiety that reached a fevered pitch in fall 2022 with the release of the National Assessment of Educational Progress results indicating a decline in reading and math scores of fourth- and eighth-grade students.[29] Dismal forecasts of learning loss were framed as both academic gaps for a generation of children and lost human capital for the overall economy. Resulting calls for accelerated academic intervention included lengthening school days and years, focusing resources on tested subjects, and restoring accountability measures.[30]

Classroom teachers recognized students' learning needs, were well aware of the missing content, witnessed students struggling to "do school," and were deeply concerned about student mental health and trauma. They agreed with the goal of content recovery but not the methods or expected pace. Akin to Satisfied Stayer Jane Farley's metaphor of two buckets of student needs, one for belonging and social-emotional well-being and the other for content knowledge, teachers invoked a Maslow-like concept of needs in asserting student well-being as a foundation for academic learning.[31] And while Ms. Farley's school had a team of social workers to whom she could refer students struggling with their mental health, many teachers lacked the support of even one mental health professional. In the 2020–2021 school year, 69 percent of US public schools experienced an increase in students seeking mental health support at school and only about half felt equipped to meet that need. In three-quarters of those schools, teachers voiced concerns about student depression, anxiety, and trauma.[32]

In summer 2022, project teachers were still deeply troubled by students' unmet needs and concerned about how to support and improve their students' well-being. The top ten challenges identified by teachers at that time were all about meeting student needs and feeling a decreased sense of professional effectiveness and well-being as a teacher. Teachers felt overworked and exhausted (70 percent), an increased cynicism about their work as teachers (63 percent), challenged to meet the needs of their most vulnerable students (60 percent), a diminished sense of success as a teacher (60 percent), and an inability to balance work with nonwork responsibilities (56 percent). Student attendance (55 percent), student engagement (52 percent), and student behavior (48 percent) were identified as major challenges for teachers who were struggling with a diminished capacity to support others, including their students (42 percent), and a feeling of isolation as they worked to meet student needs (40 percent).

The pressure to attend to test scores and accelerate the pace of academic instruction ran counter to what teachers know about how learning happens. California Mover Francisco Vargas, an urban math teacher for over thirty years, described his opposition to calls for accelerated instruction and his concern about the learning loss frame:

> I'm not hiding my head in the sand about the state of kids' academics. It's the notion that, therefore, we have to catch them up as quickly as possible which I think is misguided because it's not how learning happens. You can't just talk faster. It risks pushing teachers to take shortcuts that won't lead to any kind of learning and it focuses all our attention on scope and sequence and diagnostics and stuff like that and daily assessments, formative assessments, instead of starting with an open mind about the relationship between classroom activities and the unknown of how kids are going to step into these spaces. (July 2022)

Leaver Sam Stewart remarked that the real learning loss lay in not learning from the pandemic the need to attend to student well-being. For many teachers, the misguided laser focus on academics first and fast, the reassertion of standardized testing as a measure of that learning, and the dearth of support for mental health needs revealed a misalignment of priorities and an understanding about what real pandemic recovery required.

Many dedicated teachers, when faced with a priorities disconnect, resisted exit and turned to voice as an avenue to change. To allow himself an exit option, Mr. Stewart had to believe that continuing his efforts at voice was futile, which required a big reframing. He found both in what he described as a "painful but valuable realization" that the system that ignored him did not, from his perspective, prioritize the best interests of students or teachers. The misalignment was not just in how best to serve students but also in how much (or little) teachers should be involved in making such determinations.

REALIZATION 3: ESCALATING COSTS AND DIMINISHING REWARDS

The response and handling of pandemic-modified schooling exacerbated conditions undermining teacher commitment by decreasing occupational benefits and increasing the costs of teaching work. As the demands of the job increased, intrinsic rewards declined, balancing work and family became more challenging, and the risks associated with teaching work rose. "I didn't sign up for this" was a choral refrain in Facebook groups, teacher blogs, social media, and from the teachers' stories detailed here. As teachers encountered the new realities of pandemic teaching—as they became more aware of the waters of teaching itself—they started asking, "Is teaching worth it?"

Even before the pandemic, teachers' work was demanding, fast-paced, and stressful. It has been said that only air traffic controllers make more decisions in a day than teachers. According to federal labor data, even with the summer break, teachers work longer hours and are paid less than other working professionals. On average, teachers work about fifteen hours beyond their contracted hours per week, and 17 percent of teachers work a second job to make ends meet.[33] In the United States, low salary and long hours are top reasons given by teachers considering leaving the profession.[34]

Sacrifice is often associated with work considered "a calling," and some put teachers and the clergy in the same devotional category of those "called to serve." Teachers are understood to be community-minded and motivated by a desire to contribute meaningfully to improving students' lives and opportunities.[35] In a 1975 landmark analysis of teachers' work, the sociologist Dan Lortie theorized that teachers were primarily motivated and satisfied by intrinsic (or "psychic") rewards that were derived from the work itself. The primary psychic reward, Lortie argued, is derived from close contact with students and success in the classroom. A half century later, a large corpus of research has substantiated the importance of intrinsic rewards, especially the satisfaction of working in close proximity with students, facilitating their knowledge development, and contributing to the care and development of young people.[36]

Draws to the profession include the promise of stable work with a predictable schedule compatible with family life. Lortie theorized two relevant material benefits of teaching: job security and time compatibility. Teaching offers stable employment; teachers can count on employment stability in the form of annual teaching contracts, the potential for tenure, and the promise of health-care and retirement benefits. During economic downturns, the flow of candidates into the profession increases when occupational stability is more appealing than pay levels, particularly when jobs are unstable in other sectors.[37] The structure of teaching work is also relatively predictable; while there may be curricular or instructional changes, the core work of teaching looks the same year to year. Time compatibility refers to the notion that teaching is "family friendly" by offering the predominantly female workforce a schedule aligned with parenting and the flexibility of professional exit and reentry consistent with family needs. As recently as 2018, a teacher workforce trends report theorized that the compatibility of teaching and domestic labor continues to be a factor in the concentration of women in the teacher workforce.[38]

The pandemic intensified teachers' work by increasing workload, stress, and learning demands. Veteran teachers suddenly felt like novices, working nonstop and needing to learn and implement new methods on the spot. The stability of teaching was disrupted as teachers transitioned back and forth from remote to in-person instruction and back again as schools pushed to reopen during COVID-19 surges. The burden of multiple modality changes increased both workload and stress for nearly nine out of every ten teachers, with 30 percent contending with four or more changes. Teachers required to teach in blended hybrid faced the most challenging conditions and exhibited the highest degree of stress and overwork.[39] Those working in remote contexts experienced isolation as well as Zoom fatigue and strain from the metamorphosis of their active classroom lives into desk jobs.

Reduced proximity to and contact with students negatively affected teachers' work satisfaction. Teachers missed their students, their colleagues, and the lively realities of classroom teaching. When in 2020, Texas Mover Leanne Edwards forlornly noted, "The reason I like my job is gone," she spoke for many teachers who missed their students. Repeatedly, across the full thirty months of this study, project teachers named the care, connection, and opportunity to be part of students' growth as a major source of career satisfaction and any decline as a substantive loss in intrinsic rewards. Several other pandemic studies also found a direct relationship between teachers' sadness and low levels of student contact.[40] For some teachers it was a painful but temporary loss, but for others it was an unmitigated loss that eroded their feelings of success and satisfaction.

Arguably an elusive goal before the pandemic, work-life balance was unattainable for parenting teachers (mostly mothers) who experienced the collapse of two labor domains—professional and domestic—requiring them to simultaneously teach students while parenting children at home.[41] Torn between teaching and parenting responsibilities, many found any prioritization of one over the other layered guilt on top of overwork and exhaustion. More than half of nonparents also struggled with work-life balance. Teaching became distinctly time incompatible, magnifying workload and stress. As Massachusetts Outbound Stayer Meredith Nathan, an urban special education middle school teacher with twenty-one years' experience, put it, "I love my job, I love what I do, but the pandemic has me reevaluating my work/life balance. I've been rethinking how long I can do this and what other opportunities I could pursue that would allow me to have a job that doesn't take over my entire life" (August 2022).

Increased health risk was another increased cost. Leavers Natalie Lehrer and Rachel Larsen (Iowa) and Sophie Blum (Florida) named unnecessary COVID-19 transmission risks as a factor in their exit decisions. Dr. Blum was willing to "take a bullet" for her students if it came to that, but virus exposure felt more avoidable than the seemingly unpredictable risk of a school shooter. Teachers raised concerns about elevated exposure and transmission risk even as others declared schools low-risk zones for students.[42] More recently, epidemiology has given scientific substance to teachers' concerns with a growing body of research identifying teaching as among the occupations at a disproportionately high risk of COVID-19 infection and mortality.[43]

With the intensification of the pandemic, the teaching profession's already low levels of satisfaction and reward came into focus and, for some, dipped even lower. In teaching, salaries, status, and satisfaction are low, while workload, risk, and stress are high.[44] Some teachers came to the realization that teaching cost too much and offered too little.

Cracks in the System

In Emma Thorsen's words, "Teaching is such an emotionally charged career. We go into it knowing we will not make as much money as other professions, we will work long hours during the school year, and we will have many tough moments with our students. But there is only so much we can control. COVID showed all the cracks in the system" (June 2022).

For Emma Thorsen, the experience of pandemic-era teaching brought the cracks in the system into clear focus—particularly those in the framing and treatment of teachers and school-level leaders in the US public educational system. Her realization that "there is a finite amount of pressure, guilt, and feelings of inadequacy that someone can endure" is how she explained her decision to exit in summer 2022. The exit, voice, and loyalty frame helps us see that her decision to leave resulted from an increased awareness of dissonance in her lived professional experience that shifted her occupational understanding and attitude. Over two years of intensified effort to fill the system cracks weakened her capacity to sustain the shock of further pressure. Her exit came when she reached her breaking point, the point where the cost of teaching exceeded the rewards of the work.

Whatever the occupational outcome, teachers' perspectives on educational practice and the teaching profession were affected by their pandemic teaching experiences. For many, including the ones we have looked at most closely in this chapter, commitment was eroded as they gained new perspectives through a series of crucial realizations. Widespread distrust framed them as knaves whose goals were suspect and from whom attention to student learning necessitated coercion. The spring 2020 disruption of schooling temporarily suspended these managerial controls and fleetingly framed teachers as knights whose motives were pure, intentions trustworthy, and efforts celebrated. The fall 2020 resumption of prepandemic norms—especially a return to framing teachers as knaves—created a shock that brought the cracks to the surface of awareness for many teachers. Many teachers were distressed by what they saw as public disregard for their safety, their lives, and the health of their families. This disregard was felt by some to be largely indicative of the low status afforded teachers and their work.

Reconciling the dissonance caused by pandemic disruption took many routes, depending on both the working conditions teachers faced and the degree to which they had real voice, exit as a viable option, and the elasticity of their loyalty. Chapter 7 has attended to teachers who navigated significant pandemic teaching challenges with little reliable access to voice and variable access to exit. Their stories of eroded career commitment are a cautionary tale of the vulnerabilities created by a system where, as Outbound Stayer Meredith Nathan reflected, "People want to blame teachers for everything that is going wrong at the present time instead of the fact that leaders, policy makers, government officials, and communities have devalued and underfunded schools for years and COVID has only exacerbated those deficits" (August 2022).

In writing this chapter, we faced the dilemma that detailing these hard realities of the teaching profession could also be seen as magnifying the problems and contributing to diminishing interest in teaching. We wondered to one another, who would want to become a teacher after reading this chapter? But denying or hiding these challenges to developing and sustaining a strong and appealing teaching profession will not defuse the problems. Unspoken problems are unsolvable problems.

In chapter 8 we turn our hopeful attention to the Satisfied Stayers, those teachers whose pandemic experiences were challenging but not career changing. Satisfied Stayers typically experienced more workplace support, professional respect, and voice than Leavers and Outbound or Stuck Stayers. Better support meant more resources to draw on in navigating the challenges of pandemic teaching, including strong collaborative colleagues, supportive school leaders, and reasonable workplace demands. More voice meant professional priorities were set collaboratively and misalignments navigated with fewer negative consequences for career commitment. In the stories of the Satisfied Stayers we see solutions to the threats undermining the teaching profession—we see the conditions we need to support more teachers in going the distance.

8

Supporting and Sustaining a Crisis-Ready Profession

On January 3, 2024, Japan Airlines Flight 516 collided with a Japanese Coast Guard plane while landing at Tokyo airport. As flames erupted, the jet taxied to a stop and tilted forward with the front landing gear collapsed. Eighteen minutes after touchdown, all 367 passengers and 12 crew members were safely evacuated before flames completely engulfed the plane. Credit for averting catastrophic loss of life was attributed to a well-made plane and a well-trained and experienced crew. Good engineering of the plane's cabin slowed the spread of fire while well-trained professional staff mobilized an effective deplaning. The crew assessed the situation, maintained calm, and determined and implemented a course of action. They drew on their knowledge of plane systems, their flight experience, prior training, and rigorous emergency preparation in a high-stress environment to adapt to the particular situation: determining only three of eight slides were safe to deploy, firmly and clearly directing passengers, coordinating with other crew members, and bypassing chains of command as circumstances required.[1]

In handling the event, the crew prevented an escalation to a deadly disaster. Their response highlights the importance of on-the-ground actions in critical events. Had the crew waited for the captain's permission to deploy the slides, or been unable to assess slide safety given fire specifics, the event could have escalated to a historical disaster.

Crisis theorists classify the crew's actions, especially the collective decision to act outside of the chain of command, as emergent behavior characteristic of crisis situations—departing from norms and practices of the established order. Such adaptation requires emergency responders to draw on a repertoire of possibilities grounded in education, experience, and shared purpose. Improvisation is one way to think of emergence. It is neither completely spontaneous nor novel but does indicate decision-making and actions carried out by knowledgeable professionals drawing on their experience.

The idea of improvisation comes from the study of jazz, where "spontaneous composition of music and performance depends on the ability to draw upon a repertoire of training, experience, and a shared vision with fellow performers. Performers must be skilled in reading their cues and making sense of the performance's direction."[2] Emergency responders are similarly drawing on a repertoire of possibilities grounded in education, experience, and community knowledge when they improvise in disaster situations. Good teaching has also been associated with achieving a balance between plans and improvisation—something we will get to shortly.

As we explain in chapter 1, crises do not arise inevitably from an event. Crises occur in the complex interaction of an event, context, and response. Effective crisis response facilitates and benefits from emergent action. In his theory of emergence, influential crisis scholar E. L. Quarantelli presents emergent action as requiring a shared perception of need and the nature of that need; supportive context of shared norms, values, and beliefs; existing social relationships and trusted connections; and material and knowledge resources.[3]

Organizational and societal resilience results from transforming existing conditions that create vulnerabilities and by responding adaptively, which requires planning and experience among responders who share a culture of responsibility.[4] This is true in all crises and especially relevant in crises as long lasting and complex as the coronavirus pandemic. Writing in a 2021 agenda-setting book, addressing government and governance handling of the pandemic, leading crisis scholars characterized the pandemic as a *mega-crisis*, a transboundary crisis that "gave rise to a complex and multifaceted intersection of numerous crises."[5] They attend to several of those interesting domains, including public health, the economy, political capacity, and social inequality. To that list we add education.

This book is concerned with the degree to which the pandemic resulted in an educational crisis, especially as it relates to the teaching profession. We are not alone in our concern or attention. Many researchers are exploring the pandemic's consequences for the teaching profession, paying special attention to teacher turnover and school personnel shortages. In March 2024, characterizing the teaching profession as at an inflection point between "high levels of burnout and disillusionment" and an uncertain future, *Education Week* launched the Teacher Morale Index to measure and track professional well-being.[6] In the Suddenly Distant Research Project, we attended to teacher turnover and indicators of engagement and commitment as we considered how existing circumstances and pandemic responses shaped teachers' experiences and career outcomes. In doing so, we also considered what might be done to reduce organizational vulnerabilities and increase organizational resilience.

The coronavirus pandemic arrived at a moment when national measures of the US teaching profession's status and appeal, and teachers' satisfaction, were at a fifty-year low, while locally Americans still rated "their" schools highly.[7] Predominantly female, the teacher workforce was broadly characterized as having strong community connections and motivated by intrinsic occupational rewards from a "calling" and a pervasive professional culture of care—a commitment to teach well and care for students. Yet the schools that teachers taught in were decades into a state and federal policy frame of centrally—and increasingly politically—established content requirements coupled with high-stakes accountability tests that teachers often felt were out of alignment with their own teaching values and priorities.

From the Leavers, Outbound Stayers, and Stuck Stayers, we know that teacher commitment was negatively affected by disrespectful treatment, which was felt most profoundly, but not exclusively, in the hero to villain, knight to knave arc. Misalignments in teaching and learning values pose a significant threat to teachers' satisfaction and commitment when teacher priorities are not reflected in school planning and programs—something that is much more frequent in contexts where teachers are excluded from agenda setting. Intrinsic rewards shrink with the accumulated loss of reduced respect, undervalued expertise, and a reduced sense of efficacy from misaligned goals.

Satisfied Stayers offer us lessons for ameliorating the effect of future crises on teacher commitment and improving the future of the teaching profession. By increasing organizational and social resilience, we can improve the status and satisfaction of the teaching profession by reframing the perception and treatment of teachers as knowledgeable, trustworthy professionals. Furthermore, we must cultivate the conditions of adaptive capacity for times of crisis by supporting formalized systems of teacher voice and improving teachers' working conditions in times of calm.

INSIGHTS FROM SATISFIED STAYERS

To go the distance is to stay the intended course even when it proves difficult and challenging. In summer 2022, thirty months into the pandemic response, twenty-five of the project's seventy-five teachers had *gone the distance*, satisfied with their careers in schools with supportive working conditions. They still "love being a teacher" and find it "deeply satisfying." Relieved to be back fully in person, they rejoiced in reconnecting with students and resuming their preferred instructional methods. Satisfied Stayers' stories offer hope, both as a contrast with those of the Leavers and Outbound Stayers, and as a foundation from which to focus attention on the state of the teaching profession and to mobilize action needed to build and sustain it. That some teachers made it through the intensity of the pandemic response with their commitment intact is evidence that it is possible to create the conditions that facilitate professional engagement and commitment even in times of crisis.

Satisfied Stayers are not in and of themselves remarkable—no more so than the project teachers whose commitment was eroded and career paths altered by their pandemic teaching experience—but their working conditions were remarkable. Those stayers were found in places where teachers were professionally respected and trusted to make decisions in students' best interests—that is, treated as knights, not knaves.[8] Teachers framed as knights were treated differently at every level, presumed to act with ethical motivation and professional judgment that shielded them from overly coercive or control-oriented policies and provided them with supportive working conditions.

Crafting solutions to problems about working conditions requires a focus on improving the policies and practices that create those conditions. In the analogy that Maslach and Leiter so aptly present in their work on burnout, canary deaths in coal mines were not due to any deficiencies in the birds themselves but rather to the poor air quality and unsafe conditions that both canaries and miners faced in the mines.[9] To keep more canaries and miners alive required improved working conditions. To attract more teachers to the profession and then retain them, and to improve the education system's capacity to navigate disruptions effectively, requires creating a system premised on teachers as knights with voice and influence in schools—a system that facilitates teachers' improvisation, in their daily classrooms and in times of crisis, by striking a balance between planning and adapting.[10]

Policy Culture and Context Shaped Teacher Experience and Capacity

Three-quarters of the Satisfied Stayers worked in states that offered guidance and deferred to local discretion in educational reopening policies, offering metrics and data to inform local decision-making. This was evident in state handling of public health, the timing of in-person schooling in relation to vaccine availability, and the absence of new restrictive laws.[11] Guidance-oriented contexts were typically unreceptive to state laws banning topics related to race and gender, prioritizing local-level process over escalating state mandates.

The anthropologist Sandra Stein's work on policy culture articulates the relationship among policy makers' assumptions, societal norms, biases, and the form and foci of resulting education policies.[12] Pandemic-era control policies framed the problem as a lack of local will and commitment to resume in-person schooling. State leaders who ordered schools to reopen buildings and required teachers to report in person before vaccine availability essentially characterized teachers, and often the unions that represented them, as knaves unwilling to prioritize students and economic interests. States with a policy-guidance approach located the problem as a lack of information rather than will, operating from an assumption that school building reopening hinged on information and resources needed to enact safety protocols. These states invested in data and communication systems and tended to defer to local responses to state-issued guidance.[13]

From teachers' accounts, districts in guidance-oriented states were, in turn, better positioned to offer more flexibility to teachers. For example, New York City schools used metrics to guide modality shifts, and project teachers there reported having flexibility in individual assignments. Satisfied Stayer Tom James appreciated the flexibility to remain remote in fall 2020, allowing him to navigate his childcare responsibilities while fulfilling his teaching commitments. In summer 2021, he valued his "intellectual freedom" that resulted from being "trusted to do right by the young people we serve" and his high school's intentional de-emphasis of standardized testing. But even within a guidance-oriented state, some districts took a command orientation. Elsewhere in New York State, elementary teacher Vicky Bauer's plan to retire early was fueled by feeling "micro-managed," constrained by her urban district's insistence on uniform adherence to pacing guides. Lamenting her lack of autonomy, she said, "I went into teaching to teach kids. Well, I feel like a robot sometimes and I didn't go into teaching to be a robot." Over twenty-two years in teaching, she had seen big declines in teacher voice and tightened control over instructional practice that she found demoralizing.[14]

Tom James valued the flexibility he was afforded to pursue his learning goals, drawing on his history background, teaching experience, and knowledge of his students to craft lessons that engaged them in learning. He consistently located his commitment in the joy, respect, and dignity he felt as a teacher, "It's a joy to do this work and I feel respected and treated with dignity, so I have no reason to leave." Satisfied Stayers demonstrate that teachers are best equipped for adaptive teaching in ordinary times and for a rapid and capable response to crisis when they work in systems that convey trust in well-prepared professionals, build the infrastructures that enable those professionals to act with skill and confidence—rapidly if necessary—and provide the latitude to improvise and innovate toward shared goals.

Supporting Improvisation in a Framework of Professional Authority

Skillful improvisation is evidence of accomplished practice in multiple domains, including jazz performance, emergency response, and teaching. All three require practitioners to balance structure with creativity, and routine with spontaneity, while drawing on depths of knowledge and collaborating with others. In 2011, an edited volume devoted to the importance of skillful improvisation in teaching opened with this assertion: "Great teaching involves many structuring elements, and at the same time requires improvisational brilliance."[15] Acknowledging the stranglehold of accountability over creativity, the book explores ways teachers might endeavor to carve out spaces of improvisation within state curriculum requirements, pacing guides, and testing protocols. The book compels the question of how valuing a combination of structure and skillful improvisation could reorient the concept of accountability, rooting it more firmly in professional commitments and accomplishments.

Theorists and practitioners across fields as diverse as music, crisis response, and education align around the conditions needed to facilitate improvisation: clarity of shared purpose, knowledgeable and experienced actors, strong social networks, and loose coupling of policy and practice.[16] Loose coupling here refers to alignment in purpose shared by actors at many levels with autonomy between and among levels to determine actions—a system recognized as conducive to local adaptation.[17] In contrast, tight coupling of external accountability presumes that "mandates, incentives, and sanctions will bring schools into line with state policy and the goal of increased student performance."[18] This tight coupling is portrayed, in the foreword to *Structure and Improvisation in Creative Teaching*, by the learning scientist David Berliner, as a "great wrong . . . promoted and supported by many politicians, business people, and school administrators" who embrace manufacturing efficiency models in the "belief that structures such as algorithms, procedures, scripts, and protocols for conducting instruction will improve teaching and learning."[19] David Berliner argues that it is "misguided to apply these same ideas in the much more uncertain environment of a classroom" and, furthermore, "By failing to build and honor the improvisational repertoires of teachers so they can respond in educative ways to the unique opportunities afforded during interaction with students and curriculum, we chip away at their love of teaching . . . and restrain student growth."[20]

If good teaching and good crisis response need improvisation, and improvisation requires loose coupling, then it follows that tight coupling would inhibit the improvisation needed for good teaching and crisis response. Loose coupling does not preclude standards, planning, or structural protocols; rather, it presumes that standards are more likely to be achieved when conditions allow local adaption of plans and structures by experienced professionals. In the past, crisis response experts viewed emergence as a failure of planning, but amassed experience and research reframed the relationship between emergence and planning as interrelated: good planning, they have since concluded, prepares for and enables effective emergent response.[21]

The Importance of Workplace Structures and Systems

Teachers' satisfaction with their work owes a large debt to the kinds of workplace support that they experience on a day-to-day basis: respected and collaborative colleagues; access to relevant, useful, and timely professional learning opportunities; adequate resources to support students' needs; and capable and responsive leadership. As detailed in chapter 5, favorable elements of daily work life prior to the pandemic also proved crucial in equipping teachers to respond effectively to a crisis.

Satisfied Stayers spoke vividly of the instructional, social, and emotional support they found among close colleagues as they pivoted first to teaching from a distance and then adapted to a range of instructional configurations in the following two school years. Their experience is consistent with a large body of research that finds robust norms and practices of teacher collaboration to be a significant resource for teacher learning and instructional improvement. In such cases, teachers work together frequently, delve deeply into evidence of student learning or student struggle, and consider when and how to change their instructional practices.[22] Teachers' work together within schools may be aided by fruitful ties to external teacher networks and other sources of professional development, as it was for many of the Satisfied Stayers.[23] All fourteen focal teachers who were Satisfied Stayers named existing or new teacher networks as useful sources of support.

Iowa teacher Judy Aldrich and Florida teacher Jennifer Donegal—both Satisfied Stayers—credited their school administrators with granting teachers the autonomy to establish their own learning priorities and the time to spend learning from and with each other. Beyond the school, Satisfied Stayers took advantage of network ties and organizational affiliations they had established well before the pandemic. Carl Graham was deeply immersed in the Oregon Writing Project; Claire Macalister, a National Board–certified science teacher, participated in regular Zoom meetings hosted by the American Association of Chemistry Teachers; Jane Farley found a professional home in a national network of math and science teachers; and Tom James joined a two-week course conducted by the National Endowment for the Humanities. The wide range of teachers' external pursuits opens a window on the landscape of professional development opportunities and resources not typically made visible through research on professional development but now made evident and salient in the context of crisis response.[24]

The Satisfied Stayers' close connections to colleagues and their engagement in professional learning beyond the school certainly attest to their individual initiative and interests, but their portrayal of their workplace contexts also places substantial weight on the effectiveness and responsiveness of school and district leaders. Indeed, the quality of school-level leadership, with an emphasis on leaders who communicated well, worked collaboratively with teachers, and shared teachers' priorities, was a decisive factor in the decision of some teachers to stay and other teachers to change schools. And while we have focused here on the day-to-day conditions of work in schools, teachers, as was evident in chapter 3, were also attentive to compensation, both in the form of salary and benefits, including retirement benefits.

Satisfied Stayers tended to have strong collaborative relationships inside and beyond the school, voice in decision-making, agency in pursuing a course of professional development, and leaders who prioritize affordances for teaching and learning. Strong working conditions existed across labor contexts, but they were most often in places where policies, practices, and discourse framed teacher expertise as a valuable asset in school leadership and direction. The experience of these Satisfied Stayers provides the outline of a vision for the teaching profession in the twenty-first century.

Voice Was Felt as a Manifestation of Trust and Respect

Consistent with Hirschman's contention that exit declines in contexts where effective voice is possible, Satisfied Stayers consistently had more influence in decision-making than other teachers.[25] At every step, they felt consulted and respected; their meaningful inclusion in school planning was tangible evidence of respect.[26] Teachers valued authentic collaborative processes even when outcomes diverged from their own personal preferences. They were more likely to criticize what they viewed as performative gestures at voice, as when districts surveyed teachers but then never disclosed the results or made apparent how the results were used in decision-making. To be meaningfully consulted was to be respected and trusted.

Without trust, teachers recognized that system-level decision-making tended both to exclude them and result in control-oriented policies, further evidencing a framing of teachers as knaves. Satisfied Stayer Henry Marquez, a twenty-five-year California urban middle school teacher, contrasted the remote instruction policy of his district with that of his wife's nearby district. He had discretion in determining whether to teach from home or school while she was required to teach online from school. He understood mandated building presence as evidence that "there is not a culture of trust, the trust that the teachers are really going to do their professional best. I mean, it just doesn't seem like they're respecting the teachers and their wishes."

Many Satisfied Stayers came through the pandemic with a renewed—and at times newfound—belief in the value of their unions. Florida elementary teacher Jennifer Donegal was not a union member for her first eight years in the classroom, but the pandemic "was definitely the push" for her to join. For many, the union became essential once teachers saw the need to act collectively in response to the disruptions wrought by the pandemic.[27] Imani Johnson, an Oregon Satisfied Stayer, expressed newfound union appreciation after her local successfully fought to have teachers' collaborative planning time reinstated: "It wasn't until [the pandemic] that I really understood that sometimes you can't get what you need without a union."

Satisfied Stayers foregrounded their unions' democratic processes and willingness to address conflict. As New York City teacher Jane Farley put it, "The union put an incredible amount of pressure" on decision-makers that resulted in safe working conditions and manageable hybrid teaching modalities. Even in the weakest labor contexts, some teachers lauded their local unions' willingness to challenge flawed policies. Veteran Florida teacher Sarah Weaver remarked, "[Our local] really stepped into the fray this time and they really, really fought." Henry Marquez described a culture of trust and respect in his district arising from and contributing to a healthy mix of teachers, union representation, and district leadership: "Our union communicated with us pretty consistently, and I would say successfully, to share plans that needed teacher input and then to relay that teacher feedback to the district." In this way, his union served as a vehicle for teacher voice, and district leadership solicited this input.[28]

Two-thirds of Satisfied Stayers felt adequately represented by their local union, in contrast with fewer than half of Leavers and Outbound Stayers. Most Satisfied Stayers worked in states where unions are considered stronger, meaning better positioned to amplify collective teacher voice regarding working conditions and educational priorities. Hirschman's *exit*, *voice*, and *loyalty* framework sheds light on the relationship between teacher unionism and teachers' career commitments. The scholar Richard Freeman built upon that framework to illustrate how unionism offers employees a "voice" alternative to exit.[29] Recent studies have affirmed this relationship between teacher unionism and teacher retention, particularly for novice teachers who are at the highest risk of turnover.[30]

State-level union strength, however, was not predictive of teacher career commitment. Even districts within the same strong union state varied in orientation; similarly, strong labor contexts existed locally in weaker union states. One Satisfied Stayer, Monica Cooper, reported, "Arizona is a right to work state so there is no union involvement," while another Satisfied Stayer in the same state, Lori Perenno, credited her union with representing her well. Ms. Perenno increased her union involvement during the pandemic as she considered teacher voice essential to a well-functioning school district and unions as essential to teacher voice: "I've gotten really more involved with our union, because I see what it's doing positively. I don't think a district can function without the voices of the educators that are in those classrooms. And so, by being involved with the union, that's the only way it's going to happen."

Judging by the contrast between the Satisfied Stayers and those who left, moved, or stayed reluctantly, teacher voice matters. Effective avenues for teacher voice communicate and deepen trust and respect, reducing exit. Those avenues include most prominently teacher unions but also collaborative leadership practices at the district and school level.

Shifted Perception of the Role of Unions

Narratives that assigned blame to teacher unions for learning loss, school closures, and other educational ruptures during the pandemic abounded. One *National Review* article was titled "Teachers' Unions Deserve Much of the Blame for Pandemic-Era Learning Loss."[31] The education newspaper *The74* reported, "Members of the House's GOP majority and their witnesses used the education subcommittee gathering to lay blame on the teachers unions for delays in reopening."[32] These narratives framed teacher unions as "special-interest groups," a term conjuring powerful corporate interests wielding undue influence over decisions pertaining to the public good. These and other public discourses during the pandemic adhered to a conception of teacher unions as powerful groups pursuing a self-interested agenda—often at the expense of student needs.

An alternative paradigm understands teacher unions as "encompassing social movements advocating for public education."[33] According to this view, teacher unions defend education as a public good and resist delegitimizing regressive educational policies. This paradigm posits teachers and their unions as active agents with the capacity to make change, as they promote increased investment in public education or advocate for instructional models that meet differentiated student needs. Teacher unions have periodically fallen prey to the same corporate management methods, centralized decision-making, and bureaucratic tendencies that they purport to oppose. Yet teachers have also demonstrated how they can transform the organizing culture of their unions to advocate for change. We contend that this paradigm best captures what teacher unions actually do, as captured in the stories of the seventy-five educators within these pages. Respected progressive educator and leader Deborah Meier captured what is at stake in shifting the public perception of unions: "When all is said and done, there's another reason why we need to worry about the public's perception of unions (and our own too). Not only are strong teacher unions critical to the success of teaching and learning, they are critical to the survival of the conditions needed to support teaching and learning. They are critical to the success of the mission of public schools in a democracy: to produce citizens who can effectively rule."[34]

The framing of teacher unions as selfish, lazy, and unprofessional during the pandemic obscures the ways that educators' interests align with those of the students they teach and risks undermining an already embattled profession. Consider Carl Graham, whose union advocated against a blended hybrid teaching model that would have created an "instant opportunity gap" for remote students.

Teacher voice is essential to teacher commitment and good schooling. School leaders need to integrate teacher knowledge and expertise in school planning. Building a profession that is prepared to respond creatively, flexibly, and strategically to future crises will depend upon trusting our teachers and their voices now. Teacher unions, as the independent and democratic organizations that represent teachers, are essential to amplifying teacher voice and, ultimately, to sustaining teachers in their work.[35]

A Confluence of Enabling Conditions

Throughout this book, we have cited the example of Satisfied Stayer Jane Farley, a New York high school science teacher in a racially diverse Title I urban school at the epicenter of the COVID-19 public health crisis in spring 2020. She embodies in a single case the confluence of all the enabling conditions that functioned to the benefit of the Satisfied Stayers and at least one that others did not enjoy: relief from the state-driven standardized testing that so frustrated and constrained others.

Ms. Farley worked in a state that from the outset took public health metrics seriously and relied on them to craft requirements and recommendations for schools. She credited her school principal with anticipating and taking steps to prepare for the spring 2020 shutdown, even when district and government leaders had yet to acknowledge the likelihood of imminent closures. While many other project teachers were frustrated by inadequate attention to safety, excessive workloads, and exclusion from school decision-making, Ms. Farley praised strong union and school leadership support for safety measures and shared that teachers at her school were given the flexibility needed to adapt. Her school relied on established and "incredibly coordinated teams" of grade-level teachers to support one another through the closure and then as school gradually reopened. When students returned in person, she was able to count on the support of counselors and social workers to cope with the students' emotional and mental health difficulties. As the only secondary teacher in the study whose students were not subject to state standardized tests (in this case, the New York State Regents Examinations), she could seek meaningful balance between renewed academic learning and a supportive social and emotional climate.[36]

Like all the project teachers, Ms. Farley faced challenges during pandemic teaching. She had moments of exhaustion and doubt. She felt demoralized by polarizing conversations in the wider community. She worried that the narrative drumbeat of "learning loss" would make students feel like "damaged goods" and that the discourse of loss might be used as an excuse to ramp up testing. But in her school, secure in her voice, accustomed to teacher-led innovation, and supported by an established tradition of collaborative leadership, she felt supported, heard, and appreciated. In summer 2022, she told us she had read about problems with the teaching profession, heard others talk about them, but not experienced them herself: "When people talk about all the issues with teaching, I understand all of them, and I don't argue with all of them. I'm just like, that's not me."

It would be easy to dismiss Jane Farley as an outlier. She stands out even among Satisfied Stayers as exceptionally well positioned to go the distance. We prefer to think of her as an existence proof, a harbinger of hope: If there can be one Jane Farley then there can be many. Ms. Farley's capacity to find fulfillment in and stay committed to teaching has much to do with the supportive policy context and the "really special school community" in which she works.

We contend that framing teaching as the work of knowledgeable professionals and supplying workplace conditions consistent with that framing fuel teacher engagement in ordinary times and supply significant resources in times of crisis. Satisfied Stayers tended to have strong collaborative relationships inside and beyond the school, voice in decision-making, agency in pursuing a course of professional development, and leaders who prioritize affordances for teaching and learning. Strong working conditions existed across labor contexts, but most often in places where policies, practices, and discourse framed teacher expertise as an asset in school leadership and direction. The experience of these Satisfied Stayers provides the outline of a forward-looking vision for the teaching profession.

A VISION OF THE TEACHING PROFESSION FOR THE 21ST CENTURY

We know what needs to be done to strengthen the conditions of the teaching profession; we have known for forty years. Getting there requires that we come to terms with how a conception of teaching as complex work, and teachers as well-prepared professionals with the latitude and resources to act, has been displaced by a far more diminished conception of teachers as workers expected to follow the dictates of others. The advent of the pandemic crisis—the disruption it caused and the responses it engendered—invites a renewed focus on the nature of teaching as a profession.

The control and compliance policy frame is consistent with the growth of a centralized standards and test-based accountability model that has dominated US educational improvement efforts for more than three decades. Centralized systems of state-based testing expanded from the early 1980s through the 1990s and further solidified with the passage of No Child Left Behind (NCLB) in 2001. Yet the policy bent toward centralization and control coincided throughout those decades with a smaller movement to promote accountability rooted not in bureaucratic control but in the teacher profession itself. The 1983 publication of *A Nation at Risk*—warning of a "rising tide of mediocrity" in American schools that would threaten the nation's economy and international standing—stimulated efforts to elevate both the status and the capacity of the teacher workforce.

Formed in 1985 in response to *A Nation at Risk*, the Task Force on Teaching as a Profession responded in 1986 with *A Nation Prepared: Teachers for the 21st Century*. That blueprint conceived of teachers as "people of substantial intellectual accomplishment" who were positioned to orchestrate ambitious student learning, and it argued for a form of professional accountability that "permits teachers to decide how best to meet state and local goals for children while holding them accountable for student progress."[37] Ambitious student learning, we knew then and we know now, requires a more ambitious conception of teaching that is anything but robotic. It requires intellectual strength, adaptability, creative thinking, and collaboration.

It is no coincidence that in *The Rise and Fall of the Teaching Profession: Prestige, Interest, Preparation, and Satisfaction over the Last Half Century*, scholars at Brown University's Annenberg Institute characterized the 1980s as a window of rapidly increasing professional prestige, occupational appeal, and on-the-job satisfaction.[38] That era of professional optimism anticipated rigorous teacher preparation, salaries commensurate with the expectations of rigorous preparation, and a workplace appropriate to the work of professionals.[39] Together, these conditions would yield work

> characterized by the assumption that the job of the professional is to bring special expertise and judgment to bear on the work at hand. Because their expertise and judgment is respected and they alone are presumed to have it, professionals enjoy a high degree of autonomy in carrying out their work. They define the standards used to evaluate the quality of work done, they decide what standards are used to judge the qualifications of professionals in their field, and they have a major voice in deciding what program of preparation is appropriate for professionals in their field.[40]

This vision launched a flurry of reform initiatives—changes in teacher education policy and practice, career ladder schemes, school restructuring initiatives, experimentation with union-district relationships. For example, teachers had a prominent role in shaping subject-matter standards in the 1980s and through much of the 1990s. In 1989, the National Council of Teachers of Mathematics (NCTM) was the first professional association to publish curriculum and evaluation standards. Its release of *Curriculum and Evaluation Standards for School Mathematics* was followed by publication of *Professional Standards for Teaching Mathematics* in 1991 and by *Assessment Standards for School Mathematics* in 1995.[41] Other professional associations followed suit in the core academic domains.[42]

Yet even as teachers embraced academic standards, states moved to define standards tied to high-stakes student testing.[43] By the passage of NCLB in 2001, a standards movement that began with a strong teacher imprint and that signaled a strong investment in profession-based accountability had evolved into a government-defined, test-based system of bureaucratic accountability. Teachers have pushed back against what they view as a narrowly defined testing agenda while continuing to embrace meaningful standards and useful assessment. In 2015, the Shanker Institute published testimony provided to Congress by high school teacher Stephen Lazar.[44] Describing himself as a "proud New York City public high school teacher," Mr. Lazar—a National Board–certified teacher, local union leader, and contributor to state and national curriculum and assessment initiatives—spoke of his frustration and disappointment each year when the approaching Regents exams forced him to "turn into a bad teacher," putting aside the research projects, rich discussions, and immersion in complexity that were hallmarks of his teaching to focus on preparation for tests that "measure the wrong things." Mr. Lazar explained the need to replace annualized administration of narrowly conceived standardized tests with well-designed assessments posing "authentic tasks" that allow students to demonstrate what they know and are able to do.[45]

A Nation Prepared supplied a scenario consistent with its imagined school of the twenty-first century, a school guided by an executive committee of lead teachers, a school where teachers are supported by aides and nonteaching specialists, where a diverse teaching staff jointly devises a rich curriculum and employs a range of assessments to attend closely to student progress and struggles, and where teachers take collective responsibility for student growth and for the school's steady improvement. The report goes on to say, "This is not a utopian vision. There are schools in the United States whose staff would recognize this description as very like what they do now. But not many."[46]

In some respects, efforts to cultivate higher levels of teacher collaboration and promote teacher leadership have gained some traction. For example, the acronym PLC (professional learning community) has become commonplace, as have instructional leadership and mentorship roles.[47] Yet PLCs can be co-opted to administrative direction rather than teachers' interests. It was just such a circumstance that led Florida teacher Sarah Weaver to see PLC meetings as simply a time to "check the box" in a list of administrative tasks rather than as collaborative teacher time to advance student learning. And although highly collaborative schools do exist, they are still too rare. Fewer than one-third of project teachers—primarily Satisfied Stayers—described strongly collaborative school cultures prior to the pandemic, but their accounts underscore the importance of doing more to make such schools commonplace.

A vision of the teaching profession expressed by 1980s reforms spawned a range of initiatives that conveyed a sense of momentum. And yet we must reckon with a certain irony: the conditions to which this vision responded have proved stubbornly persistent.[48] Authors of *A Nation Prepared* lamented then and might well lament now that schools were "suffused with bureaucracy," places where "an endless array of policies succeed in constraining the exercise of the teacher's independent judgment on almost every matter of moment."[49]

Resistance to systemic change is persuasively attributed to *inherited terrains* of multiple, often competing and contested, purposes and policies of public education.[50] Any reform vision or policy shift must contend with the preexisting landscape. Considering the implications of her own study of teachers' work during the COVID-19 pandemic in Canada, Nina Bascia cautions that recommendations for change cannot assume some kind of blank canvas, or *tabula rasa*, on which to paint. Others have sounded similar caveats; as one essay on policy change warned, "Policies do not land in a vacuum; they land on top of other policies."[51] There are underlying logics at play, often not articulated, but framing and driving systems nonetheless: teachers as knights or knaves, good teaching as uniform pacing or as structures that enable improvisation, attention on more resilient canaries or on better working conditions.

Today finds us on the heels of a massive disruption to schooling navigated by a teaching profession that has yet to be fully framed as respected "people of substantial intellectual accomplishment," entrusted with defining standards and assessing outcomes in support of improvisational teaching of ambitious student learning. For some teachers, notably the Leavers and Outbound Stayers, the experience of pandemic teaching brought into relief the deprofessionalized reality of their working conditions. The Satisfied Stayers offer a contrast case—a clear reminder that the conditions of commitment are possible even in an inherited terrain that includes bureaucratic control, managerialism, and external accountability. There are lessons here for improving educational crisis response, ameliorating the effect of future crises on teacher commitment, and improving the future of the teaching profession. By increasing organizational and social resilience, and reducing vulnerability, we can improve the professional status of teaching so that it attracts and retains professional teachers. Resuscitating a professionalism reform movement will require that we reframe the public and political perception of teachers as knowledgeable, trustworthy professionals and cultivate the conditions of emergence in times of crisis and calm by supporting formalized systems of teacher voice, recognizing the policy and working conditions needed to facilitate both teacher voice and improvisational teaching. Just as teachers in this book sought to exercise voice as an avenue to change, so we have the capacity to advocate for the schools and the conditions of the teaching profession we envision.

THE TEACHING PROFESSION IN A POST-COVID WORLD

Fundamentally, this is a book about the teaching profession, as it has been, as it is, and how it could be. Pandemic-era teaching highlights the need to reconceptualize teachers' work discursively, organizationally, and systemically. Teachers demonstrated remarkable professional initiative and creativity throughout the crisis, employing knowledge, skill, and judgment to pursue what they considered the best interests of their students. Their actions embodied effective emergency response by on-the-ground responders drawing on expert knowledge and local context needs assessments. Preparation for future crises means cultivating the adaptive capacity of schools for an agile response to the unexpected.[52]

Adaptive capacity requires organizations to develop shared purpose, trust, resources, distributed leadership, and a culture of capitalizing on experience.[53] The imperative we face now is how to improve the adaptive capacity of schools, particularly the conditions that support teacher adaptation, without eroding professional commitment. We need to fix the mines so we can save the canaries. Building adaptive capacity requires shifting discursive framing of teachers from knaves to knights; fostering school working conditions that capitalize on teacher expertise and experience; and cultivating an educational policy culture to support these changes. We view this as a set of broadly strategic points of departure, pointing to areas where it might profitably focus but refraining from the more detailed choices and decisions best made by individuals, groups, and organizations close to the action—including teachers whose voice we have highlighted throughout.

Discursive Reframing: Promote Messaging Consistent with Teaching as a Profession

Consciously communicating respect for teachers, as professionals trusted to guide schooling, requires attention to language and implicit messaging. During the pandemic, concerns that teachers might not prioritize students' needs led to policies that constrained teacher adaptation and communicated distrust, framing teachers as knaves. Unquestionably, there are knaves in all occupations and organizations, but creating policies on the presumption of knavery will create conditions not conducive to supporting teachers as professionals. Every dismissive or pejorative statement—from politicians, school board members, in the media, or by parents on Facebook—further diminishes the standing of the teaching profession and takes a toll on teachers. In any profession, there may be reason to disparage certain individuals; there is good reason for malpractice suits in medicine and for calls to dismiss incompetent or unethical teachers. However, sweeping, negative portrayals of teachers fail to do justice to the knowledge, skill, care, and effort that most teachers bring to their work on a day-to-day basis—and undermine the overall image and regard for the profession.

The retrospective policy, media, and public analysis of what has been termed pandemic *learning loss* has consistently sought to attribute declines in national academic assessment measures to schools' decisions to delay a return to in-person schooling while relying on remote or hybrid configurations.[54] But such an attribution—and the associated recommendation to intensify and accelerate academic instruction—is simplistic at best, ignoring confounding factors like the variation in what "hybrid" instruction configurations required of teachers and students, the relative stability (or instability) of instructional modality over the course of the academic year, as well as the relationship between students' academic progress and the social, emotional, and mental health problems they experienced during an extended pandemic.[55]

Many teachers considered learning loss to be a misdiagnosis with a potential for damage. As detailed in chapter 7, project teachers recognized the symptoms—students' quite evident academic learning needs and struggles—but traced them not only to interrupted instruction but also to pandemic-related trauma. Jane Farley in New York worried that the learning loss narrative would make students feel like "damaged goods," while Carl Graham in Oregon explained that "learning doesn't work like that," and trying to accelerate the pace of curriculum coverage would only deepen students' anxiety. To bolster students' academic development would instead require reestablishing students' sense of belonging, safety, and overall well-being. To make a medical comparison, shortness of breath is a symptom of both asthma and heart failure, but the treatments to restore clear airways differ greatly and a misdiagnosis can have a catastrophic outcome. Treating heart failure with an asthma inhaler will neither restore breath nor address the real underlying cardiac cause of the symptom. Similarly, treating social and emotional trauma with intensified academics will not likely increase student learning and may very well exacerbate the underlying trauma, as evidenced in low school attendance and increased student behavior problems.[56]

The messages conveyed to and about teachers are potent signals of the regard in which teachers are held and have immediate import for practicing teachers—as evidenced by project teachers who left, moved, or stayed; they also suggest the potential for longer term and more widespread consequences for the appeal and satisfactions of the teaching profession. We call upon readers to use care when discussing educational challenges, avoid blanket blaming of teachers, counter negative depictions by amplifying powerful moments of learning facilitated by committed teachers, interrogate policies and programs for implicit messaging, and avoid simplistic framings of educational problems that sideline teachers and curtail comprehensive solutions. Sustaining a profession of teachers requires a conscious and intentional discursive representation of teaching as a respected profession.

Reconfigure Systemic Support for a Profession of Teachers

Our observations have led us to question, as others have done before us, the wisdom of a state-driven accountability system in which teachers are subject to tight managerial controls rather than called upon and authorized to share more directly the responsibility for the quality of teachers and teaching.[57] This points to a reconfiguration and rebalancing of professional authority, government policy and regulation, and responsiveness to the parents, children, and other citizens who have a stake in the public education system.[58] The centering of teacher voice is consistent with crisis theories that highlight the limits of top-down management and contingency planning in adaptive capacity.[59] Reconfiguring systemic support requires school leaders and policy makers to actively include teachers as professional experts and to recognize the value of a guidance and local discretion model in organizational effectiveness.[60]

Enable teacher voice. Authentically including teachers' voice in policy making and the daily work of schools is essential to conveying respect for teaching as a profession, for sustaining professional teachers' commitment, and ensuring good crisis response. A shift in accountability authority from politics to professional expertise will develop adaptation capacities.

Recognize the systemic role of unions. In the current ecology of schools, unions are the collective voice of teachers. As such, unions help retain loyal teachers by ensuring they have a vehicle for voice, minimizing the risk of exit. When districts and unions are at odds, unions amplify the priorities, needs, and commitments of teachers, as they did in helping teachers fend off proposals for the most demanding forms of hybrid instruction that were detrimental to teaching and learning. There is also value in conceiving of district-union relationships well beyond the usual focus on "the contract," on whether state law allows for collective bargaining and permits or prohibits strikes.[61] The pandemic showed how local unions could emerge as effective influences even in weak labor states and how local unions varied in their relationships with districts and communities even in strong labor states.

Facilitating a shift in policy culture requires states and districts to step back from command-and-control systems to make room for adaptation. A system's capacity to manage the unexpected is characterized by "deference to expertise" over "deference to hierarchy."[62] In a guidance model, the central authority provides vision, communicates clear goals, sources and distributes resources equitably, and facilitates information sharing. In adaptive systems, the balance among central and distributed units of decision-making nets the benefits of centralized clarity of goals and flow of information and decentralized awareness of local contexts and expertise.[63] Supporting school-level collaborative practices, framing teachers as trustworthy and respected professionals, requires a shift in state-level policies to facilitate local enactment of goals. Preparation for future crisis response starts with cultivating the conditions of an adaptive teaching profession and elevating teachers to the status of respected professionals entrusted with authority and influence.

Organize for Adaptive Capacity

Both good teaching and effective emergency response are facilitated by the same adaptive conditions: the best way to prepare for future crises is to cultivate the adaptive capacity of schools and teachers for an agile response to the unexpected. Adaptive capacity is the underlying organizational ability to adapt, meaning "adjusting behavior and changing priorities in the pursuit of goals."[64] Crisis research identifies factors that build adaptive capacity, including shared purpose, distributed leadership, and capitalizing on experience.[65] These factors, together with prior research on strong, learning-focused teacher groups and the experiences of the Satisfied Stayers, point to the importance of collaborative workplace culture, collaborative leadership, and the conditions that must be established for teacher collaboration to flourish.[66]

Support teachers' collaborative work. The pandemic experience underscored the advantage that accrued to teachers accustomed to frequent and productive interaction with their teacher colleagues and other school-based professionals. Collaborative workplace cultures provided teachers with trusted networks of colleagues with whom they built off a shared sense of purpose to adapt their practice. Teachers immersed in close workplace collaborations had a markedly better pandemic experience than teachers with weak ties to colleagues or, in extreme cases, what could be considered a toxic workplace. This has implications for teacher preparation and mentorship, the preparation and support of school administrators, and the organization of the professional workday, workweek, and work year, including acknowledging collaboration in the school schedule and recognizing collaboration as a legitimate source of professional development. Effective teacher collaboration benefits from structural supports like common planning time, physical proximity, and collective participation in professional development. Beyond such structural support, teachers in effective collaborative groups cultivate shared norms and practices conducive to probing questions, in-depth attention to problems of practice, and an open-minded consideration of new ideas.

Organize schools for distributed leadership. Recent decades have witnessed a shift from a single-minded focus on the principal as school leader to a conception of distributed leadership with a focus on collaborative leadership practices.[67] Project teachers' experiences and previous studies have demonstrated a relationship among teachers' involvement in decision-making, their organizational and professional commitment, and the organization's capacity to adapt.[68] Yet it would be a mistake to view a shift from a deference to hierarchy to a deference to professional expertise and to a deeply collaborative culture as within easy reach where such a culture does not already exist.[69] First, teachers must be able to count on school administrators who enable collaboration without endeavoring to control it. Teachers work within a hierarchical structure where managerialist orientations toward teachers and their work have solidified in recent decades. Even where teachers are provided with structured time to meet together during the workweek, the use of that time may be defined by school or district administrators rather than by teachers themselves—a situation that has been termed "contrived collegiality."[70] Schools can facilitate shared leadership by building on established traditions, like instructional leadership teams, committing to authentic rather than performative forms of shared decision-making, and developing the capacities of principals and teachers to lead collaboratively.

Plan for the Next One. Adaptation in crises requires a preexisting underlying capacity. Schools should turn now to teachers to identify the changes needed to reinvent and reenvision—and to fortify against a future crisis, as France did in its response to the 2003 heat wave disaster in Paris. Seizing this opportunity requires learning from the experience of those on-the-ground responders who acted quickly and creatively to manage the massive disruption that a crisis presents. A pandemic crisis that stretched over two years should yield lessons for the future. Teachers are extraordinarily well positioned (along with local school and district leaders) to mine those lessons and help prepare for disruptions to come. Teachers' experience of an abrupt closure of schools despite numerous advance warning signs underscores the importance of emergency contingency planning at multiple levels. Their experience of the unanticipated and lingering consequences of "do no harm" policies—the precipitous decline in student participation and motivation—might, as some project teachers advised, stimulate educators and policy makers to rethink a system in which participation and motivation are so wedded to grades and testing.

Improvisation is built on a foundation of planning and a repertoire of knowledge practices. It could prove prescient to establish some forum and process for capturing the collective insights of principal actors in the service of mitigating future disasters. Appropriate convenors (individually or jointly) include state school board associations, departments of education, teacher unions or associations, administrator associations, and local school boards and unions. It is no accident that the adoption of a National Heatwave Plan in France in 2004, directly on the heels of the 2003 disaster, enabled it to better navigate a subsequent, potentially disastrous, heat wave event. Education could learn from the example set by France.

Access to Meaningful, Multilevel Data on the Teacher Workforce

Federal and state departments of education need to collaborate to develop more robust and reliable sources of teacher workforce data that permit analysis within and between states. The insufficient availability of data on school and state level teacher retention, turnover, and staffing vacancies, and the variation in measures, impede analysis and understanding of teacher workforce issues. While we assembled annual state-level teacher turnover data for five of nine states (see figure 7.1), variable definitions of *turnover* and *year* parameters made comparisons difficult. As for availability, some states publicly publish annual turnover rates, and some freely and expediently release these data upon request, while others have complicated bureaucratic and political processes to gain access—with access not guaranteed—and a few charge significant fees for teacher turnover data. This needs to change. States need to make information on teacher workforce patterns publicly available in a timely manner that school leaders, the public, researchers, and policy makers can rely on. These data should not identify individual teachers but should permit school-level analysis. Among our nine states, Massachusetts, New York, Arizona, and Kentucky all had interactive dashboards with comprehensive information on teacher turnover. Texas does not provide an interactive dashboard but does provide comprehensive information online.[71]

A great deal of policy attention has attended to what constitutes a well-qualified teacher while the specifics of a well-resourced school are opaque. Knowing the distribution of novice and experienced teachers by school, together with the school-level turnover rate, would permit analysis over time and between schools that could inform the decisions of state and local leaders, teacher unions, and teachers themselves.

Additionally, research on the relative well-being, satisfaction, and stability of the teaching profession must reach beyond patterns of exit and shortage as a measure of workforce problems. As evidenced by the experiences of Outbound and Stuck Stayers, there are many reasons demoralized teachers might remain in classrooms. Considerations beyond occupational persistence must factor into considerations of workforce health. And finally, research on teachers' work must be disaggregated by state and district in ways that illuminate context variations within and between states. Reports on US teachers' experiences, perceptions of their working conditions, and career plans are minimally useful in the aggregate, especially in assertions about "American teachers" as a whole without locating them in relation to meaningful context specifics related to state policy, compensation and other working conditions, union strength, and more.

CRISIS AS CATALYST

There is an old proverb that *a change is as good as a rest* for revitalizing attention and energy. The pandemic disruption was undeniably a change: a shock to our world that disrupted every system and shifted perspectives and priorities of people, individually and collectively. For some teachers, that shock created or exacerbated working conditions they found unsustainable. Satisfied Stayers, however, offer a powerful alternative possibility of working conditions—respect, voice, and professional authority—that sustained them through a prolonged crisis and provided a vision of how to take the teaching profession from its prepandemic fifty-year low to an aspirational new hundred-year high.

The question before us is will we act on what we have learned? Having seen the cracks in the framing of the teaching profession, will the lessons they reveal motivate policy and social change needed to secure teacher engagement and commitment, in times of calm and in times of crisis? Much of what we have suggested here is a call to revive and extend the vision of a vibrant, committed, and respected profession of teachers endowed with trust and authority. We have reasons to feel optimistic that the teaching profession is at an inflection point where trust and regard will rise reciprocally with improved working conditions.

A source of hope and optimism may be found in historical precedents of large-scale societal change emerging out of crisis. Historians have associated the Black Death of 1348–1350 with the emergence of the cultural renaissance. Emerging from the scourge of the plague, "Europe's Renaissance, or 'rebirth,' was forged in the crucible of its terrible, yet transcendent, ordeal with the Black death."[72] The mortal toll is understood to have transformed survivors' perceptions and values, undermined their religious beliefs, inspired artistic expression, and changed the realities of work; for example, population loss drove up wages. Other crises have been associated with significant social, cultural, and economic change, like the passage of New Deal legislation to form a social safety net in the United States following the Depression, the creation of England's National Health Service after World War II, and the postwar expansion of higher education access in both countries. In a 2017 research brief on the benefits of crises, the Brookings Institution identified new levels of cooperation, unexpected systemic change, dramatic policy shifts, and increased resilience for the next event.[73]

The coronavirus pandemic has already transformed the ways in which people work, where they live, and their priorities in how to distribute their time. In education, it has raised questions about the purposes of schooling, the needs of students that go well beyond academic learning, and what is essential about teachers' work. It seems completely reasonable to imagine that this crisis could catalyze a transformation in how public education—and the teachers upon which it relies—could best serve the public good. Such a transformation must achieve the right balance of professional authority, government regulation and policy setting, and responsiveness to a citizenry with a significant stake in the strength of its public schools. This transformation will only be as powerful as the teaching profession it envisions and empowers.

Appendix

Table A.1 Study participants

Name (pseudonym)	Career code 2022*	Years experience in 2020	State	Race**	Community	Level and subject
Charlotte Adams	M	9	TX	Wh	Suburb	HS: Science
Judy Aldrich	SS	16	IA	Wh	Rural	MS: Science
Victor Andrei	OS	30	OR	Lat	Suburb	HS: Social Studies
Denise Arlington	OS	13	MA	Wh	Suburb	MS: Science
Vicky Bauer	SS	22	NY	Wh	Urban	Elementary
Robin Beach	L	3	TX	Wh	Urban	Elementary
Dr. Sophie Blum	L	6	FL	Wh	Urban	HS: Science
Taylor Brennan	L	4	IA	Lat; Wh	Suburb	HS: Language Arts
Frances Carter	L	11	KY	Wh	Rural	MS: Language Arts
Ruth Cartwright	ST	13	IA	Wh	Suburb	HS: Social Studies
Monica Cooper	SS	19	AZ	PNS	Rural	HS: Special Education

(*Continued*)

Table A.1 Study participants (*Continued*)

Name (pseudonym)	Career code 2022*	Years experience in 2020	State	Race**	Community	Level and subject
Noelle Cruz	M	3	OR	Lat; Ind; Wh	Rural	HS: Language Arts
Liz Darcie	SS	10	CA	Wh	Other	PreK
Brittany Davlin	L	5	IA	Wh	Suburb	Elementary
Summer Diaz	M	6	CA	Wh	Suburb	MS: Language Arts
Michael Donovan	OS	15	MA	Wh	Urban	HS: Science
Jennifer Donegal	SS	8	FL	Wh	Other	Elementary
Cora Donner	L	15	AZ	Wh	Suburb	HS: Vocational
Bob Dover	SS	27	MA	Wh	Suburb	HS: Language Arts
Chelsea Doyle	OS	4	KY	Wh	Rural	HS: Social Studies
Evelyn Dworkin	SO	6	FL	Wh	Other	MS: Special Education
Leanne Edwards	M	10	TX	Wh	Suburb	MS: Language Arts
John Evans	SO	13	MA	Wh	Rural	HS: Social Studies
Jane Farley	SS	6	NY	Wh	Urban	HS: Chemistry
Janet Featherstone	OS	20	FL	Lat	Rural	HS: Language Arts
Rowan Finchley	M	6	KY	Wh	Suburb	MS: Art
Clara French	SS	1	TX	As, PI	Suburb	Elementary
Stacey Garcia	SS	12	AZ	Bl; Wh	Urban	HS: Science
Carl Graham	SS	17	OR	PNS	Urban	Elementary
Don Granger	SS	27	TX	Wh	Rural	HS: Language Arts

Leonardo Hall	OS	24	NY	Wh	Urban	HS: Social Studies
Julia Harper	SS	9	KY	Wh	Suburb	Elementary
Linnea Harris	SS	13	CA	As; Wh	Rural	Elementary
Ava Hoffman	SS	23	OR	Wh	Suburb	Elementary
Jessica Holm	L	9	NY	Wh	Urban	Elementary
Tom James	SS	11	NY	Wh	Urban	HS: Social Studies
Imani Johnson	SO	9	OR	Bl; Lat	Suburb	Elementary
Amelia Jones	SS	6	NY	Wh	Urban	Elementary
Layla Karim	OS	1	OR	As; Wh	Rural	MS: English Language Develop-ment
Emily Kline	OS	4	MA	Wh	Rural	HS: Science
Alice Kovak	SS	14	FL	Wh	Suburb	Elementary
Rachel Larsen	L	4	IA	Wh	Rural	HS: Social Studies
Amanda LaScala	OS	15	CA	Bl; Wh	Suburb	Elementary
Natalie Lehrer	L	6	IA	Wh	Rural	HS: Science
Sherry Lincoln	SO	14	CA	Bl	Urban	HS: Language Arts
Amy Locke	OS	9	AZ	Wh	Urban	HS: Science
Claire Macalister	SS	20	TX	Wh	Rural	HS: Science
Tobias Maccini	OS	24	MA	Wh	Rural	Elementary
Fred Marino	SS	15	AZ	Wh	Suburb	HS: Science
Henry Marquez	SS	25	CA	Lat	Urban	MS: Social Studies
Susan Mazur	M	21	AZ	Wh	Rural	HS: Math
Gail Miller	L	6	KY	Wh	Urban	Elementary
Carla Morrison	OS	8	MA	Wh	Suburb	Elementary
Addison Myers	OS	13	KY	Wh	Suburb	HS: Language Arts
Meredith Nathan	OS	21	MA	Wh	Urban	MS: Special Education
Eve Nowak	SN	22	NY	Wh	Suburb	HS: Science

(*Continued*)

Table A.1 Study Participants (*Continued*)

Name (pseudonym)	Career code 2022*	Years experience in 2020	State	Race**	Community	Level and subject
Morgan O'Neil	OS	5	OR	Wh	Suburb	MS: Language Arts
Lori Perenno	SS	10	AZ	Wh	Suburb	Elementary
Richard Rozman	U	5	KY	Wh	Urban	MS: Language Arts
James Sampson	SS	20	OR	Wh	Rural	HS: Language Arts
Leslie Spark	M	14	FL	Wh	Rural	MS: Math
Jeff Stevens	SS	20	CA	Wh	Suburb	Elementary
Sam Stewart	L	9	IA	Wh	Rural	MS: Social Studies
Joanna Suarez	SN	14	MA	Lat	Urban	HS: Vocational
Emma Thorsen	L	3	KY	Wh	Suburb	Elementary
Francisco Vargas	M	29	CA	Lat	Urban	MS: Math
Nancy Walsh	SS	22	KY	Wh	Suburb	Elementary
Sarah Weaver	OS	21	FL	PI; Wh	Urban	HS: Social Studies
Charles Welk	SN	17	FL	Bl; Lat; Wh	Suburb	MS: Social Studies
Elizabeth Winters	LU	22	MA	Wh	Suburb	PreK
Vivian Woods	ST	13	OR	Bl; Ind; Wh	Suburb	HS: Social Studies
Nella Worth	M	2	TX	Wh	Urban	Elementary
Casey Wright	SS	20	CA	Wh	Urban	HS: Language Arts
Ruth Yamaguchi	L	6	OR	As	Suburb	PreK
Michelle Yang	LU	10	NY	As	Urban	HS: Math

* L = Leaver; LU = Leaver Unrelated; M = Mover; SS = Satisfied Stayer; OS = Outbound Stayer; ST = Stuck Stayer; SO = Stayer Other; SN = Stayer N/A; U = Unknown
** Bl = Black; Wh = White; Ind = Indigenous/First Nations; Lat = Latinx; As = Asian; PI = Pacific islander; PNS = Prefer Not to Say

Notes

Chapter 1

1. News and research throughout 2023 warned of lingering effects on teacher shortages and students' learning and well-being. For example, see Moriah Balingit, "Teacher Shortages Have Gotten Worse: Here's How Schools Are Coping," *Washington Post*, August 24, 2023, https://www.washingtonpost.com/education/2023/08/24/teacher-shortages-pipeline-college-licenses/; Matt Barnum, "Recent School Year Saw Little Academic Recovery, New Study Finds," *Chalkbeat*, July 10, 2023, https://www.chalkbeat.org/2023/7/11/23787212/nwea-learning-loss-academic-recovery-testing-data-covid/. Yet by fall 2023, some reports noted modest improvements in student attendance and tempered the alarm over learning loss. See Evie Blad, "Student Attendance Rates Show Signs of Rebounding," *EducationWeek*, October 18, 2023, https://www.edweek.org/leadership/student-absenteeism-remains-at-a-crisis-level-but-shows-signs-of-rebounding/2023/10; David Wallace-Wells, "American Students Outperformed Much of the World During the Pandemic," *New York Times*, December 13, 2023, https://www.nytimes.com/2023/12/13/opinion/learning-loss-test-results-covid.html.
2. Matthew A. Kraft and Melissa A. Lyon, "The Rise and Fall of the Teaching Profession: Prestige, Interest, Preparation, and Satisfaction over the Last Half Century," Annenberg Institute EdWorkingPaper: 22–679 (November 2022), Brown University, Providence, RI, November 2022, https://doi.org/10.26300/7b1a-vk92.
3. In a book based on teacher surveys, interviews, and focus groups, Marshall and Pressley argue that "long-term school closures were a mistake, possibly the biggest educational policy mistake of the past century." David Marshall and Tim Pressley, *Lessons of the Pandemic: Disruption, Innovation, and What Schools Need to Move Forward* (New York: Guilford, 2024), 125.
4. See Jack Schneider and Jennifer Berkshire, *A Wolf at the Schoolhouse Door: The Dismantling of Public Education and the Future of School* (New York: New Press, 2023); Steven C. Ward, *Neoliberalism and the Global Restructuring of Knowledge and Education* (New York: Routledge, 2014); David F. Labaree, "Public Schools for Private Gain: The Declining American Commitment to Serving the Public Good," *Phi Delta Kappan* 100, no. 3 (October 2018): 8–13.

5. The effect of the pandemic on teacher attrition is a contested topic. Some scholars predict significant pandemic-related consequences for the national teacher supply. See John Schmitt and Katherine DeCourcy, *The Pandemic Has Exacerbated a Long-Standing National Shortage of Teachers* (Washington, DC: Economic Policy Institute, 2022), https://www.epi.org/publication/shortage-of-teachers/; Melissa Kay Diliberti and Heather L. Schwartz, *Districts Continue to Struggle with Staffing, Political Polarization, and Unfinished Instruction: Selected Findings from the Fifth American School District Panel Survey* (Santa Monica, CA: RAND, 2022), https://www.rand.org/pubs/research_reports/RRA956-13.html. Others contend that the forecast of pandemic-related shortages has been overblown and not substantiated in workforce data. See Dan Goldhaber and Roddy Theobald, "Teacher Attrition and Mobility in the Pandemic," *Educational Evaluation and Policy Analysis* 45, no. 4 (December 2023): 682–87.
6. Emma Garcia, Eunice Han, and Elaine Weiss, "Determinants of Teacher Attrition: Evidence from District-Teacher Matched Data," *Education Policy Analysis Archives* 30, no. 25 (March 2022): 4.
7. Garcia, Han, and Weiss, "Determinants of Teacher Attrition," 20.
8. The importance of working conditions for teacher retention has long been established in research on teachers' work. See Richard M. Ingersoll, "Teacher Turnover and Teacher Shortages: An Organizational Analysis," *American Educational Research Journal* 38, no. 3 (Fall 2001): 499–534; Susan Moore Johnson, "The Workplace Matters: Teacher Quality, Retention, and Effectiveness," working paper (Washington, DC: National Education Association Research Department, July 2006).
9. Roger E. Kasperson and Jeanne Kasperson, eds., *The Social Contours of Risk* (New York: Earthscan, 2005); E. L. Quarantelli, Arjen Boin, and Patrick Lagadec, "Studying Future Disasters and Crises: A Heuristic Approach," in *Handbook of Disaster Research*, ed. H. Rodriguez, W. Donner, and J. E. Trainor (New York: Springer, 2018), 61–86; Ortwin Renn, William J. Burns, and Paul Slovic, "The Social Amplification of Risk: Theoretical Foundations and Empirical Applications," *Journal of Social Issues* 48, no. 4 (Winter 1992): 137–60; Kathleen Tierney, *Disasters: A Sociological Approach* (Hoboken, NJ: Wiley, 2019).
10. Richard C. Keller, *Fatal Isolation: The Devastating Paris Heat Wave of 2003* (Chicago: University of Chicago Press, 2015).
11. Peter Ford, "Heat Waves: How France Has Cut Death Toll 90% Since 2003," *Christian Science Monitor*, November 4, 2019, https://www.csmonitor.com/World/Europe/2019/1104/Heat-waves-How-France-has-cut-death-toll-90-since-2003.
12. Kevin Fox Gotham and Miriam Greenberg, *Crisis Cities: Disaster and Redevelopment in New York and New Orleans* (Oxford: Oxford University Press, 2014), 135–36.
13. Gotham and Greenberg, *Crisis Cities*, 136.
14. Andy Horowitz, "Hurricane Betsy and the Politics of Disaster in New Orleans's Lower Ninth Ward, 1965–1967," *Journal of Southern History* 80, no. 4 (November 2014): 893–934.
15. Andy Horowitz, *Katrina: A History, 1915–2015* (Cambridge, MA: Harvard University Press, 2020).
16. Gotham and Greenberg, *Crisis Cities*, 161–66.
17. Quarantelli, Boin, and Lagadec, *Studying Future Disasters and Crises*, 68.

18. Chris Ansell, Arjen Boin, and Ann Keller, "Managing Transboundary Crises: Identifying the Building Blocks of an Effective Response System," *Journal of Contingencies and Crisis Management* 18, no. 4 (December 2010): 195–207. Crisis theorists consistently highlight the relevance of emergent actors and networks across levels in transboundary crisis response.
19. Matthew A. Kraft, Nicole S. Simon, and Melissa Arnold Lyon, "Sustaining a Sense of Success: The Protective Role of Teacher Working Conditions During the COVID-19 Pandemic," *Journal of Research on Educational Effectiveness* 14, no. 4 (July 2021): 20; Veronica M. O'Toole and Myron D. Friesen, "Teachers as First Responders in Tragedy: The Role of Emotion in Teacher Adjustment Eighteen Months Post-Earthquake," *Teaching and Teacher Education* 59, no. 1 (October 2016): 57–67.
20. Thomas A. Birkland, "Focusing Events, Mobilization, and Agenda Setting," *Journal of Public Policy* 18, no. 1 (January–April 1998): 53–74.
21. Rob A. DeLeo, K. Taylor, Deserai A. Crow, and Thomas A. Birkland, "During Disaster: Refining the Concept of Focusing Events to Better Explain Long-Duration Crises," *International Review of Public Policy* 3, no. 1 (March 2021): 5–28.
22. See Nina Bascia, *Teachers' Work During the Pandemic* (New York: Routledge, 2023) for a discussion of the dominance of a narrow, technical conception of teaching held by decision-makers prior to and during the pandemic and the relative inattention to socioemotional, intellectual, and sociopolitical dimensions of teachers' work.
23. Susan L. Moffitt, Michaela Krug O'Neill, and David K. Cohen, *Reforming the Reform: Problems of Public Schooling in the American Welfare State* (Chicago: University of Chicago Press, 2023).
24. Betty Achinstein and Rodney T. Ogawa, "(In)Fidelity: What the Resistance of New Teachers Reveals About Professional Principles and Prescriptive Educational Policies," *Harvard Educational Review* 76, no. 1 (April 2006): 30–63.
25. The intersection of managerialist reforms, work intensification, and loss of teachers' professional autonomy has been analyzed by a number of scholars. See Katrijn Ballet, Geert Kelchtermans, and John Loughran, "Beyond Intensification Towards a Scholarship of Practice: Analyzing Changes in Teachers' Work Lives," *Teachers and Teaching: Theory and Practice* 12, no. 2 (April 2006): 209–29; Jenny Ozga, "Deskilling a Profession: Professionalism, Deprofessionalisation and the New Managerialism," in *Managing Teachers as Professionals in Schools*, ed. Hugh Busher and Rene Saran (London: Routledge, 1995), 21–37; and Teresa Fisher-Ari, Kara Kavanagh, and Anne Martin, *Urban Teachers Struggling Within and Against Neoliberal, Accountability-Era Policies* (Philadelphia: Penn GSE Perspectives on Urban Education, 2018).
26. See Richard M. Ingersoll and Gregory J. Collins, "The Status of Teaching as a Profession," in *Schools and Society: A Sociological Approach to Education*, ed. Jeanne H. Ballantine, Joan Z. Spade, and Jenny M. Stuber (Newbury Park, CA: Pine Forge, 2018), 199–213; Sandra Acker, "Women and Teaching: A Semi-Detached Sociology of a Semi-Profession," in *Gender, Class and Education*, ed. Stephen Walker and Len Barton (London: Routledge, 1983), 123–39. Ingersoll and Collins conclude that teaching is a semiprofession in that it lacks characteristics that sociology has established as characteristic of professions, including substantial workplace and professional authority, relatively high compensation, and occupational prestige. Sandra Acker highlights

gender's role in the status difference between professions and semiprofessions, including teaching and nursing.

27. Sylvia Allegretto, *The Teacher Pay Penalty Has Hit a New High* (Washington, DC: Economic Policy Institute, 2022). Accounting for inflation, teacher wages have been relatively flat since the late 1990s. From 1996 to 2021, teachers' weekly wages only rose $45 while other college graduates' weekly wages increased $445.
28. OECD, "Boosting the Prestige and Standing of the Profession," in *TALIS 2018 Results (Volume II): Teachers and School Leaders as Valued Professionals* (Paris: OECD, 2018), https://doi.org/10.1787/db0bca51-en. For a detailed but concise overview of the relationship among occupational respect, prestige, satisfaction, and working conditions, see https://read.oecd-ilibrary.org/education/talis-2018-results-volume-ii_db0bca51-en#page4.
29. Amber M. Winkler, Janie Scull, and Dara Zeehandelaar, *How Strong Are U.S. Teacher Unions? A State-by-State Comparison* (Washington, DC: Thomas B. Fordham Institute, 2012), https://fordhaminstitute.org/national/research/how-strong-are-us-teacher-unions-state-state-comparison.
30. Eric Blanc, *Red State Revolt: The Teachers' Strike Wave and Working-Class Politics* (London: Verso, 2019). The Red for Ed movement is the name of the surge of teachers in several traditionally Republican-dominated (red) states, including Arizona, West Virginia, Oklahoma, and Kentucky, who defied legal restrictions on teacher strikes and walked out of their classrooms to demand improved teaching conditions in 2018.
31. Ed Fuller, *Trends in Enrollment in US Teacher Preparation Programs: 2009–2021* (Penn State: Center for Education Evaluation and Policy, Research Brief 2023-6, June 2023). Enrollment in teacher preparation has been in decline, dropping from 684,119 in 2008 to 397,691 in 2018. However, variations exist across states: Texas, Washington, Mississippi, and Arizona all saw increased enrollment during this period of overall decline.
32. The importance of school-level working conditions for teacher job satisfaction and retention is well documented: Susan Moore Johnson, *Where Teachers Thrive: Organizing Schools for Success* (Cambridge, MA: Harvard Education Press, 2020); Karen J. DeAngelis and Jennifer B. Presly, "Toward a More Nuanced Understanding of New Teacher Attrition," *Education and Urban Society* 43, no. 5 (September 2011): 598–626.
33. Moffitt, O'Neill, and Cohen, *Reforming the Reform.*
34. Michael Dimock and Richard Wike, *America is Exceptional in the Nature of Its Political Divide* (Washington, DC: Pew Research Center, 2020).
35. Eli Finkel et al., "Political Sectarianism in America," *Science* 370, no. 6516 (October 2020): 533–36.
36. Amber Hye-Yon Lee, "Social Trust in Polarized Times: How Perceptions of Political Polarization Affect Americans' Trust in Each Other," *Political Behavior* 44, no. 3 (March 2022): 1533–54.
37. Jonathan E. Collins, "The Politics of Reopening Schools: Explaining Public Preferences Reopening Schools and Public Compliance with Reopening Orders During the COVID-19 Pandemic," *American Politics Research* 51, no. 2 (March 2023): 232.
38. Jon Valant, "School Reopening Plans Linked to Politics Rather Than Public Health," *Brookings Commentary*, July 29, 2020.

39. Matt Grossman, Sarah Reckhow, Katherine O. Strunk, and Meg Turner, "All States Close but Red Districts Reopen: The Politics of In-Person Schooling During the COVID-19 Pandemic," Annenberg Institute EdWorkingPaper: 21-355 (February 2021), Brown University, Providence, RI, https://edworkingpapers.com/ai21-355.
40. Grossman, Reckhow, Strunk, and Turner, "All States Close but Red Districts Reopen," 17.
41. Lora Bartlett, "I've Studied Teachers for 20 Years. The Pandemic Was Their Ultimate Challenge," *EducationWeek*, July 19, 2021, https://www.edweek.org/teaching-learning/opinion-ive-studied-teachers-for-20-years-the-pandemic-was-their-ultimate-challenge/2021/07.
42. In addition, the coprincipal investigators included Lina Darwich, Associate Professor at Lewis and Clark College, whose work focuses on social and emotional dimensions of teachers' work lives. Data collection and preliminary analysis were also aided by a small group of research assistants.
43. The research team did not explicitly take dominant political affiliation or orientation (red/blue designation) into account in selecting states. However, the sampling criterion of labor strength proved to be closely tied to political orientation more broadly, with weak labor states tending to be those commonly identified as red and strong labor states commonly seen as blue.
44. Winkler, Scull, and Zeehandelaar, *How Strong Are U.S. Teacher Unions?*.
45. During the data analysis process, these nine states were subsequently categorized in two groups. Oregon, California, New York, and Massachusetts were categorized as stronger labor states, ranked 2nd, 6th, 9th, and 21st, respectively. Arizona, Florida, Texas, Kentucky, and Iowa were categorized as weaker labor states, ranked 51st, 50th, 44th, 28th, and 27th, respectively.
46. See Anthony S. Bryk, Penny Bender Sebring, Elaine Allensworth, Stuart Luppescu, and John Q. Easton, *Organizing Schools for Improvement* (Chicago: University of Chicago Press, 2010); Milbrey Wallin McLaughlin and Joan E. Talbert, *Professional Communities and the Work of High School Teaching* (Chicago: University of Chicago Press, 2001); Elizabeth DeBray, Gail Parson, and Katrina Woodworth, "Patterns of Response in Four High Schools Under State Accountability Policies in Vermont and New York," *Teachers College Record* 103, no. 8 (December 2001): 170–92; Deborah Alvarez, "'I Had to Teach So Hard': Traumatic Conditions and Teachers in Post-Katrina Classrooms," *High School Journal* 94, no. 1 (Fall 2010): 28–39; Kraft, Simon, and Lyon, "Sustaining a Sense of Success"; O'Toole and Friesen, "Teachers as First Responders in Tragedy," 57–67.
47. That fear is borne out both in our own study and in studies completed by RAND and others. See Elizabeth D. Steiner and Ashley Woo, *Job-Related Stress Threatens the Teacher Supply: Key Findings from the 2021 State of the US Teacher Survey* (Santa Monica, CA: RAND, 2021); Elizabeth D. Steiner, Ashley Woo, Aarya Suryavanshi, and Christopher Redding, *Working Conditions Related to Positive Well-Being in Five States* (Santa Monica, CA: RAND, 2023); Andrea Westphal, Eva Kalinowski, Clara Josepha Hoferichter, and Miriam Vock, "K–12 Teachers' Stress and Burnout During the COVID-19 Pandemic: A Systematic Review," *Frontiers in Psychology* 13 (September 2022): 1–29; Rebecca J. Collie, "COVID-19 and Teachers' Somatic Burden, Stress, and Emotional Exhaustion: Examining the Role of Principal Leadership and Workplace

Buoyancy," *AERA Open* 7, no. 1 (January 2021): 1–15; Marshall and Pressley, *Lessons of the Pandemic.*

Chapter 2

1. All teacher names are pseudonyms.
2. In summer 2020, we asked teachers about new content taught after March 13. Our findings are consistent with RAND findings based on large-scale survey data that teachers provided "more review and less coverage of new content than usual." Laura S. Hamilton, Julia H. Kaufman, and Melissa Kay Diliberti, *Teaching and Leading Through a Pandemic: Key Findings from the American Educator Panels Spring 2020 COVID-19 Surveys* (Santa Monica, CA: RAND, 2020), https://www.rand.org/pubs/research_reports/RRA168-2.html.
3. Before spring 2020, the terms *synchronous* and *asynchronous* instruction were anomalies in K–12 educational vernacular, but with the move to remote teaching they became the standard for clarifying the type of instructional modality in a remote context. Synchronous instruction happened live with teachers and students meeting via a virtual platform like Zoom. Asynchronous instruction provided materials and tasks posted by teachers that students could access and complete independently.
4. Olga Khazan, "The School Reopeners Think America is Forgetting About Kids," *Atlantic*, June 25, 2020, https://www.theatlantic.com/health/archive/2020/06/will-schools-reopen-fall/613468/; Nicole Russell, "I Can't Keep Doing This, Please Open the Schools," *Atlantic*, July 27, 2020, https://www.theatlantic.com/ideas/archive/2020/07/please-open-schools/614605/; Emily Oster, "Schools Are Not Superspreaders," *Atlantic*, October 9, 2020, https://www.theatlantic.com/ideas/archive/2020/10/schools-arent-superspreaders/616669/.
5. Just as in-person teaching grew over the course of the 2020–2021 school year, remote teaching steadily decreased from 79 percent of teachers teaching in a remote/online modality at the start of the school year to 23 percent by the end of the year. However, even teachers who were teaching in person spent some time teaching remotely to support quarantining students. Remote teaching was a reality for all teachers in the 2020–2021 school year.
6. In spring 2020, only 45 percent of teachers held synchronous class meetings, but by November 2020, thirty-seven of thirty-nine teachers in a remote modality were teaching entirely synchronously (eighteen teachers) or a mix of asynchronous and synchronous instruction (nineteen teachers).
7. In November 2020, 74 percent of remote-teaching teachers (29) reported Zoom fatigue as a significant challenge.
8. In fall 2020–2021, only 4 percent of project teachers were completely in person; another 17 percent were in a hybrid configuration with the teacher in person with some students and other students still online. By the end of the school year, 77 percent (fifty-three of sixty-nine) teachers were teaching mostly or fully in person.
9. The CDC recommended six feet of spacing. Ms. Donegal's district adopted three feet and mandated masking as mitigation strategies.
10. For details on various hybrid teaching models and their significance for teachers' work, see Lora Bartlett, "Specifying Hybrid Models of Teachers' Work During COVID-19," *Educational Researcher* 51, no. 2 (March 2022): 152–55.

11. Almost all teachers (92 percent) were teaching in-person and nearly two-thirds (63 percent) were able to use all or most of their preferred teaching methods.
12. OECD relied on findings from a survey of member countries for this report: "Before the pandemic, less than half of the primary and secondary teachers felt "well prepared" or "very well prepared" to use ICT in their own teaching." OECD, *The State of Global Education: 18 Months into the Pandemic* (Paris: OECD Publishing, 2021), 26.
13. The "second shift" is a term coined by the sociologist Arlie Hochschild to describe the phenomenon of women shouldering domestic labor, including childcare, after working their first shift as paid labor outside the home. Arlie Hochschild with Anne Machung, *The Second Shift: Working Families and the Revolution at Home* (New York: Penguin, 2012).
14. Eighty-seven percent of the thirty-one teachers had a remote working spouse and only 23 percent had partners who shared or assumed the majority of the family caregiving.
15. In spring 2020, 74 percent of the parenting teachers experienced an extended workday compared to 45 percent of teachers without dependent children at home. This statistic is consistent with other reports of working parents published during the pandemic. Ohio State researchers used the term "parental burnout" to describe the phenomenon facing parents during the pandemic. The research found that 66 percent of parents exhibited signs of burnout during the pandemic. Risk factors that exacerbated burnout among parents included 1) being female, 2) the number of children in the home, and 3) having a child with a learning disability or special needs. These risk factors were also reflected in the parenting teachers who suffered higher degrees of overwork and stress during pandemic teaching. See Kate Gawlick and Bernadette Mazurek Melnyk, *Pandemic Parenting: Examining the Epidemic of Working Parental Burnout and Strategies to Help* (Columbus: Ohio State University, 2022); Molly Wiant Cummins and Grace Ellen Brannon, "Mothering in a Pandemic: Navigating Care Work, Intensive Motherhood, and COVID-19," *Gender Issues* 39, no. 2 (June 2022): 123–41.

Chapter 3

1. Not all states track teacher turnover, but available data show rising attrition as of 2021–2022 and provide evidence that stated intention to leave is significantly predictive of subsequent behavior. See chapter 7 for patterns in five of the nine focal states where state-level data were available. Also see Dan Goldhaber and Roddy Theobald, "Teacher Attrition and Mobility in the Pandemic," *Educational Evaluation and Policy Analysis* 45, no. 4 (December 2023): 682–87; Erica Harbatkin, Tuan D. Nguyen, Katharine O. Strunk, Jason Burns, and Alex Moran, "Should I Stay or Should I Go (Later)? Teacher Intentions and Turnover in Low-Performing Schools and Districts Before and During the COVID-19 Pandemic," Annenberg Institute EdWorkingPaper: 23–815 (April 2023), Brown University, Providence, RI, https://doi.org/10.26300/d7dh-kq82; Tuan D. Nguyen, Chanh B. Lam, and Paul Bruno, "Is There a National Teacher Shortage? A Systematic Examination of Reports of Teacher Shortages in the United States," Annenberg Institute EdWorkingPaper: 22-631 (August 2022), Brown University, Providence, RI, https://doi.org/10.26300/76eq-hj32. In addition, National Education Association surveys showed a dramatic increase in educators' thinking about leaving the profession, from 37 percent in August 2021 to 55 percent in January 2022. See Tim Walker, "Survey: Alarming Number of Educators May Soon Leave the Profession," *NEA*

Today, February 1, 2022, https://www.nea.org/nea-today/all-news-articles/survey-alarming-number-educators-may-soon-leave-profession.

2. One teacher did not provide information on his career plans.
3. Soheyla Taie, Laurie Lewis, and Julie Merlin, *Teacher Attrition and Mobility: Results from the 2021–22 Teacher Follow-up Survey to the National Teacher and Principal Survey* (Washington, DC: National Center for Education Statistics, US Department of Education, 2023). According to this report issued in December 2023 by NCES, "84% of public-school teachers remained at the same school during the 2020–21 and 2021–22 school years ('stayers'), 8% moved to a different school between the 2020–21 and 2021–22 school years ('movers'), and 8% left the teaching profession ('leavers')." In the national data, early career teachers were more likely to move schools, and only 6 percent of movers left because they were dissatisfied with the way the school or district supported them during the pandemic.
4. This corresponds to broader patterns of turnover. See Andrew Camp, Gema Zamarro, and Josh McGee, "Teacher Turnover During the COVID-19 Pandemic," Annenberg Institute EdWorkingPaper: 23–757 (April 2023), Brown University, Providence, RI, https://doi.org/10.26300/akme-z405; Andrew Bacher-Hicks, Olivia L. Chi, and Alexis Orellana, "Two Years Later: How COVID-19 Has Shaped the Teacher Workforce," *Educational Researcher* 52, no. 4 (May 2023): 219–29; Melissa Kay Diliberti and Heather L. Schwartz, *Educator Turnover Has Markedly Increased, But Districts Have Taken Actions to Boost Teacher Ranks: Selected Findings from the Sixth American School District Panel Survey* (Santa Monica, CA: RAND, 2023), https://www.rand.org/pubs/research_reports/RRA956-14.html; Melissa Kay Diliberti, Elizabeth D. Steiner, Julia H. Kaufman, Ashley Woo, and Heather L. Schwartz, "Five Charts That Tell Us About the State of Public Education Right Now," *RANDBlog*, August 28, 2023, https://www.rand.org/pubs/commentary/2023/08/five-charts-that-tell-us-about-the-state-of-public.html.
5. Two additional teachers left for reasons unrelated to the pandemic: one to take a scheduled retirement and a second to raise a family.
6. After signaling in spring 2020 that districts could determine their own local "Return to Learn Plans," Iowa governor Kim Reynolds announced in the summer that schools must be at least 50 percent in person. Iowa's state policy context is covered more fully in chapter 4.
7. "IA HF802 | 2021–2022 | 89th General Assembly," June 8, 2021. Described as "a bill for an act providing for requirements related to racism or sexism trainings at, and diversity and inclusion efforts by, governmental agencies and entities, school districts, and public postsecondary educational institutions," https://legiscan.com/IA/research/HF802/2021.
8. Richard M. Ingersoll, "Teacher Turnover and Teacher Shortages: An Organizational Analysis," *American Educational Research Journal* 38, no. 3 (Fall 2001): 499–534; Leib Sutcher, Linda Darling-Hammond, and Desiree Carver-Thomas, "Understanding Teacher Shortages: An Analysis of Teacher Supply and Demand in the United States," *Education Policy Analysis Archives* 27, no. 35 (April 2019); Huriya Jabbar, Jennifer J. Holme, K. Trautmann, and J. S. Rodriguez, "COVID-19, Organizational Social Capital, and Organizational Resiliency in Schools," paper presented at the annual meeting of the American Educational Research Association, San Diego, April 2022.
9. We did not count district-initiated transfers as moves for the purpose of this analysis.

10. The value of teacher pensions as a component of teacher compensation, together with their impact on teacher recruitment and retention and overall public education funding remains a complicated topic. See Dan Goldhaber and Kristian L. Holden, "How Much Do Teachers Value Compensation Deferred for Retirement? Evidence from Defined Contribution Rate Choices," *Educational Researcher* 52, no. 2 (March 2023): 80–89; Kata Mihaly and Michael Podgursky, "Teacher Pensions: An Overview," *Educational Researcher* 52, no. 2 (March 2023): 57–62.
11. In Florida, teachers are part of the Florida Retirement System, formed in 1970, which includes all state employees. See https://www.teacherpensions.org/state/florida.
12. Ms. Featherstone's comment points to likely student consequences if teachers suffer burnout. Christina Maslach and Michael Leiter describe a burnout profile as consistent exhaustion, cynical distancing from others, and a sense of low efficacy; they characterize someone fitting a disengaged profile as someone consistently cynical about their jobs and with diminished motivation, even if they still believe they are doing a good job. See Christina Maslach and Michael P. Leiter, *The Burnout Challenge: Managing People's Relationships with Their Jobs* (Cambridge, MA: Harvard University Press, 2022).
13. See "The Retirement Process for Public Employees," Mass.gov, https://www.mass.gov/guides/the-retirement-process-for-public-employees.
14. The dissatisfied teachers in this study likely represent a sizable group of public school teachers. See S. Doan, E. D. Steiner, and R. Pandey, *Teacher Well-Being and Intentions to Leave in 2024: Findings from the 2024 State of the American Teacher Survey* (Santa Monica, CA: RAND, 2024).

Chapter 4

1. *The Proclamation on Declaring a National Emergency Concerning the Novel Coronavirus Disease (COVID-19) Outbreak*, issued on March 13, 2020, specifically references the WHO declaration: "On March 11, 2020, the World Health Organization announced that the COVID-19 outbreak can be characterized as a pandemic, as the rates of infection continue to rise in many locations around the world and across the United States," https://trumpwhitehouse.archives.gov/presidential-actions/proclamation-declaring-national-emergency-concerning-novel-coronavirus-disease-covid-19-outbreak/. Two of the nine project states, Oregon and Kentucky, acted on March 12 to recommend school closures. Of the remaining seven states, all had acted to order or recommend school closures by March 19. In some states, including California, Iowa, New York, and Texas, large urban school districts had already taken steps to close, perhaps influenced by news from national public health organizations and agencies.
2. President Trump formed a White House Task Force on January 29, 2020, but its formation did not spur action by the states. A critique issued in May 2020 by the Brookings Institution urged the end of the task force, arguing that "White House task forces are never a substitute for government agencies that have expertise, authority, and operational capability. . . . In times of crisis the White House is not 'operational.' It has to rely on other agencies to actually do things. . . . A final reason for the White House to get out of the way is that when the White House runs the show, responses are bound to become politicized." Elaine Karmack, "Get Rid of the White House Coronavirus Task Force Before It Kills Again," *Brookings Commentary*, May 7, 2020.

3. Technology infrastructure was more common in urban districts, raising the question of how rural and small-town districts and communities might be better equipped with technology resources and expertise for crisis response.
4. This is not to suggest that the impulse toward broader change reflected a shared vision of the future. For example, the vastly expanded system of online education and plethora of digital tools envisioned by tech entrepreneurs and some public officials met with skepticism among educators, while teachers' hopes to reduce or abandon the heavy reliance on standardized testing gained little traction among policy makers. See Susanna Loeb, "How Effective Is Online Learning? What the Research Does and Doesn't Tell Us," *EducationWeek*, March 20, 2020; Paul Reville, "Coronavirus Gives Us an Opportunity to Rethink K–12 Education," *Boston Globe*, April 9, 2020; Yong Zhao, "COVID-19 as a Catalyst for Educational Change," *Prospects* 49 (June 2020): 29–33; Fernando M. Reimers and Andreas Schleicher, *Schooling Disrupted, Schooling Rethought: How the COVID-19 Pandemic Is Changing Education* (Paris: OECD, 2020); Libby Stanford, "Educators Feel Growing Pressure for Students to Perform Well on Standardized Tests," *EducationWeek*, September 1, 2023.
5. Derek Thompson, "The Truth About Kids, School, and COVID-19," *Atlantic*, January 28, 2021.
6. Lora Bartlett, "Specifying Hybrid Models of Teachers' Work During COVID-19," *Educational Researcher* 51, no. 2 (March 2022): 152–55.
7. Project data from the November 2020 teacher survey (N=73). These figures are consistent with national data. A "household pulse" survey conducted by the United States Census Bureau between November 25 and December 7, 2020, found that 87 percent of the more than fifty million responding households with school-age children reported that the children were enrolled in some form of distance learning, with varying levels and types of personal contact with a teacher. United States Census Bureau, Household Pulse Survey (December 14, 2020), https://www.census.gov/data/tables/2020/demo/hhp/hhp20.html. National data nonetheless mask some significant contextual variation. For example, see Andrew M. Camp and Gema Zamarro, "Determinants of Ethnic Differences in School Modality Choices During the COVID-19 Crisis," *Educational Researcher* 51, no. 1 (January/February 2022): 6–16.
8. The term "flatten the curve" originated in the context of public health and epidemiology, specifically in the early days of the COVID-19 pandemic. The concept refers to slowing down the rate of infection to ensure that the health-care system does not become overwhelmed by a sudden surge in cases. By spreading out the number of infections over a more extended period, the goal is to "flatten" the epidemiological curve. The term was first used in a 2007 CDC paper on prepandemic planning guidance (https://stacks.cdc.gov/view/cdc/11425) and was applied initially to the COVD-19 pandemic in a February 29, 2020, article (https://www.economist.com/briefing/2020/02/29/covid-19-is-now-in-50-countries-and-things-will-get-worse). The term gained widespread attention in March 2020, when it was used by public health officials and experts to emphasize the importance of implementing measures such as lockdowns, social distancing, and other preventive actions.
9. See "President Donald J. Trump Is Supporting America's Students and Families by Encouraging the Safe Reopening of America's Schools," The White House, August 12,

2020, https://trumpwhitehouse.archives.gov/briefings-statements/president-donald-j-trump-supporting-americas-students-families-encouraging-safe-reopening-americas-schools/.

10. American Academy of Pediatrics, "COVID-19 Planning Considerations: Guidance for School Re-entry," June 25, 2020, 1.
11. As early as April 2020, the American Federation of Teachers had issued the "Plan to Safely Reopen American Schools and Communities." It called for specific measures, including COVID-19 testing and resources to support proactive screening and case tracing, comprehensive access to and use of personal protective equipment, smaller class sizes, and social distancing. See https://www.aft.org/our-community/reopen-schools/safely-reopening-americas-schools-and-communities.
12. See the July 10, 2020, news release at https://www.aap.org/en/news-room/news-releases/aap/2020/pediatricians-educators-and-superintendents-urge-a-safe-return-to-school-this-fall/.
13. https://www.aap.org/en/news-room/news-releases/aap/2020/pediatricians-educators-and-superintendents-urge-a-safe-return-to-school-this-fall/.
14. Valerie Strauss, "The Case for Treating Teachers Around the World as Essential Front-Line Workers," *Washington Post*, July 21, 2020.
15. Kentucky Labor Force Update, November 2020, https://www.cisa.gov/publication/guidance-essential-critical-infrastructure-workforce.
16. Daniel Victor, Lew Serviss, and Azi Paybarah, "In His Own Words, Trump on the Coronavirus and Masks," *New York Times*, October 2, 2020, https://www.nytimes.com/2020/10/02/us/politics/donald-trump-masks.html.
17. Victor, Serviss, and Paybarah, "In His Own Words, Trump on the Coronavirus and Masks."
18. Arizona Office of the Governor, Executive Order 2020-51 (Arizona: Open for Learning), July 23, 2020; California Department of Public Health, *COVID-19 Industry Guidance: Schools and School-Based Programs*, July 17, 2020, https://files.covid19.ca.gov; New York State Education Department, *Recovering, Rebuilding, and Renewing: The Spirit of New York's Schools: Reopening Guidance*, July 16, 2020, 17, https://nysed.gov; Oregon Department of Education and Oregon Health Authority, *Ready Schools, Safe Learners*, July 29, 2020, 30, https://www.oregon.gov/ode/students-and-family/healthsafety/pages/rssl-guidance.aspx.
19. Massachusetts Department of Elementary and Secondary Education, *Initial Fall School Reopening Guidance*, June 25, 2020, 8.
20. *Reopening Florida's Schools and the CARES Act*, Florida Department of Education, June 11, 2020, 6.
21. Florida Department of Education archive, summarizing the guidance for 2020–2021, https://www.fldoe.org/covid-19/info-guidance/archive.stml.
22. Iowa Office of the Governor, Proclamation of Disaster Emergency, July 17, 2020, https://www.huschblackwell.com/iowa-state-by-state-covid-19-guidance.
23. Texas Education Agency, *SY 20-21 Public Health Planning Guidance*, July 28, 2020.
24. *Reopening Florida's Schools and the CARES Act*.
25. *Reopening Florida's Schools and the CARES Act*.

26. Iowa Department of Education, *Reopening Guidance for Schools*, June 25, 2020, 1; Texas Education Agency, *SY 20-21 Public Health Planning Guidance*, 1.
27. Daniel Cassady, "Despite DeSantis, Nearly One-Third of Florida Counties Require Masks," *Forbes*, July 23, 2020; Adam Dean, Jamie McCallum, Simeon Kimmel, and Atheendar Venkatermani, "Iowa School Districts Were More Likely to Adopt COVID-19 Mask Mandates Where Teachers Were Unionized," *Health Affairs* 40, no. 8 (August 2021): 1270–76.
28. Arizona, California, Kentucky, Massachusetts, New York, and Oregon.
29. Oregon Department of Education and the Oregon Health Authority, *Ready Schools, Safe Learners: Community COVID-19 Metrics*, July 28, 2020, 1. Detailed guidance appeared in the document *Ready Schools, Safe Learners: Guidance for School Year 2020-21*, first issued in early June 2020 and updated regularly.
30. California Department of Public Health, COVID-19 Industry Guidance: Schools and School-Based Programs, July 17, 2020, 1, https://files.covid19.ca.gov.
31. Arizona Office of the Governor, Executive Order 2020-51, July 23, 2020.
32. *Ready Schools, Safe Learners*, July 29, 2020, 7.
33. March 2021 is arguably a late date to prioritize teachers for the vaccine given the widespread interest in a return to in-person schooling and the calls to maximize safety measures in reopening buildings.
34. Kentucky and Arizona, both considered weaker labor states, also adopted a stance of caution, guidance, and local discretion, reflecting countervailing within-state political pressures.
35. The pandemic crisis intersected in summer 2020 with protests following the murder of George Floyd. See https://www.edweek.org/leadership/how-the-murder-of-george-floyd-changed-k-12-schooling-a-collection.
36. The organization PEN America coined the term "educational gag orders" to characterize a range of proposed or enacted state laws that "target discussions of race, racism, gender, and American history, banning a series of 'prohibited' or 'divisive' concepts for teachers and trainers operating in K–12 schools, public universities, and workplace settings.. . . In short: They are educational gag orders," https://pen.org/report/educational-gag-orders/. See also Ashley Woo, Melissa Kay Diliberti, and Elizabeth D. Steiner, *Policies Restricting Teaching About Race and Gender Spill Over into Other States and Localities: Findings from the 2023 State of the American Teacher Survey* (Santa Monica, CA: RAND, 2024).
37. *Ready Schools, Safe Learners*, 10, 36.
38. Richard C. Keller, *Fatal Isolation: The Devastating Paris Heat Wave of 2003* (Chicago: University of Chicago Press, 2015).
39. The absence of contingency planning in the weeks prior to the school closures should not suggest that formal emergency plans may be sufficient to aid a response to crisis. Ansell, Sorensen, and Torfing (2021) advise that responders to transboundary crises and problems of "turbulence" cannot rely on pre-existing plans, structures, and processes, but must be equipped for flexible and adaptive responses. See C. Ansell, E. Sorensen, and J. Torfing, "The COVID-19 Pandemic as a Game-Changer for Public Administration and Leadership? The Need for Robust Governance Responses to Turbulent Problems," *Public Management Review* 23, no. 7 (2021): 949–60.

Chapter 5

1. A cumulative body of research dating back to the 1970s has established the influence of key workplace conditions that enable teachers to pursue school improvement, cope with major policy shifts, or respond effectively to exogenous shocks like natural disasters. See Seymour Sarason, *The Culture of the School and the Problem of Change* (Boston: Allyn & Bacon, 1971); Anthony S. Bryk, Penny Bender Sebring, Elaine Allensworth, Stuart Luppescu, and John Q. Easton, *Organizing Schools for Improvement* (Chicago: University of Chicago Press, 2010); Elizabeth DeBray, Gail Parson, and Katrina Woodworth, "Patterns of Response in Four High Schools Under State Accountability Policies in Vermont and New York," *Teachers College Record* 103, no. 8 (2001): 170–92; Matthew A. Kraft, Nicole S. Simon, and Melissa Arnold Lyon, "Sustaining a Sense of Success: The Protective Role of Teacher Working Conditions During the COVID-19 Pandemic," *Journal of Research on Educational Effectiveness* 14, no. 4 (July 2021): 727–69.
2. Susan Moore Johnson, *Where Teachers Thrive: Organizing Schools for Success* (Cambridge, MA: Harvard Education Press, 2019).
3. Christina Maslach and Michael Leiter identify six domains of organizational life associated with burnout risk: workload, control, reward, community, fairness, and values. See Christina Maslach and Michael P. Leiter, "Understanding Burnout: New Models," in *Handbook of Stress and Health: A Guide to Research and Practice*, ed. Cary L. Cooper and James Campbell Quick (Oxford: Wiley Blackwell, 2017), 36–56; Christina Maslach and Michael P. Leiter, *The Burnout Challenge: Managing People's Relationships with Their Jobs* (Cambridge, MA: Harvard University Press, 2022).
4. A collaborative ethos extended beyond teachers to encompass other specialists in some schools. Nearly half of teachers surveyed in March 2021 had found very useful or somewhat useful support from librarians, counselors, school psychologists, or school social workers. However, we have limited data on this aspect of the pandemic response.
5. For an introduction to the use of social network theory in the study of educational change, see Alan J. Daly, ed., *Social Network Theory and Educational Change* (Cambridge, MA: Harvard Education Press, 2010). For research focusing specifically on social media networks, see Annika Bergviken Rensfeldt, Thomas Hillman, and Neil Selwyn, "Teachers 'Liking' Their Work? Exploring the Realities of Teacher Facebook Groups," *British Educational Research Journal* 44, no. 2 (February 2018): 230–50; Nick Kelly and Amy Antonio, "Teacher Peer Support in Social Network Sites," *Teaching and Teacher Education* 56 (May 2016): 138–49; Maria Macia and Iolanda Garcia, "Informal Online Communities and Networks as a Source of Teacher Professional Development: A Review," *Teaching and Teacher Education* 55 (2016): 291–307.
6. Following the spring 2020 shutdown, more than 150 new Facebook groups emerged, with a combined membership of more than five hundred thousand teachers. While many of these groups were organized around safety concerns and reopening plans such as Kentucky Teachers in the Know (22,316 members in July 2020) or Iowa Educators for a Safe Return to School (19,755 members in July 2020), others were focused on professional learning and instructional collaboration. On the role of networks in crisis response, see E. L. Quarantelli, Arjen Boin, and Patrick Lagadec, "Studying Future Disasters and Crises: A Heuristic Approach," in *Handbook of Disaster Research*, ed. H. Rodriguez, W. Donner and J. E. Trainor (New York: Springer, 2018), 61–86.

7. Brian Rowan, "Commitment and Control: Alternative Strategies for the Organizational Designs of Schools," in *Review of Research in Education*, ed. Courtney B. Cazden (Washington, DC: AERA, 1990), 353–92.
8. Studies of school leadership during the pandemic attest to the increased levels of stress experienced by school principals. See Ashley Woo and Elizabeth Steiner, *The Well-Being of Secondary School Principals One Year into the COVID-19 Pandemic* (Santa Monica, CA: RAND, 2022); Elizabeth D. Steiner et al., *Restoring Teacher and Principal Well-Being Is an Essential Step for Rebuilding Schools: Findings from the State of the American Teacher and State of the American Principal Surveys* (Santa Monica, CA: RAND, 2022).
9. Twelve of the thirty-six focal teachers reported one or more changes in principal and four reported a change in superintendent. Because teachers were not explicitly asked about administrator turnover, actual turnover may have been higher.
10. One focal teacher was excluded from this analysis because she did not participate in the final two interviews.
11. Two teachers were considering leaving despite strong working conditions. Veteran science teacher Michael Donovan, who stepped away from various teacher leadership roles during the pandemic, was "keeping my options open." Yet upon the return to school, he took pride in developing ambitious new science partnerships with outside organizations for his students. High school social studies teacher Chelsea Doyle was pondering a possible move into administration but remained engaged in teaching and was well supported by colleagues and school leaders.
12. For research on the relationship between teacher workload and measures of well-being, see John Jerrim and Sam Sims, *Teacher Workload and Well-Being: New International Evidence from the OECD TALIS Study* (London: UCL Institute of Education, 2018).
13. Susan I. Stone and Jessica Charles, "Conceptualizing the Problems and Possibilities of Interprofessional Collaboration in Schools," *Children & Schools* 40, no. 3 (July 2018): 185–92.
14. Andy Hargreaves, "Contrived Collegiality: The Micropolitics of Teacher Collaboration," in *The Politics of Life in Schools: Power, Conflict, and Cooperation*, ed. Joseph Blase (Newbury Park, CA: SAGE, 1991).
15. Anit Somech and Ronit Bogler, "Antecedents and Consequences of Teacher Organizational and Professional Commitment," *Educational Administration Quarterly* 38, no. 4 (2002): 555–77; Richard Ingersoll, Philip Sirinides, and Patrick Dougherty, "Leadership Matters: Teachers' Roles in School Decision Making and School Performance," *American Educator* (Spring 2018): 13–17, 39.

Chapter 6

1. Albert O. Hirschman, *Exit, Voice & Loyalty: Response to Decline in Firms, Organizations, and States* (Cambridge, MA: Harvard University Press, 1970); Hirschman acknowledges that loyalty can be a complicating factor, with some making the decision to stay in an unsatisfactory situation even when voice is scarce; see *Exits, Voices and Social Investment* by Keith Dowding and Peter John (Cambridge: Cambridge University Press, 2012) for their refinements of exit and an empirical look at exit and voice in the public sector, including private and collective.
2. This analysis of teacher voice is drawn from a synthesis of the full data set, with particular emphasis on 1) the summer 2020 teacher interviews (N=75) with attention to

the spring response and the fall return plans, including teacher satisfaction with the plans and their degree of input in the planning; 2) the summer 2021 teacher survey (N=69) questions about respect and influence; 3) and the summer 2022 interviews with focal teachers (N=33).

3. In the July 2021 survey, sixty-nine teachers responded to questions about teacher influence in district- and school-level decision-making during the 2020–2021 school year. Fifty-one percent disagree that their school decision-making was informed by teachers' experience, judgment, and perspective, with only 26 percent strongly disagreeing, while 67 percent disagree regarding district decision-making, with 46 percent strongly disagreeing.
4. Amber M. Winkler, Janie Scull, and Dara Zeehandelaar, *How Strong Are U.S. Teacher Unions? A State-by-State Comparison* (Washington, DC: Thomas B. Fordham Institute, 2012), https://eric.ed.gov/?id=ED537563.
5. In 1931, federal soldiers were dispatched to tamp down the Harlan County mine workers strike, sparking almost a decade of struggle that became known as "Bloody Harlan." See Paul F. Taylor, *Bloody Harlan: The United Mine Workers of America in Harlan County, Kentucky, 1931–1941* (Lanham, MD: University Press of America, 1989). In 1973, Harlan County coal miners went on strike for thirteen months for the right to unionize with the United Mine Workers and were again met with state violence. See Lynda Ann Ewen, *Which Side Are You On? The Brookside Mine Strike in Harlan County, Kentucky, 1973–1974* (Chicago: Vanguard, 1979); Dave Jamieson and Travis Waldron, "America's Growing Teacher Strikes Were Decades in the Making," *HuffPost*, April 8, 2018, www.huffpost.com/entry/americas-growing-teacher-strikes-were-decades-in-the-making_n_5ac8f468e4b0337ad1e8979c.
6. "Burbio's K–12 School Opening Tracker," Burbio, 2022, https://about.burbio.com/school-opening-tracker.
7. In 2018, teachers in Arizona, West Virginia, Oklahoma, Kentucky, Colorado, and North Carolina defied legal restrictions on teacher strikes and led statewide walkouts to demand improved teaching conditions and higher investment in public education. See Erin Dyke and Brendan Muckian-Bates, *Rank-and-File Rebels: Theories of Power and Change in the 2018 Education Strikes* (Denver: University Press of Colorado, 2023); Rebecca Tarlau, "Networked Movements and Bureaucratic Unions: The Structure of the 2018 #RedForEd Teachers' Strikes," *ILR Review* 76, no. 5 (2023): 833–63; Eric Blanc, *Red State Revolt: The Teachers' Strike Wave and Working-Class Politics* (New York: Verso, 2019).
8. Tarlau, "Networked Movements and Bureaucratic Unions"; Blanc, *Red State Revolt*.
9. For an extended discussion of Arizona teacher organizing during the COVID-19 pandemic, see Riley Collins, "Countering Fragmentation, Cultivating Solidarity: Arizona Teacher Organizing During the COVID-19 Pandemic," *Globalisation, Societies and Education* (January 2024): 1–11.
10. Blanc, *Red State Revolt*.
11. In Iowa Code, chapter 20, the newly restricted scope of teacher bargaining had other swift consequences. By 2019, just two years after the law passed, over 170 Iowa school districts had removed some or all of the language pertaining to permissive—or non-mandated—topics in bargaining agreements; in 130 of those districts, all permissive language was removed, according to Randy Richardson, former executive director of the Iowa State Education Association.

12. Colin Gordon, "Hope in the Heartland: The Struggle for Public-Sector Collective Bargaining in Iowa," LAWCHA, November 15, 2017, lawcha.org/2017/11/15/hope-heartland-struggle-public-sector-collective-bargaining-iowa/.
13. In summer 2020, all but two of the seventy-five teachers entered the study with the intention of remaining in the profession. The two exceptions with previous exit plans included one Massachusetts teacher who retired and one New York teacher who left for family-related reasons.
14. Of the seventy-five teachers in the whole sample, six were excluded from this calculation because one or both measures were missing. The summer 2020 plan satisfaction and input analysis is based on the responses of the remaining sixty-nine teachers; one 2022 Satisfied Stayer did not respond to the 2020 questions about 2020 reopening plans and influence; hence, we can only report on twenty-four of the twenty-five.
15. Respect and influence scores, individual and averaged by category, were determined by weighting the closed survey responses then adding them together. Responses ranged from *strongly agree* to *strongly disagree* to a series of declarative statements (e.g., "This past school year, I felt respected as a professional by my principal"). Individual responses were then averaged across the sample and within groups to allow comparison. More detail on the weighting and calculations are described in the appendix.

Chapter 7

1. David Foster Wallace, *This Is Water: Some Thoughts on a Significant Occasion, About Living a Compassionate Life* (New York: Little, Brown, 2009).
2. Both are terms coined to describe shifts in worker orientations and expectations. The US "quit rate" reached a twenty-year high in November 2021 as many left their jobs in what came to be known as "The Great Resignation." Kim Parker and Juliana Menasce Horowitz, "Majority of Workers Who Quit a Job in 2021 Cite Low Pay, No Opportunities for Advancement, Feeling Disrespected" (Washington, DC: Pew Research Center, March 9, 2022), https://www.pewresearch.org/short-reads/2022/03/09/majority-of-workers-who-quit-a-job-in-2021-cite-low-pay-no-opportunities-for-advancement-feeling-disrespected/; Heidi Batiste, "Management in Times of Crisis: A Qualitative Exploration of the Great Resignation from a Social Exchange Perspective," *Compensation & Benefits Review* (2024): 08863687231221854. "Quiet quitting" described the rebalancing many did to not work beyond their paid hours and commitments in order to create more room for personal and family life. Lauren Aratani, "While Some Say Quiet Quitting is Over, the Spirit of It May Carry into 2023," *Guardian*, January 2, 2023; Nicholas Bloom, *The Great Resistance: Getting Employees Back to the Office* (Stanford, CA: Stanford Institute for Economic Policy Research, July 2022), https://siepr.stanford.edu/publications/work/great-resistance-getting-employees-back-office.
3. Albert O. Hirschman, *Exit, Voice & Loyalty: Response to Decline in Firms, Organizations, and States* (Cambridge, MA: Harvard University Press, 1970).
4. Hirschman, *Exit, Voice & Loyalty*, 83.
5. Hirschman, *Exit, Voice & Loyalty*, 92.
6. Christina Maslach and Michael P. Leiter, *The Burnout Challenge: Managing People's Relationships with Their Jobs* (Cambridge, MA: Harvard University Press, 2022).
7. Because of state data differences, data are reported here by annual percentage change rather than actual turnover rates.

8. Although teacher turnover and shortage data are limited by uneven availability and definitional variations, many sources coalesce to support an understanding that turnover was generally lower or flat in 2020 and then rose to levels above the pre–COVID-19 rates. See Patricia Saenz-Armstrong, *State of the States 2021: State Reporting of Teacher Supply and Demand Data* (Washington, DC: National Council on Teacher Quality, 2021), https://files.eric.ed.gov/fulltext/ED617872.pdf, for a comprehensive analysis of the limits of state and national teacher workforce data. The exit timing of the Suddenly Distant fifteen Leavers fits with the overall state patterns: two exits of seventy-five in 2020, six of seventy-three in 2021, and seven of sixty-seven in 2022—small numbers but still a relatively large change from years one to two and a small but still increasing change between years two and three.
9. Melissa Kay Diliberti and Heather L. Schwartz, *Educator Turnover Has Markedly Increased, but Districts Have Taken Actions to Boost Teacher Ranks: Selected Findings from the Sixth American School District Panel Survey* (Santa Monica, CA: RAND, 2023), https://www.rand.org/pubs/research_reports/RRA956-14.html.
10. GBAO, "Poll Results: Stress and Burnout Pose Threat of Educator Shortages," January 31, 2022, https://www.nea.org/sites/default/files/2022-02/NEA%20Member%20COVID-19%20Survey%20Summary.pdf.
11. See Julian Le Grand, *Motivation, Agency, and Public Policy: Of Knights and Knaves, Pawns and Queens* (Oxford: Oxford University Press, 2003).
12. Sara Li, "National Teacher Appreciation Day: Educators Are Standing by Students During Coronavirus," *Teen Vogue*, May 12, 2020, https://www.teenvogue.com/story/how-teachers-helping-students-during-coronavirus.
13. Gabrielle Fonrouge, "Hero of the Day: Queens Teacher Battled Coronavirus but Never Took a Day Off," *New York Post*, May 8, 2020, https://nypost.com/2020/05/08/hero-of-the-day-queens-teacher-battled-coronavirus-but-never-took-a-day-off/.
14. See, for example, Pamela McCable, "Lee County Teachers Are Already Zooming In on New Norm That Is Virtual Learning," *Fort Meyers News Press*, March 26, 2020, https://www.news-press.com/story/news/education/2020/03/26/coronavirus-florida-lee-teachers-zoom-new-norm-virtual-learning/2901854001/, and Jeffery Solocheck, "Teaching Kindergarten at a Distance: What a Rookie and Veteran Learned," *Tampa Bay Times*, March 9, 2020, https://www.tampabay.com/news/health/2020/04/27/teaching-kindergarten-at-a-distance-what-a-rookie-and-a-veteran-learned/.
15. Aurelie Corinthios, "Jimmy Fallon Dedicates Song to Teachers During Coronavirus: They 'Should Make a Billion Dollars,' " *People*, May 6, 2020, https://people.com/tv/jimmy-fallon-song-teacher-appreciation-week/.
16. Valerie Earnest, "I'm Over the Teacher Hate," *Cedar Rapids Moms*, March 22, 2021, https://crmoms.com/in-and-around-cedar-rapids/covid19/im-over-the-teacher-hate/.
17. Dana Goldstein and Eliza Shapiro, " 'I Don't Want to Go Back': Many Teachers Are Fearful and Angry Over Pressure to Return," *New York Times*, July 11, 2020, https://www.nytimes.com/2020/07/11/us/virus-teachers-classrooms.html; Eric Rogers, "Anti-mask Protesters Rally as Brevard School Board Indefinitely Extends Mask Mandate," *Florida Today*, October 28, 2020, https://www.floridatoday.com/story/news/education/2020/10/28/protesters-rally-school-board-indefinitely-extends-mask-mandate/3754184001/.

18. See for example, Emma Platoff and Aliyya Swaby, "Texas Schools Tell Teachers with Medical Risks They Must Return to Classrooms During the Pandemic," *Texas Tribune*, October 20, 2020, https://www.texastribune.org/2020/10/20/texas-schools-teachers-coronavirus-pandemic/. National polls indicated parents and teachers were aligned in their concerns about reopening and a preference for remote instruction. See Anya Kamenetz and Laura Isensee, "Most Teachers Concerned About In-Person School; 2 in 3 Want to Start the Year Online," *NPR Morning Edition*, August 6, 2020, https://www.npr.org/2020/08/06/898584176/most-teachers-concerned-about-in-person-school-2-in-3-want-to-start-the-year-online.
19. Caitlin Oprysko, "Not Dangerous: DeVos Defends Schools Reopening According to CDC Guidelines," *Politico*, July 12, 2020, https://www.politico.com/news/2020/07/12/betsy-devos-schools-reopen-357840.
20. This public comment was made at the February 8, 2021, school board meeting at Perkiomen Valley School District in Collegeville, Pennsylvania—see the three-minute clip starting at 3:23:19, https://www.youtube.com/watch?v=1Z5oGLj5SgA, and widespread online conversations about it on Reddit, https://www.reddit.com/r/Teachers/comments/loooit/disheartening_to_hear_a_parent_say_teachers_lives/, and on Facebook with over five hundred reposts and two hundred comments by teachers from all over the country.
21. Rebecca Martinson, "I Won't Return to the Classroom, and You Shouldn't Ask Me To," *New York Times*, July 18, 2020, https://www.nytimes.com/2020/07/18/opinion/sunday/covid-schools-reopen-teacher-safety.html.
22. See Madeline Will, "Has the Public Turned on Teachers?," *Education Week*, January 25, 2021, https://www.edweek.org/teaching-learning/has-the-public-turned-on-teachers/2021/01.
23. In an elaboration on the Knights and Knaves framing, Le Grand associates policy orientations with assumed motivations: policies premised on trust for knights and mistrust for knaves. Julian Le Grand, "Knights and Knaves Return: Public Service Motivation and the Delivery of Public Services," *International Public Management Journal* 13, no. 1 (2010): 56–71.
24. See teacher work intensification concept as outlined by Magali Sarfatti Larson, "Proletarianization and Educated Labor," *Theory and Society* 9, no. 1 (1980): 131–75, and further developed by Michael W. Apple and Kenneth Teitelbaum, "Are Teachers Losing Control of Their Skills and Curriculum?," *Journal of Curriculum Studies* 18, no. 2 (1986): 177–84; Michael W. Apple, "Controlling the Work of Teachers," *Knowledge, Power, and Education* (New York: Routledge, 2012), 116–31; Andy Hargreaves, "Teachers' Work and the Politics of Time and Space," *International Journal of Qualitative Studies in Education* 3, no. 4 (1990): 303–20; Katrijn Ballet, Geert Kelchtermans, and John Loughran, "Beyond Intensification Towards a Scholarship of Practice: Analysing Changes in Teachers' Work Lives," *Teachers and Teaching* 12, no. 2 (2006): 209–29. Teacher control over curricular and other classroom decisions began eroding in the 1980s with implications for teacher deskilling. Sarbani Chakraborty, "Deskilling of the Teaching Profession," *Sociology of Education: An A-to-Z Guide*, ed. Chakraborty (Thousand Oaks, CA: SAGE, 2013), 184–86.
25. Betty Achinstein and Rodney Ogawa, "(In)fidelity: What the Resistance of New Teachers Reveals About Professional Principles and Prescriptive Educational Policies," *Harvard Educational Review* 76, no. 1 (2006): 30–63; Stephen J. Ball, "The Teacher's Soul

and the Terrors of Performativity," *Journal of Education Policy* 18, no. 2 (2003): 215–28; Lora Bartlett, "Expanding Teacher Work Roles: A Resource for Retention or a Recipe for Overwork?," *Journal of Education Policy* 19, no. 5 (2004): 565–82.

26. On the SDRP survey in March 2021 (n=71), sixty-five reported resumed testing, and of those fifty disapproved, fourteen were undecided/withholding judgment till they had more info, and one approved. Of the remaining six, three taught in places without testing and three gave only partial answers.
27. Of fifteen Leavers, ten disapproved, two were neutral/undecided, one taught in a place without testing, and two did not respond as they had left teaching; six of eight responding Movers also expressed disapproval; the other two reserved judgment.
28. The Baker Act is Florida legislation regarding emergency mental health services and detention for people experiencing mental health crises. In 2020–2021, there was a 7 percent increase in child referrals. See Annette Christy et al., "The Baker Act: Fiscal Year 2021–2022 Report" (Tampa: University of South Florida, Department of Mental Health Law and Policy, 2023), https://www.usf.edu/cbcs/baker-act/documents/ba_usf_annual_report_2021_2022.pdf.
29. See Karyn Lewis and Megan Kuhfeld, "Education's Long COVID: 2022–23 Achievement Data Reveal Stalled Progress Toward Pandemic Recovery" (Portland, OR: Center for School and Student Progress at NWEA, 2023), https://www.nwea.org/uploads/Educations-long-covid-2022-23-achievement-data-reveal-stalled-progress-toward-pandemic-recovery_NWEA_Research-brief.pdf, and Bastian A. Betthäuser, Anders M. Bach-Mortensen, and Per Engzell, "A Systematic Review and Meta-analysis of the Evidence on Learning During the COVID-19 Pandemic," *Nature Human Behaviour* 7, no. 3 (2023): 375–85.
30. Eric A. Hanushek, "Generation Lost: The Pandemic's Lifetime Tax," *Education Next*, October 6, 2023, https://www.educationnext.org/generation-lost-the-pandemics-lifetime-tax/; Rick Hess, "Schools Need to Reclaim Lost Learning Time. Here's How to Start (Opinion)," *Education Week*, October 17, 2022; Michael J. Petrilli, "We Can Fight Learning Loss Only with Accountability and Action," *New York Times*, September 5, 2023.
31. See the Jane Farley profile in chapter 3.
32. National Center for Education Statistics, "Roughly Half of Public Schools Report That They Can Effectively Provide Mental Health Services to All Students in Need," May 31, 2022, https://nces.ed.gov/whatsnew/press_releases/05_31_2022_2.asp.
33. See Madeline Will, "Long Hours, Second Jobs: New Federal Data Give a Snapshot of the Teaching Profession," *Education Week*, December 13, 2022, https://www.edweek.org/teaching-learning/long-hours-second-jobs-new-federal-data-give-a-snapshot-of-the-teaching-profession/2022/12.
34. Elizabeth D. Steiner, Ashley Woo, and Sy Doan, *All Work and No Pay—Teachers' Perceptions of Their Pay and Hours Worked: Findings from the 2023 State of the American Teacher Survey* (Santa Monica, CA: RAND, 2023), https://www.rand.org/pubs/research_reports/RRA1108-9.html.
35. Teaching locally is a persistent feature of teacher labor markets. Donald Boyd, Hamilton Lankford, Susanna Loeb, and James Wyckoff use the term "the draw of home" to describe teachers' preferences for working in close proximity to where they grew up: "The Draw of Home: How Teachers' Preferences for Proximity Disadvantage Urban Schools," *Journal of Policy Analysis and Management* 24, no. 1 (2005): 113–32.

36. In 2023, RAND reported that teachers cited their ability to positively affect students as a major reason to stay in teaching: Sy Doan, Elizabeth D. Steiner, Rakesh Pandey, and Ashley Woo, *Teacher Well-Being and Intentions to Leave: Findings from the 2023 State of the American Teacher Survey* (Santa Monica, CA: RAND, 2023), https://www.rand.org/pubs/research_reports/RRA1108-8.html. For intrinsic rewards, see Janina Roloff Henoch, Uta Klusmann, Oliver Lüdtke, and Ulrich Trautwein, "Who Becomes a Teacher? Challenging the 'Negative Selection' Hypothesis," *Learning and Instruction* 36 (2015): 46–56; Manuela Heinz, "Why Choose Teaching? An International Review of Empirical Studies Exploring Student Teachers' Career Motivations and Levels of Commitment to Teaching," *Educational Research and Evaluation* 21, no. 3 (2015): 258–97; Leigh McLean, Michelle Taylor, and Manuela Jimenez, "Career Choice Motivations in Teacher Training as Predictors of Burnout and Career Optimism in the First Year of Teaching," *Teaching and Teacher Education* 85, no. 1 (2019): 204–14.
37. Recessions attract more qualified candidates, as people are more attracted to teaching when nonteaching job opportunities are limited and the stability of teaching becomes more attractive. Markus Nagler, Marc Piopiunik, and Martin R. West, "Weak Markets, Strong Teachers: Recession at Career Start and Teacher Effectiveness," *Journal of Labor Economics* 38, no. 2 (2020): 453–500.
38. Richard M. Ingersoll, Elizabeth Merrill, Daniel Stuckey, and Gregory Collins, *Seven Trends: The Transformation of the Teaching Force–Updated October 2018* (Philadelphia: CPRE, 2018), https://repository.upenn.edu/handle/20.500.14332/8354.
39. Lora Bartlett, "Specifying Hybrid Models of Teachers' Work During COVID-19," *Educational Researcher* 51, no. 2 (2022): 152–55.
40. Hannele Marjatta Niemi and Päivi Kousa, "A Case Study of Students' and Teachers' Perceptions in a Finnish High School During the COVID Pandemic," *International Journal of Technology in Education and Science* 4, no. 4 (2020): 352–69; Hilary Naa-Afi Tackie, "DISRUPTION: Finding Humanizing Opportunities in the COVID-19 Impacted Classroom" (PhD diss., University of Chicago, 2022); Justin Reich, Christopher J. Buttimer, Dan Coleman, Richard D. Colwell, Farah Faruqi, and Laura R. Larke, "What's Lost, What's Left, What's Next? Lessons Learned from the Lived Experiences of Teachers During the 2020 Novel Coronavirus Pandemic," EdArXiv, July 22, 2020, doi:10.35542/osf.io/8exp9; Lisa E. Kim, Rowena Leary, and Kathryn Asbury, "Teachers' Narratives During COVID-19 Partial School Reopenings: An Exploratory Study," *Educational Research* 63, no. 2 (2021): 252; Nathan D. Jones, Eric M. Camburn, Benjamin Kelcey, and Esther Quintero, "Teachers' Time Use and Affect Before and After COVID-19 School Closures," *Aera Open* 8 (2022): 23328584211068068.
41. See the section "The Additional Challenges for Parenting Teachers" in chapter 2.
42. Apoorva Mandavilli, "Schoolchildren Seem Unlikely to Fuel Coronavirus Surges, Scientists Say," *New York Times*, October 22, 2020, https://www.nytimes.com/2020/10/22/health/coronavirus-schools-children.html.
43. See Miriam Mutambudzi et al., "Occupation and Risk of Severe COVID-19: Prospective Cohort Study of 120 075 UK Biobank Participants," *Occupational and Environmental Medicine* 78, no. 5 (2021): 307–14; See Marissa G. Baker, Trevor K. Peckham, and Noah S. Seixas, "Estimating the Burden of United States Workers Exposed to Infection or Disease: A Key Factor in Containing Risk of COVID-19 Infection," *PloS One* 15, no. 4 (2020): e0232452; Theocharis Kromydas et al., "Occupational Differences in the

Prevalence and Severity of Long-COVID: Analysis of the Coronavirus (COVID-19) Infection Survey," *Occupational and Environmental Medicine* 80, no. 10 (2023): 545–52.

44. Sylvia Allegretto, "The Teacher Pay Penalty Has Hit a New High: Trends in Teacher Wages and Compensation Through 2021" (Washington, DC: Economic Policy Institute, 2023). In analyzing the teacher pay gap, Allegretto found teachers' wages relatively flat since the late 1990s; the weekly wage for teachers has only risen $45 from 1996 to 2021. The teacher pay penalty refers to the difference of pay for teachers when compared to similarly educated professionals. The weekly wage for other college graduates rose from $1,564 to $2,009 over the same period—a $445 increase. In 2023, Kentucky teachers earned close to $10,000 less than 2008 when adjusted for inflation, a 14.2 percent real wage decline. See Dustin Pugel, "Kentucky Average Teacher Pay Fails to Keep Up with Inflation in Most Districts, Remains Far Behind 2008 Levels," *Kentucky Center for Economic Policy*, December 15, 2023.

Chapter 8

1. Motoko Rich and Hisako Ueno, "As Flames Surged, Order Prevailed Inside a Japan Airline Jet," *New York Times*, January 3, 2024; "Crew's Quick Decisions Behind Safe Escape from Burning JAL Plane," *Kyodo News*, January 5, 2024.
2. Tricia Wachtendorf and James M. Kendra, "Improvising Disaster in the City of Jazz: Organizational Response to Hurricane Katrina," Social Science Research Council, June 11, 2006, https://items.ssrc.org/understanding-katrina/improvising-disaster-in-the-city-of-jazz-organizational-response-to-hurricane-katrina/; it is inspired by P. F. Berliner, *Thinking in Jazz: The Infinite Art of Improvisation* (Chicago: University of Chicago, 1994); and it is advanced in organizational behavior by Karl E. Weick, "Improvisation as a Mindset for Organizational Analysis," *Organization Science* 9, no. 5 (1998): 543–55.
3. Enrique Quarantelli, "Emergent Behaviors and Groups in the Crisis Time of Disasters," in *Individuality and Social Control: Essays in Honor of Tamotsu Shibutani*, ed. Kian Kwan (Greenwich, CT: JAI, 1996), 47–68.
4. Thomas E. Drabek and David A. McEntire, "Emergent Phenomena and the Sociology of Disaster: Lessons, Trends and Opportunities from the Research Literature," *Disaster Prevention and Management* 12, no. 2 (2003): 97–112; Quarantelli, "Emergent Behaviors and Groups in the Crisis Time of Disasters," https://udspace.udel.edu/items/a506fac1-477d-41ae-9e55-acf3ad20d49c; Mark Pelling, *Adaptation to Climate Change: From Resilience to Transformation* (New York: Routledge, 2011).
5. Arjen Boin, Allan McConnell, and Paul T. Hart, *Governing the Pandemic: The Politics of Navigating a Mega-Crisis* (Cham, Switzerland: Palgrave Macmillan, 2021), https://doi.org/10.1007/978-3-030-72680-5.
6. The initial overall score of –13 indicates teachers are feeling more negative than positive—with variation by subject, grade, experience, etc. Holly Kurtz, Sterling C. Lloyd, and Vanessa Solis, "Introducing the Teacher Morale Index," *Education Week*, March 6, 2024, https://www.edweek.org/teaching-learning/introducing-the-teacher-morale-index/2024/03.
7. Martin R. West, "Why Do Americans Rate Their Local Public Schools So Favorably?," *Brookings*, October 23, 2014, https://www.brookings.edu/articles/why-do-americans-rate-their-local-public-schools-so-favorably/.

8. See Julian Le Grand, *Motivation, Agency, and Public Policy: Of Knights and Knaves, Pawns and Queens* (Oxford: Oxford University Press, 2003), chapter 7.
9. Christina Maslach and Michael P. Leiter, *The Burnout Challenge: Managing People's Relationships with Their Jobs* (Cambridge, MA: Harvard University Press, 2022).
10. M. Lampert and F. Graziani, "Instructional Activities as a Tool for Teachers' and Teacher Educators' Learning," *Elementary School Journal* 109, no. 5 (2009): 491–509. Lampert and Graziani examined the role of structure and improvisation in managing the complexities of ambitious academic instruction. Citing prior research on improvisation in theater and music, they studied how one program of teacher preparation equipped novice teachers with a set of instructional activities and routines that served as "a stable and rehearsable backdrop for the dynamic work of responding to student thinking," (493).
11. See chapter 4.
12. Sandra J. Stein, *The Culture of Education Policy* (New York: Teachers College, 2004). Analyzing the origins of the Elementary and Secondary Education Act (ESEA), Stein makes evident policy makers' deficit framing of family poverty, citing legislators' derogatory references to low-income students and attributing this cultural deficit framing to misguided policy attention.
13. Our thinking is also informed by George Lakoff and Sam Ferguson, *The Framing of Immigration* (Berkeley, CA: The Rockridge Institute, 2006).
14. For more on the moral imperative of teachers and relation to career paths, see Doris A Santoro, *Demoralized: Why Teachers Leave the Profession They Love and How They Can Stay* (Cambridge, MA: Harvard Education Press, 2018).
15. R. Keith Sawyer, "What Makes Good Teachers Great," in *Structure and Improvisation in Creative Teaching*, ed. R. Keith Sawyer (Cambridge: Cambridge University Press, 2011), 2.
16. Paul F. Berliner, *Thinking in Jazz: The Infinite Art of Improvisation* (Chicago: University of Chicago Press, 1994); Quarantelli, "Emergent Behaviors and Groups in the Crisis Time of Disasters"; Michael H. Glantz and Ivan J. Ramírez, "Improvisation in the Time of Disaster," *Environment: Science and Policy for Sustainable Development* 60, no. 5 (2018): 4–17; Tricia Wachtendorf and James M. Kendra, "Improvising Disaster in the City of Jazz: Organizational Response to Hurricane Katrina," Social Science Research Council, June 11, 2006; Sawyer, "What Makes Good Teachers Great."
17. Karl E. Weick, "Educational Organizations as Loosely Coupled Systems," *Administrative Science Quarterly* 21, no. 1 (1976): 1–19.
18. Martin Carnoy, Richard Elmore, and Leslie S. Siskin, eds., *The New Accountability: High Schools and High-Stakes Testing* (New York: Taylor & Francis, 2003), 56. This study of accountability reforms in four states found schools' responses to and alignment with states' *external* accountability policy had much to do with the schools' *internal* systems of and capacity for accountability.
19. David C. Berliner, "Foreword" in *Structure and Improvisation in Creative Teaching*, ed. R. Keith Sawyer, xiii.
20. Berliner, "Foreword," xvi.
21. Quarantelli, "Emergent Behaviors and Groups in the Crisis Time of Disasters"; James Kendra and Tricia Wachtendorf, *Improvisation, Creativity and the Art of Emergency Management*, Preliminary Paper #357 (Newark: University of Delaware, Disaster

Research Center, 2006); Michael H. Glantz and Ivan J. Ramírez, "Improvisation in the Time of Disaster," *Environment: Science and Policy for Sustainable Development* 60, no. 5 (2018): 4–17.

22. Research in recent years has specified aspects of "pedagogically productive talk" in teacher work groups, aided by advances in video-based research methods and discourse analysis. For example, see Adam Lefstein, Nicole Louie, Aliza Segal, and Ayelet Becher, "Taking Stock of Research on Teacher Collaborative Discourse: Theory and Method in a Nascent Field," *Teaching and Teacher Education* 88 (2020): 1–13; Adam Lefstein, Dana Vedder-Weiss, and Aliza Segal, "Relocating Research on Teacher Learning: Toward Pedagogically Productive Talk," *Educational Researcher* 49, no. 5 (2020): 360–68; Ilana Seidel Horn and Judith Warren Little, "Attending to Problems of Practice: Routines and Resources for Professional Learning in Teachers' Workplace Interactions," *American Educational Research Journal* 47, no. 1 (October 2010): 181–217; Judith Warren Little, "Inside Teacher Community: Representations of Classroom Practice," *Teachers College Record* 105, no. 6 (August 2003): 913–45.
23. Cynthia E. Coburn, Jennifer L. Russell, Julia Heath Kaufman, and Mary Kay Stein, "Supporting Sustainability: Teachers' Advice Networks and Ambitious Instructional Reform," *American Journal of Education* 119, no. 1 (November 2012): 137–82; Michael Huberman, "Networks That Alter Teaching: Conceptualizations, Exchanges and Experiments," *Teachers and Teaching: Theory and Practice* 1, no. 2 (1995): 193–211; Judith Warren Little, "Professional Learning and School-Network Ties: Prospects for School Improvement," *Journal of Educational Change* 6 (September 2005): 277–83.
24. Much of the research on teachers' professional development remains situated in the context of formal programs offered by districts or by other professional development providers, although some researchers have argued persuasively for taking a broad view of what should count as professional development. See Hilda Borko, "Professional Development and Teacher Learning: Mapping the Terrain," *Educational Researcher* 33, no. 8 (November 2004): 3–15; Laura M. Desimone, "Improving Impact Studies of Teachers' Professional Development: Toward Better Conceptualizations and Measures," *Educational Researcher* 38, no. 3 (April 2009): 181–99.
25. For a discussion of Albert O. Hirschman's theory of exit, voice, and loyalty, see chapters 6 and 7.
26. See chapter 6 for data on respect, influence, and satisfaction as experienced by Satisfied Stayers.
27. Here we focus on formal unions as a vehicle for voice. See chapter 6 for elaborations on other sources of voice.
28. See Julia E. Koppich, *Grappling with COVID's Impact on Education: Labor and Management Confront the Crisis* (San Francisco: CDE Foundation, 2021), www.cdefoundation.org/calmireport.
29. Richard B. Freeman, "The Exit-Voice Tradeoff in the Labor Market: Unionism, Job Tenure, Quits, and Separations," *Quarterly Journal of Economics* 94, no. 4 (1980): 643–73.
30. E. S. Han, "The Myth of Unions' Overprotection of Bad Teachers: Evidence from the District–Teacher Matched Data on Teacher Turnover," *Industrial Relations: A Journal of Economy and Society* 59, no. 2 (2020): 316–52; Yujin Choi and Il Hwan Chung, "Voice Effects of Public Sector Unions on Turnover," *Public Personnel Management* 45, no. 2 (2016): 213–33.

31. Walter Blanks Jr., "Teachers' Unions Deserve Much of the Blame for Pandemic-Era Learning Loss," *National Review*, September 6, 2022, www.nationalreview.com /2022/09/teachers-unions-deserve-much-of-the-blame-for-pandemic-era-learning-loss/.
32. Linda Jacobson, "A Hearing on Learning Loss and a Preview of the Election Battle to Come," *The74*, July 28, 2023, www.the74million.org/article/a-hearing-on-learning -loss-and-a-preview-of-the-election-battle-to-come/.
33. Julián Gindin and Leslie Finger, "Promoting Education Quality: The Role of Teachers' Unions in Latin America," paper commissioned for the EFA Global Monitoring Report, 2013. See also John McCollow, "Teacher Unions," in *Oxford Research Encyclopedia of Education*, ed. George Noblit (Oxford: Oxford University Press, 2017); examples of scholarship aligning with this second paradigm include Erin Dyke and Brendan Muckian-Bates, *Rank-and-File Rebels: Theories of Power and Change in the 2018 Education Strikes* (Fort Collins, CO: WAC Clearinghouse, 2023) and Joseph A. McCartin, Marilyn Sneiderman, and Maurice BP-Weeks, "Combustible Convergence: Bargaining for the Common Good and the #RedforEd Uprisings of 2018," *Labor Studies Journal* 45, no. 1 (2020): 97–113.
34. Deborah Meier, "On Unions and Education," *Dissent*, February 14, 2023, https://www .dissentmagazine.org/article/on-unions-and-education/.
35. See Howard Stevenson and Alison Gilliland, "The Teachers' Voice: Teacher Unions at the Heart of a New Democratic Professionalism," in *Flip the System* (Abingdon: Routledge, 2015): 108–19.
36. Jane Farley's school was part of the New York Performance Standards Consortium, formally established in 1998 with the goal of advancing "practitioner-developed, student-focused, and externally reviewed assessment" as an alternative to standardized exams. Consortium schools are exempt from the New York State Regents exams; they build internal accountability and satisfy external accountability through assessments developed collaboratively by teachers. See Ann Perron, Mary Reid, Douglas B. Reeves, Allan Luke, and Lucy West, *Teacher Moderation Collaborative Assessment of Student Work* (Toronto, ON: Curriculum Services Canada, 2007); Michelle Fine and Karyna Pryiomka, *Assessing College Readiness Through Authentic Student Work: How the City University of New York and the New York Performance Standards Consortium Are Collaborating Toward Equity* (Palo Alto, CA: Learning Policy Institute, 2020).
37. *A Nation Prepared: Teachers for the 21st Century* (New York: Carnegie Forum on Education and the Economy, 1986), 25, https://ncee.org/book-report/a-nation-prepared -teachers-for-the-21st-century/.
38. Matthew A. Kraft and Melissa Arnold Lyon, "The Rise and Fall of the Teaching Profession: Prestige, Interest, Preparation, and Satisfaction over the Last Half Century," Annenberg Institute EdWorkingPaper: 22–679, Brown University, 2022.
39. Pawlewicz has argued persuasively that quality of teachers has been a school reform focus since the 1800s, and the profession is often blamed for any frustrations with school purpose, form, or function. Diana D'Amico Pawlewicz, *Blaming Teachers: Professionalization Policies and the Failure of Reform in American History* (New Brunswick, NJ: Rutgers University Press, 2020).
40. *A Nation Prepared*, 36.
41. The NCTM timeline notes *A Nation at Risk* as a "historical milestone," https://www .nctm.org/100timeline/.

42. Peter West, "NSTA Begins Effort to Create Science Standards," *EducationWeek*, May 15, 1991. There is no indication NSTA itself published the first science standards in the 1990s; standards were published by the National Academy of Sciences in 1996. The National Council for the Social Studies (NCSS) published curriculum standards in 1997, followed by the *NCSS National Standards for Social Studies Teachers* and the *NCSS/NCATE Program Standards for the Initial Preparation of Teachers of Social Studies* (https://www.socialstudies.org/standards/national-curriculum-standards-social-studies). The National Council of Teachers of English (NCTE) and the International Reading Association (IRA) jointly published *The Standards for the English Language Arts* in 1996 (https://ncte.org/resources/standards/ncte-ira-standards-for-the-english-language-arts/).
43. Richard J. Coley and Margaret E. Goertz, *Educational Standards in the 50 States:1990* (Princeton, NJ: Educational Testing Service, 1990).
44. Stephen Lazar, "Fixing Our Broken System of Testing and Accountability: The Reauthorization of ESEA," *Shanker Blog*, January 21, 2015, https://www.shankerinstitute.org/blog/fixing-our-broken-system-testing-and-accountability-reauthorization-esea. See also Valerie Strauss, "Teacher Tells Congress: 'The Federal Incentives in Education Are Wrong,'" *Washington Post*, January 21, 2015, https://www.washingtonpost.com/news/answer-sheet/wp/2015/01/21/teacher-tells-congress-the-federal-incentives-in-education-are-wrong/.
45. Assessments aligned to the Next Generation Science Standards and the C3 Framework (College, Career, and Civic Life Framework for Social Studies) were named as examples during the testimony. It is crucial to note that Mr. Lazar was not arguing for abandoning an ESEA requirement for student assessment, but to be "more intelligent in our approach" and to retain the capacity for disaggregating student results to preserve a focus on equity.
46. *A Nation Prepared*, 51.
47. See chapters 1 and 5.
48. Others have argued that the 1980s rise of school choice movement emerged out of a lack of trust in public schools and an orientation to market economics. See Bruce Fuller, Richard F. Elmore, and Gary Orfield, *Who Chooses? Who Loses? Culture, Institutions, and the Unequal Effects of School Choice* (New York: Teachers College Press, 1996).
49. *A Nation Prepared*, 39.
50. Susan L. Moffitt, Michaela Krug O'Neill, and David K. Cohen, *Reforming the Reform: Problems of Public Schooling in the American Welfare State* (Chicago: University of Chicago Press, 2023); for competing purposes, see also David Labaree, "Public Goods, Private Goods: The American Struggle Over Educational Goals," *American Educational Research Journal* 34, no. 1 (1997): 39–81; Samuel Bowles and Herbert Gintis, *Schooling in Capitalist America: Educational Reform and the Contradictions of Economic Life* (New York: Basic Books, 1976); Jean Anyon, "Social Class and the Hidden Curriculum of Work," *Journal of Education* 162, no. 1 (1980): 67–92.
51. Linda Darling-Hammond, "Instructional Policy into Practice: The Power of the Bottom over the Top," *Educational Evaluation and Policy Analysis* 12, no. 3 (1990): 233–41.
52. Alexander Cedergren and Henrik Hassel, "Building Organizational Adaptive Capacity in the Face of Crisis: Lessons from a Public Sector Case Study," *International Journal of Disaster Risk Reduction* 100 (2024): 104235.

53. David D. Woods, "Essentials of Resilience, Revisited," in *Handbook on Resilience of Socio-Technical Systems*, ed. Matthias Ruth and Stefan Goessling-Reisemann (Northampton, MA: Elgaronline, 2019), 52–65.
54. For example, see Sarah Mervosh, Claire Cain Miller, and Francesca Paris, "What the Data Says About Pandemic School Closures, Four Years Later," *New York Times*, March 18, 2024, https://www.nytimes.com/2024/03/18/upshot/pandemic-school-closures-data.html; Sarah Mervosh, "The Pandemic Erased Two Decades of Progress in Math and Reading," *New York Times*, September 1, 2022, https://www.nytimes.com/2022/09/01/us/national-test-scores-math-reading-pandemic.html.
55. Lora Bartlett, "Specifying Hybrid Models of Teachers' Work During COVID-19," *Educational Researcher* 51, no. 2 (2022): 152–55; see also chapter 2 of this book and figure 2.1 in particular for number of instructional mode changes.
56. Sarah Mervosh and Francesca Paris, "Why School Absences Have 'Exploded' Almost Everywhere," *New York Times*, March 29, 2024, https://www.nytimes.com/interactive/2024/03/29/us/chronic-absences.html.
57. See Marilyn Cochran-Smith and Susan Lytle, "Troubling Images of Teaching in No Child Left Behind," *Harvard Educational Review* 76, no. 4 (December 2006): 668–97.
58. For an example of institutional change that resulted over time in a combination of professional authority, government regulation and oversight, and responsiveness to the consumer health movement, see W. Richard Scott, Martin Ruef, Peter J. Mendel, and Carol A. Caronna, *Institutional Change and Healthcare Organizations: From Professional Dominance to Managed Care* (Chicago: University of Chicago Press, 2000).
59. Arjen Boin and Allan McConnell, "Preparing for Critical Infrastructure Breakdowns: The Limits of Crisis Management and the Need for Resilience," *Journal of Contingencies and Crisis Management* 15, no. 1 (March 2007): 50–59.
60. C. Ansell, E. Sorensen, and J. Torfing, "The COVID-19 Pandemic as a Game-Changer for Public Administration and Leadership? The Need for Robust Governance Responses to Turbulent Problems," *Public Management Review* 23, no. 7 (2021): 949–60. Ansell, Sorensen, and Torfing argue that increasingly complex problems and turbulent events require "that we make public institutions and programs more flexible and agile so that they can transform and adapt themselves in response to turbulence and scale their problem-solving efforts up and down" (954) and that "control-fixated administrative steering systems must give way to trust-based systems that allow more room for decentralized flexibility, innovation, and adaptation, thereby preparing public organizations to deal with turbulence."
61. For one example, see Julia E. Koppich and Charles Taylor Kerchner, *The Trust Agreement Project: Broadening the Vision of School Labor-Management Relations* (Berkeley: University of California Policy Analysis for California Education, 1988).
62. Karl E. Weick and Kathleen M. Sutcliffe, *Managing the Unexpected: Assuring High Performance in an Age of Complexity* (San Francisco: Jossey-Bass, 2001).
63. David J. Yu et al., "Toward General Principles for Resilience Engineering," *Risk Analysis* 40, no. 8 (August 2020): 1509–37.
64. Woods, "Essentials of Resilience, Revisited," 52–65.
65. Cedergren and Hassel, "Building Organizational Adaptive Capacity in the Face of Crisis."

66. See Susan Moore Johnson, *Where Teachers Thrive: Organizing Schools for Success* (Cambridge, MA: Harvard Education Press, 2019); Anthony S. Bryk, Penny Bender Sebring, Elaine Allensworth, Stuart Luppescu, and John Q. Easton, *Organizing Schools for Improvement* (Chicago: University of Chicago Press, 2010); Milbrey Wallin McLaughlin and Joan E. Talbert, *Professional Communities and the Work of High School Teaching* (Chicago: University of Chicago Press, 2001). McLaughlin and Talbert find long-standing norms of individualism, privacy, and noninterference are not conducive to strong teacher learning communities; furthermore, they distinguish between teacher learning communities that "collaborate to re-invent practice" and traditional teacher communities that unite to "enforce traditions."
67. James P. Spillane, Richard Halverson, and John B. Diamond, "Towards a Theory of Leadership Practice: A Distributed Perspective," *Journal of Curriculum Studies* 36, no. 1 (2004): 3–34.
68. Joo-Ho Park, North Cooc, and Kang-Ho Lee, "Relationships Between Teacher Influence in Managerial and Instruction-Related Decision-Making, Job Satisfaction, and Professional Commitment: A Multivariate Multilevel Model," *Educational Management Administration & Leadership* 51, no. 1 (January 2023); Richard Ingersoll, Philip Sirinides, and Patrick Dougherty, "Leadership Matters: Teachers' Roles in School Decision Making and School Performance," *American Educator* (Spring 2018): 13–17, 39.
69. Pawlewicz, *Blaming Teachers*, 179–82; see epilogue for discussion of how teacher "professionalism" reforms have historically been subverted to silence and control teachers in the name of efficiency and regulation.
70. Andy Hargreaves, "Contrived Collegiality: The Micropolitics of Teacher Collaboration," in *The Politics of Life in Schools: Power, Conflict, and Cooperation*, ed. Joseph Blase (Newbury Park, CA: SAGE, 1991), 939–70.
71. The remaining four states either provided no public information on teacher turnover (California, Florida), no information disaggregated by year (Oregon), or made information available only by special request (Iowa).
72. John Aberth, *The Black Death: The Great Mortality of 1348–1350: A Brief History with Documents* (Boston: Bedford, 2005), 5.
73. Maria Langan-Riekhof, Arex B. Avanni, and Adrienne Janetti, "Sometimes the World Needs a Crisis: Turning Challenges into Opportunities," *Brookings Research*, April 10, 2017, https://www.brookings.edu/articles/sometimes-the-world-needs-a-crisis-turning-challenges-into-opportunities/.

Acknowledgments

This book was made possible by the seventy-five teachers who shared pandemic teaching stories with the Suddenly Distant Research Project. It was a privilege to navigate the pandemic with them, to Zoom to an Iowa farmhouse and then to a New York City studio in the same day and to hear the similarities and differences of teachers across the country. We deeply appreciate the time they dedicated to sharing their knowledge, insights, and experiences with us during a time of massive disruption, uncertainty, and stress. We hope they see their experiences and insights —their struggles and their breakthroughs —well captured in this book.

The Suddenly Distant Research Project (SDRP) included four principal investigators, a doctoral research associate, a classroom teacher, two undergraduate research assistants, and three project advisors. This is a project of its time, launched during the early shutdown days of spring 2020, and collaboratively conducted online from our respective homes. To this day, the whole team has yet to be in the same physical space and it wasn't until April 2022 that five core team members gathered together. It was a joyous occasion, meeting together and presenting the project's early findings at the American Educational Research Association's Annual meeting in San Diego, CA.

Dr. Lina Darwich, associate professor at Lewis & Clark Graduate School, was integral to the project's development, data collection, and

Photograph of the Suddenly Distant research team. Pictured here from left to right: Riley Collins, Alisun Thompson, Lina Darwich, Lora Bartlett, Judith Warren Little.

analysis, bringing to the project her research expertise in social and emotional learning, especially as it pertains to teacher-student relationships.

As research assistants, classroom teacher Iris Hinds Weaver and UC Santa Cruz undergraduates Lila Harte and Luis Ramirez were indispensable in assembling the data that allowed us to map the state and teacher community contexts. We appreciate their dogged determination in finding information sources, careful attention to data indexing, and contributions to the project insights.

We are indebted to our project advisors for pushing our thinking: Dr. Jessica Charles, Director of Scholarship on Educator Practice at Bank Street Graduate School of Education, made a pivotal contribution to our thinking when she suggested that we look at the pandemic through the lens of theory and research on disasters and crises; Dr. Julia Koppich, an expert on labor-management relations and co-author of two books, *A Union of Professionals* and *United Mind Workers: Unions and Teaching in the Knowledge Society,* guided our thinking on unions, reminding us of the importance of the local level in considerations of union strength; and Dr. Ilana Horn, Professor of Math Education in the Department of Teaching and Learning at Vanderbilt University, kept us attuned to how the pandemic mattered to the learning opportunities that teachers seized and the instructional adaptations they made.

We appreciate the financial support provided by Lewis & Clark Graduate School, the University of Puget Sound, and the Center for Social Transformation at the University of California, Santa Cruz.

About the Authors

Lora Bartlett is an Associate Professor of Education at the University of California, Santa Cruz. Her research advances and develops knowledge related to teachers' professional commitment, conceptions of teacher professionalism, and composition of the teacher workforce. Her work unpacks notions of teachers' work held by individuals, professional communities, organizations, and policy makers and the consequences of those, often competing, conceptual interactions for creating and maintaining a professional teacher workforce. As a teacher, she has taught secondary school in the United States and England, prepared automobile assembly-line workers for the high school equivalency exam, and received an outstanding teaching award from the University of California. Bartlett publishes both academic and public-facing work in a diversity of publications including *EdWeek*, *Educational Researcher*, *Teachers' College Record*, *Journal of Educational Policy Analysis*, and *Review of Research in Education*. She is the author of the 2014 book *Migrant Teachers: How American Schools Import Labor*, published by Harvard University Press. Bartlett has held fellowships and received research support from, for example, the British Foreign Office, the Sloan Center for Work and Family, and the National Science Foundation.

Alisun Thompson is an Assistant Professor of Education and teacher educator at the University of Puget Sound in Tacoma, Washington. Her research focuses on the contours of the teacher workforce and the conditions that attract, support, and retain teachers in the profession. She is particularly interested in how early career teachers develop and sustain their commitment to equity and justice-oriented teaching practices, and her work attends to both the professional, organizational, and personal conditions that contribute to that process. With nearly two decades' experience in public schools, she draws on her work as a middle school teacher, literacy coach, and school board president in attending to the policy and system conditions needed to sustain a vibrant workforce. Her work as a teacher educator focuses on preparing teachers for both their work in classrooms and also for professional and organizational membership. She is published in the *Northwest Journal of Teacher Education* and *Teachers College Record*, as well as in peer-edited books (chapters) published by Harvard Education Press, Lexington Books, and Brill Sense.

Judith Warren Little is the Carol Liu Professor (Emerita) of Education Policy at the Berkeley School of Education at the University of California, Berkeley. She is a sociologist whose research focuses on teachers' work and careers, the organizational and policy contexts of teaching, and teachers' professional development. In particular, she investigates the policies and resources that support or constrain teacher learning in both formal professional development and informal workplace settings. She has also pursued an interest in national and international developments in the composition, quality, distribution, and preparation of the teacher workforce and has participated in cross-field studies of education for the professions. In 2021, she chaired the planning committee for COVID-19 and the Teacher Workforce, a two-day workshop of the National Academies of Sciences, Engineering, and Medicine. Little is an elected member of the National Academy of Education, an elected Fellow of the American Educational Research Association, and a recipient of the Frank H. Klassen Award for leadership and scholarly contributions in teacher education from the International Council on Education for Teaching (ICET).

Riley Collins is a doctoral student at the University of California, Santa Cruz. Her research interests center on US teacher labor organizing and shifts in teachers' work in the context of COVID-19. Her dissertation draws on social reproduction feminism to examine twentieth- and twenty-first-century teacher organizing in Chicago and New Orleans. Prior to entering the doctoral program, she was a high school teacher in Jefferson Parish, Louisiana, where she was a dual language Spanish-English math teacher and a Louisiana State Teacher Leader. She then worked for the San Francisco Unified School District and City College of San Francisco supporting teachers, paraeducators, and substitute teachers. Her work is published in *Globalisation, Societies and Education*, and the *International Encyclopedia of Education.*

Index